Essential Series

Springer

London
Berlin
Heidelberg
New York
Barcelona
Hong Kong
Milan
Paris
Singapore
Tokyo

Ian Palmer

Essential
Java 3D *fast*

**Developing 3D Graphics
Applications in Java**

Springer

Ian Palmer, BSc, MSc, DPhil
EIMC, University of Bradford, Bradford, BD7 1DP

Series Editor
John Cowell, BSc (Hons), MPhil, PhD
Department of Computer Science, De Montfort University, The Gateway,
Leicester LE1 9BH

British Library Cataloguing in Publication Data
Palmer, I. C. (Ian C.)
    Essential Java 3D fast: developing 3D graphics applications
    in Java. – (Essentials)
    1. Java (Computer program language) 2. Computer graphics
    I. Title
    006.6'93
    ISBN 1852333944
Library of Congress Cataloging-in-Publication Data
Palmer, Ian, 1966-
    Essential Java3D fast/Ian Palmer.
       p. cm. — (Essential series)
    Includes bibliographical references and index.
    ISBN 1-85233-394-4 (alk. paper)
    1. Java (Computer program language 2. Computer graphics.
    I. Title. II. Essential series (Springer-Verlag)
    QA76.73.J38 P34 2001
    006.6'633—dc21   00-052660

ISBN 1-85233-394-4 Springer-Verlag London Berlin Heidelberg
A member of BertelsmannSpringer Science+Business Media GmbH
http://www.springer.co.uk

© Springer-Verlag London Limited 2001
Printed in Great Britain

Typesetting: Camera-ready by author
Printed and bound at The Cromwell Press, Trowbridge, Wiltshire
34/3830-543210 Printed on acid-free paper SPIN 10784923

Contents

Contents

Chapter

1

Introduction

Introduction

Java has grown rapidly from a small project at Sun Microsystems to be one of the most widely known and used programming languages. This has resulted in Java being used for a wide variety of applications, ranging from simple Web-based games to large-scale business software. Several extensions to the core Java language have been developed, both by Sun themselves and by third parties. These cover an extensive range of application areas and one of the areas that has been the focus of a great deal of activity is that of computer graphics. Libraries have been produced that support both 2D and 3D graphics. For example, the Advanced Imaging library has been developed to support image processing-type applications. In the 3D area, there have been a number of libraries that offer 3D functionality, such as the Magician library that provided wrappers around OpenGL functions. Development work on these has been reduced recently since the release of Java 3D.

What is Java 3D?

Java 3D is a set of libraries that offer many features for developing Java programs that incorporate 3D graphics. It has been developed by Sun and so has the credibility of being developed by the original creators of Java itself. This is one of the reasons that work on alternative 3D solutions has been reduced: anyone developing a 3D application in Java can be relatively confident that the end user is more likely to have Java 3D installed than any other 3D package.

Java 3D shares many features with existing 3D graphics libraries, and so a lot of the features will probably be familiar to you. There are no completely new concepts incorporated in Java 3D, although quite a few are implemented in novel ways. If you are relatively new to 3D graphics, then you should consult a textbook aimed at introducing the basic concepts of 3D. Some examples of suitable books are given in the Reference section at the end of the book.

Running Java 3D programs

To compile and run the Java 3D programs such as those presented in this book, you'll need both the Java SDK and the Java 3D libraries. These, together with supporting documentation and some demonstration code, can be downloaded from the Sun Web site. At the time of writing, the Java 2 SDK is at version 1.3, whilst Java 3D is at version 1.2.1. Both these are under constant revision, both to add features and to fix bugs, and it is likely that as you read this there is a new version on the Web site. Despite this, the underlying concepts will be the same. This does of course mean that it is essential to read the documentation that comes with the distribution that you install to find any changes that may have been made to the language or the libraries.

Familiarity with Java is assumed, so we won't cover details of how to compile and run programs. If you are not comfortable with Java itself, then you should read a text aimed at improving your Java skills. A good example would be *Essential Java 2 Fast* by John Cowell that is published as part of the same series as this book. There are a several other books on Java, and a visit to your local bookshop should yield a book that suits your learning style. Some introductory texts on Java can be found in the Reference section.

How to use this book

This book has been written to be read from start to finish. However, it is possible to read some chapters in isolation if you only want to study that particular aspect. It is recommended that if you are completely new to Java 3D then you read Chapters 1 to 4. This will give you the basics of how to construct simple programs, create geometry and define lights and surface properties so that you can see the objects in the scene. Chapter 5 introduces more information about transformations and how to group objecs together. Chapters 6 and 7 introduce dynamics elements to your programs, such as animation and interaction. These will allow you to produce much more powerful and useful programs. Chapter 8 introduces some varied topics that will allow you to bring more realism into your work. The final chapter brings together a number of techniques into a single game.

Most of the chapters' examples are self-contained and will run straight from the text. All of the source code is also included in Appendix A, with each program in its entirety. These are grouped by the chapter in which they appear, so it should be easy to find the appropriate code listing. The code in the appendix contains comments at appropriate places to explain the workings of the code. This means that another way to use this book would be to start with the programs listed in the appendix and then refer to the relevant chapter text if you are having problems. It's up to you which learning style suits you best.

The source code is also downloadable from the book web site along with some basic documentation for the classes. This can be reached from http://www.ijpalmer.co.uk/.

Chapter 2

Our First Java 3D Program

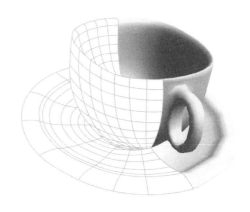

Introduction

The best way to learn any programming language is by writing programs. To be able to write Java 3D programs you must first be able to write Java programs. As we said in Chapter 1, the examples we'll be presenting here assume a working knowledge of Java and some background in 3D graphics. Only concepts that are new in Java 3D will be explained. We'll start by explaining some of the concepts that are fundamental to a Java 3D program. Next we'll write a very simple program that displays a static cube from a fixed viewpoint. In further chapters we'll modify and add features to this program to learn the other features of Java 3D.

The Scene Graph

Before we create our first Java 3D program we need to understand how the 3D world that we'll be creating is structured. Java 3D shares the concept of a *scene graph* with many other types of 3D programming languages and file formats, perhaps most notably VRML [Hartman 1996] and OpenInventor [Silicon Graphics 1993]. A scene graph is a structure that holds the information about the scene, including the geometric data, the appearance definition and the viewing parameters amongst other things. Figure 2.1 shows the scene graph of a simple Java 3D scene.

The root node of the graph is an instance of the **VirtualUniverse** node class. There will normally be only one of these in a Java 3D program. The **VirtualUniverse** references a list of **Locale** objects that contain the rest of the scene information. A **Locale** node specifies a location in the virtual universe at which the rest of the scene content exists. There may be multiple **Locale** nodes for each program. Although the **Locale** node in the example is shown as a child of the **VirtualUniverse** node, this is not explicitly the case. A **VirtualUniverse** merely maintains a list of **Locale** objects that are active in the current program. It is useful, however, to think of the **Locale** objects as being implicit children of the **VirtualUniverse**.

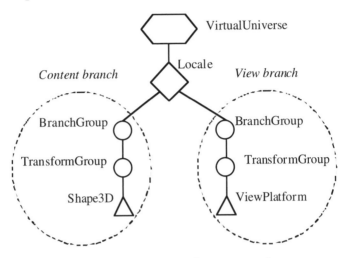

Figure 2.1 A simple scene graph.

Each **Locale** contains a number of **BranchGroup** nodes. Again, these are not explicitly children of the **Locale**, but it is useful to think of them as such. Typically there will be two **BranchGroup** objects as shown in Figure 2.1, one of which stores the scene content and the other of which stores the definition of the view parameters.

The View Branch

The view branch positions the viewpoint in the scene and defines the way in which the scene is displayed. It is very flexible and its features have been specially designed for use in VR applications. This includes support for specialised input and output equipment such as head-tracking hardware and stereoscopic displays. We will not consider these advanced features here and will concentrate on the nodes that set up our viewing parameters for a standard computer system with a single monitor, keyboard and mouse.

The first node in this branch is the **BranchGroup** node that we have already mentioned. Below this is **TransformGroup** that positions our view in the universe. This stores a transformation that affects the nodes below it in the graph, such as a translation along the *x*-axis of 5 units. We will study this in more detail later. The next node is the **ViewPlatform** that defines the coordinate system for the view. This node actually references some other objects, as shown in Figure 2.2.

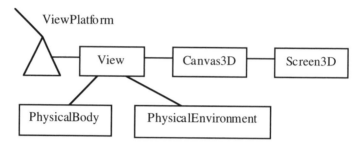

Figure 2.2 The objects referenced by the ViewPlatform.

The **View** object holds information on how to render the scene. It references a **Canvas3D** object that extends the AWT (Abstract Window Toolkit) **Canvas** object with data and methods that relate to 3D representations. This in turn references a **Screen3D** object that extends the AWT **Screen** object. This will not usually be altered by the user and is automatically created by the corresponding **Canvas3D**.

The **PhysicalBody** node stores information about the actual physical characteristics of the user. Such information would be used with advanced display and input devices, for example the separation of a user's eyes could be used to generate correct stereoscopic displays. The **PhysicalEnvironment** node stores information about the physical surroundings of the user, one use of which may be for position tracking equipment. Although we will not be considering these advanced features, the Java 3D viewing model needs these nodes to be present. In our applications we'll just create them with their default parameters, add them to our view branch and forget about them.

The Content Branch

The **BranchGroup** node of this branch of the scene graph contains the actual 3D content of the scene, as well as other elements such as sound nodes. Below this is a **TransformGroup** that allows us to position the geometry in our 3D world in the same way as the corresponding node in the view branch. There may be more than one **TransformGroup** for a given content branch.

The **Shape3D** node is where the geometric information for our scene exists. There will typically be many **Shape3D** nodes in a scene graph (possibly each below its own **TransformGroup**), each representing a distinct object. The node also contains the appearance definition of the object. It contains two separate nodes to store this information, a geometry node and an appearance node, as shown in Figure 2.3. We'll study these important nodes in more detail in Chapters 3 and 4.

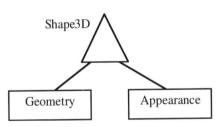

Figure 2.3 The components of the Shape3D node.

The *SimpleWorld* Program

In our first program, we are going to construct a simple scene containing a single cube, defining the content and view branch nodes as necessary. Later we will learn how to modify these to produce more complex worlds and to give a deeper understanding of each node type in the scene graph. For now we'll content ourselves with creating possibly the simplest world we can. When we've finished, the program should produce a display as shown in Figure 2.4.

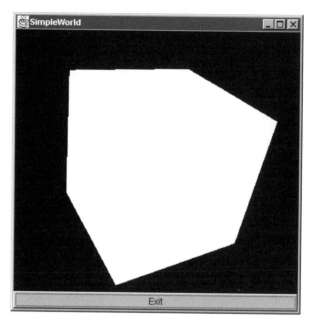

Figure 2.4 The output of the first program.

First, we will define the view branch of the graph. This begins by creating the **BranchGroup** node that forms the root of this branch. We next create a **TransformGroup** with a transformation that moves our viewpoint back along the z-axis (so that we can see the cube we will be creating). The **ViewPlatform** is then defined, and these are combined with the required parent-child relationships using the **addChild** method.

The **ViewPlatform** requires a **View** attached to it, which in turn references the **Canvas3D** that is used to display the scene. These are created and the **View** is attached to the **ViewPlatform**. We also create the **PhysicalBody** and **PhysicalEnvironment** nodes and attach these. The default parameters are used for most of the constructors. The code that achieves this is given below.

```java
protected BranchGroup buildViewBranch(Canvas3D c) {
    BranchGroup viewBranch = new BranchGroup();
    Transform3D viewXfm = new Transform3D();
    viewXfm.set(new Vector3f(0.0f,0.0f,5.0f);
    TransformGroup viewXfmGroup = new TransformGroup(viewXfm);
    ViewPlatform myViewPlatform = new ViewPlatform();
    viewXfmGroup.addChild(myViewPlatform);
    viewBranch.addChild(viewXfmGroup);
    View myView = new View();
    PhysicalBody mybody = new PhysicalBody();
    PhysicalEnvironment myEnvironment = new PhysicalEnvironment();
    myView.setPhysicalBody(myBody);
    myView.setPhysicalEnvironment(myEnvironment);
    myView.addCanvas3D(c);
    myView.attachViewPlatform(myViewPlatform);
    return viewBranch;
}
```

Next we create the content branch. Again, this begins with creating a **BranchGroup** node that is the root of this branch. We then create the **TransformGroup**, in this case with a rotation about the y-axis and the x-axis to twist and tilt the cube slightly so that we can actually see that the shape is 3D. We then add the shape itself, which we'll create in a separate method. The code to create the content branch is shown below.

```java
protected BranchGroup buildContentBranch(Node shape) {
    BranchGroup contentBranch = new BranchGroup();
    Transform3D rotateCube = new Transform3D();
    rotateCube.set(new AxisAngle4d(1.0,1.0,0.0,Math.PI/4.0));
    TransformGroup rotationGroup = new TransformGroup(rotateCube);
    contentBranch.addChild(rotationGroup);
    rotationGroup.addChild(shape);
    return contentBranch;
}
```

Finally, we need to create the geometry of the cube to add to our content branch. To do this we are going to have to use some classes that we will meet in full later. An easy way to create a cube is to create a **Shape3D** object with a set

of six four-sided faces. The six faces are defined in a
QuadArray. The array is treated as a sequence of sets of
four vertices, each set defining a quadrilateral polygon.
The other component of a **Shape3D** is the **Appearance** and
in our simple example we will merely create an instance
with the default parameters which will create a flat white
surface to the cube. The code to build a cube of unit size
centred on the origin of our universe is given below.

```
protected Shape3D buildShape() {
    float[] cubeFaces = {
        1.0f, -1.0f, 1.0f, 1.0f, 1.0f, 1.0f, -1.0f, 1.0f, 1.0f, -1.0f, -1.0f, 1.0f,
        -1.0f, -1.0f, -1.0f, -1.0f, 1.0f, -1.0f, 1.0f, 1.0f, -1.0f, 1.0f, -1.0f, -1.0f,
        1.0f, -1.0f, -1.0f, 1.0f, 1.0f, -1.0f, 1.0f, 1.0f, 1.0f, 1.0f, -1.0f, 1.0f,
        -1.0f, -1.0f, 1.0f, -1.0f, 1.0f, 1.0f, -1.0f, 1.0f, -1.0f, -1.0f, -1.0f, -1.0f,
        1.0f, 1.0f, 1.0f, 1.0f, 1.0f, -1.0f, -1.0f, 1.0f, -1.0f, -1.0f, 1.0f, 1.0f,
        -1.0f, -1.0f, 1.0f, -1.0f, -1.0f, -1.0f, 1.0f, -1.0f, -1.0f, 1.0f, -1.0f, 1.0f
    };
    QuadArray cubeData = new QuadArray(24, QuadArray.COORDINATES);
    cubeData.setCoordinates(0, cubeFaces);
    return new Shape3D(cubeData, new Appearance());
}
```

The *cubeFaces* array stores the vertex data, each group of
three values defining a single vertex. The *cubeData* uses
these vertices to define a set of six quadrilateral polygons.
The **QuadArray** constructor's parameters define the
number of vertices (in this case 6 _ 4) and the type of data
that we will be defining. In this simple case we're only
defining the coordinates associated with our faces. Other
options would include vertex normals, colours and texture
information. We then set the vertices using the
setCoordinates method, starting from position 0 in the
array of data. Finally, we create the actual **Shape3D** node
with the face information and a new **Appearance** node.

We can now put all these elements together in a class
SimpleWorld that extends the AWT class **Frame**. The
constructor for our application is shown below.

```
public SimpleWorld() {
    VirtualUniverse myUniverse = new VirtualUniverse();
    Locale myLocale = new Locale(myUniverse);
    myLocale.addBranchGroup(buildViewBranch(myCanvas3D));
    myLocale.addBranchGraph(contentBranch(buildCube()));
```

```
    setTitle("SimpleWorld");
    setSize(400,400);
    setLayout(new BorderLayout());
    add("Center", myCanvas3D);
    setVisible(true);
}
```

This creates a **VirtualUniverse** and its associated **Locale**. It then creates and adds the view and content branches using the methods that we have defined above. The **Canvas3D** that is associated with the **ViewPlatform** is then added to the **Frame**.

The full program is listed below. The final additions are the necessary **import** statements, the **main** method and a button to exit the application.

```
import javax.media.j3d.*;
import javax.vecmath.*;
import java.awt.*;
import java.awt.event.*;
public class SimpleWorld extends Frame implements ActionListener {
    protected Canvas3D myCanvas3D = new Canvas3D(null);
    protected Button myButton = new Button("Exit");

    protected BranchGroup buildViewBranch(Canvas3D c) {
        BranchGroup viewBranch = new BranchGroup();
        Transform3D viewXfm = new Transform3D();
        viewXfm.set(new Vector3f(0.0f,0.0f,5.0f);
        TransformGroup viewXfmGroup = new TransformGroup(viewXfm);
        ViewPlatform myViewPlatform = new ViewPlatform();
        viewXfmGroup.addChild(myViewPlatform);
        viewBranch.addChild(viewXfmGroup);
        View myView = new View();
        PhysicalBody myBody = new PhysicalBody();
        PhysicalEnvironment myEnvironment = new PhysicalEnvironment();
        myView.setPhysicalBody(myBody);
        myView.setPhysicalEnvironment(myEnvironment);
        myView.addCanvas3D(c);
        myView.attachViewPlatform(myViewPlatform);
        return viewBranch;
    }

    protected BranchGroup buildContentBranch(Node shape) {
```

```
        BranchGroup contentBranch = new BranchGroup();
        Transform3D rotateCube = new Transform3D( );
        rotateCube.set(new AxisAngle4d(1.0,1.0,0.0,Math.PI/4.0));
        TransformGroup rotationGroup = new TransformGroup(rotateCube);
        contentBranch.addChild(rotationGroup);
        rotationGroup.addChild(shape);
        return contentBranch;
    }
    protected Node buildShape() {
        float[] cubeFaces = {
                1.0f, -1.0f,  1.0f, 1.0f,  1.0f,  1.0f,
               -1.0f,  1.0f,  1.0f, -1.0f, -1.0f,  1.0f,
               -1.0f, -1.0f, -1.0f, -1.0f,  1.0f, -1.0f,
                1.0f,  1.0f, -1.0f, 1.0f, -1.0f, -1.0f,
                1.0f, -1.0f, -1.0f, 1.0f,  1.0f, -1.0f,
                1.0f,  1.0f,  1.0f, 1.0f, -1.0f,  1.0f,
               -1.0f, -1.0f,  1.0f, -1.0f,  1.0f,  1.0f,
               -1.0f,  1.0f, -1.0f, -1.0f, -1.0f, -1.0f,
                1.0f,  1.0f,  1.0f, 1.0f,  1.0f, -1.0f,
               -1.0f,  1.0f, -1.0f, -1.0f,  1.0f,  1.0f,
               -1.0f, -1.0f,  1.0f, -1.0f, -1.0f, -1.0f,
                1.0f, -1.0f, -1.0f, 1.0f, -1.0f,  1.0f
        };
        QuadArray cubeData = new QuadArray(24,QuadArray.COORDINATES);
        cubeData.setCoordinates(0, cubeFaces);
        return new Shape3D(cubeData, new Appearance());
    }
    public void actionPerformed(ActionEvent e) {
        dispose();
        System.exit(0);
    }
    public SimpleWorld() {
        VirtualUniverse myUniverse = new VirtualUniverse();
        Locale myLocale = new Locale(myUniverse);
        myLocale.addBranchGraph(buildViewBranch(myCanvas);
        myLocale.addBranchGraph(buildContentBranch(buildShape()));
        setTitle("SimpleWorld");
        setSize(400,400);
        setLayout(new BorderLayout());
        add("Center", myCanvas3D);
        add("South", myButton);
        myButton.addActionListener(this);
        setVisible(true);
    }
```

```
public static void main(String[] args) {
    SimpleWorld sw = new SimpleWorld();
}
}
```

This seems like a lot of work to create a simple static cube, but now that we have met some of these classes we can begin to build upon these to create more complex scenes. We'll meet most of these classes in more detail later, so don't worry if not all the features we've discussed are completely clear at this stage. What is important at this stage is to understand how we've put the scene together and what role each component performs in the code.

Summary

In this chapter we have learnt how out to create a very simple Java 3D file. This has necessitated that we learn about the basic scene graph components and how to create the components to define a view and a shape consisting of a geometry and an appearance. Many of the components of this program will be met again later, but next we will look at how to create other shapes, including loading geometry from files created in other applications.

Chapter

3

Creating Shapes

Introduction

In our first program, we created a simple cube from a set of quadrilateral faces. This is the simplest way to create a cubic shape using the basic set of Java 3D libraries. There are no geometric primitives, such as cubes, spheres or cylinders, in the Java 3D libraries. The primary method of creating shapes is through polygonal meshes of one type or another. There are, however, some primitive shapes included in one of the extension libraries included with the standard distribution. The final way of forming shapes is to load in a shape description from an external file. This is possible using some additional classes supplied in the utility libraries. Using one of these three approaches it should be possible to create most of the shapes that are required in an application. We'll look at each of these approaches in turn, starting with the geometric primitives.

Geometric primitives in the utility library

The classes for these are included in the library **com.sun.j3d.util.geometry**. The class names, together with examples and descriptions, are given in Table 3.1. It is relatively simple to use these, and we will start by recreating our program from the previous chapter using the **Box** class instead of creating our cube from a set of six quadrilateral faces.

Table 3.1 The primitive geometry classes.

Geometry class		Description
Box.class		A cubic shape, length, width and height defined in the constructor.
ColorCube.class		A cube with a different colour on each face.
Cone.class		A cone, height and radius defined in the constructor, resolution in vertical and horizontal directions can be specified.
Cylinder		A cylinder, height and radius defined, resolution in vertical and horizontal directions can be specified.
Sphere.class		Sphere, radius and resolution defined.
Text2D.class		Creates a rectangle with a texture map on it representing the text defined, font, style and size can be defined.

The main difference is in the *buildCube* method. This has to be changed to:

```
protected Node buildShape() {
    return new Box(1.0f, 1.0f, 1.0f, new Appearance());
}
```

As you can see, this is much simpler than in our previous program and produces the same output. The only other line that we need to add is the import line for the utility library:

```
import com.sun.j3d.utils.geometry.*;
```

We can also easily replace the cube with one of the other primitives, e.g. for the cone:

```
protected Node buildShape() {
    return new Cone(1.0f, 2.0f, 0, new Appearance());
}
```

This will generate the output shown in Figure 3.1. The third parameter, which is set to zero, specifies whether the program should automatically generate surface normals for the shape. For now, as we are not using the lighting model to display the object, we'll set this to zero and so not generate any normals. Later we'll see how we can use this parameter to set up the correct normals for rendering a more realistic version.

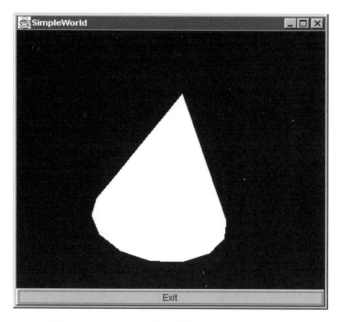

*Figure 3.1 Example of the **Cone** primitive.*

Obviously, these primitives can be combined to create complex objects in a similar way to Constructive Solid Geometry systems. Plate 1 shows an example created entirely from primitives in this way.

Geometry arrays

Geometry arrays are similar to geometric data structures in many graphics systems. They primarily consist of a set of arrays that contain coordinates, colours, normals and texture coordinates that are combined to form different types of geometry. The different types are given in Table 3.2.

To learn how these work, we'll first look at one example, the **QuadArray** class.

Using the QuadArray class

We've used this class before in our first program. This class is used to define sets of quadrilateral polygons. The data that is inherited from the parent class of all the array shapes, **GeometryArray** is:

- Coordinates: these specify the vertices making up the shape.
- Colours: defining the colours of each vertex.
- Normals: these specify the direction of the shape's surface at the vertices.
- Texture coordinates: defines the coordinates used for texture mapping operations.

Not all these sets of data need to be contained in every instance of a subclass of the **GeometryArray** class. The minimum is the coordinate information, and for a shaded representation we need to define the normals. We'll now look at how we create a simple **QuadArray** using this minimum data.

Table 3.2 Geometry array types.

Class	Description	Example
PointArray	Draws the coordinates defined as single points.	
LineArray	Draws lines defined by pairs of points in the coordinate array.	
TriangleArray	Draws triangles defined by sets of three coordinates in the array.	
QuadArray	Draws quadrilaterals defined by sets of four coordinates in the array.	
LineStripArray	Draws connected line segments. A parameter defines how many segments make up each set of connected line segments.	
TriangleFanArray	Draws a 'fan' of connected triangles. A parameter defines how many triangles are in a set of triangles.	
TriangleStripArray	Draws a 'strip' of connected triangles. A parameter defines how many triangles are in a set of triangles.	
IndexedLineArray	Draws a connected set of line segments.	
IndexedPointArray	Draws a set of points.	
IndexedQuadArray	Draws a set of quadrilaterals defined by sets of four consecutive coordinates.	
IndexedTriangleArray	Draws a set of triangles defined by sets of three consecutive coordinates.	

We first create an empty **QuadArray** that we'll use for our shape:

```
QuadArray quadCube = new QuadArray(24, QuadArray.COORDINATES);
```

The first parameter specifies how many vertices there are in the entire shape. The second parameter specifies what data will be actually contained in the shape, in this case only the vertex coordinate data will be included. In our first program we defined this data in an array of floating point numbers, each set of three sequential numbers representing one vertex coordinate. This time we'll define the vertex data in an array of **Point3f** objects, each **Point3f** being one vertex coordinate:

```
Point3f[] cubeCoordinates = {new Point3f( 1.0f, -1.0f,  1.0f),
                             new Point3f( 1.0f,  1.0f,  1.0f),
                             new Point3f(-1.0f,  1.0f,  1.0f),
                             new Point3f(-1.0f, -1.0f,  1.0f),
                             new Point3f(-1.0f, -1.0f, -1.0f),
                             new Point3f(-1.0f,  1.0f, -1.0f),
                             new Point3f( 1.0f,  1.0f, -1.0f),
                             new Point3f( 1.0f, -1.0f, -1.0f),
                             new Point3f( 1.0f, -1.0f, -1.0f),
                             new Point3f( 1.0f,  1.0f, -1.0f),
                             new Point3f( 1.0f,  1.0f,  1.0f),
                             new Point3f( 1.0f, -1.0f,  1.0f),
                             new Point3f(-1.0f, -1.0f,  1.0f),
                             new Point3f(-1.0f,  1.0f,  1.0f),
                             new Point3f(-1.0f,  1.0f, -1.0f),
                             new Point3f(-1.0f, -1.0f, -1.0f),
                             new Point3f( 1.0f,  1.0f,  1.0f),
                             new Point3f( 1.0f,  1.0f, -1.0f),
                             new Point3f(-1.0f,  1.0f, -1.0f),
                             new Point3f(-1.0f,  1.0f,  1.0f),
                             new Point3f(-1.0f, -1.0f,  1.0f),
                             new Point3f(-1.0f, -1.0f, -1.0f),
                             new Point3f( 1.0f, -1.0f, -1.0f),
                             new Point3f( 1.0f, -1.0f,  1.0f)};
```

In this case, we're defining 24 vertex coordinates (6 sides of the cube, each with 4 vertices). We next use these arrays to set the **QuadArray** data:

```
quadCube.setCoordinates(0, cubeCoordinates);
```

This sets the data for the shape using the array we've defined starting from the first data element of the array.

The IndexedQuadArray: defining quads

Now let's make the cube using the **IndexedQuadArray** class. This creates a set of quadrilateral faces from vertices, but the faces are defined by indices into an array of vertices. This allows a single vertex to be reused in more than one quadrilateral face, unlike the **QuadArray** which requires that each face is defined by a unique set of four consecutive vertices. Firstly an empty instance of an **IndexedQuadArray**:

```
IndexedQuadArray indexedCube = new IndexedQuadArray(8,
    IndexedQuadArray.COORDINATES | 24);
```

This defines that our shape has a total of 8 vertices, that we are only going to define the vertices and that we are going to specify 24 vertices (4 sides for each of the 6 faces) as shown in Figure 3.2.

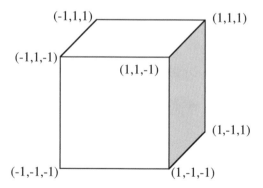

Figure 3.2 Vertex definitions for a cube.

We next create the array of vertices that will be used for our shape. In this case we only need eight of each since each vertex will be shared by three faces:

```
Point3f[] cubeCoordinates = {new Point3f( 1.0f, 1.0f, 1.0f),
                new Point3f(-1.0f, 1.0f, 1.0f),
```

```
new Point3f(-1.0f,-1.0f, 1.0f),
new Point3f( 1.0f,-1.0f, 1.0f),
new Point3f( 1.0f, 1.0f,-1.0f),
new Point3f(-1.0f, 1.0f,-1.0f),
new Point3f(-1.0f,-1.0f,-1.0f),
new Point3f( 1.0f,-1.0f,-1.0f)};
```

Next we need to define the indices into the vertex arrays. The coordinate index array consists of a set of integers, each set of four consecutive values specifying the positions in the coordinate array of the vertices of one side of the shape:

```
int coordIndices[] = {0,1,2,3,4,5,6,7,0,3,5,4,1,2,6,7,0,4,7,1,2,6,5,3};
```

We then define the shape from these by defining the vertices and the normals from this data:

```
indexedCube.setCoordinates(0, cubeCoordinates);
indexedCube.setCoordinateIndices(0, coordIndices);
```

When all this is put together, the function that creates the **Shape3D** node becomes:

```
protected Shape3D buildShape() {
    IndexedQuadArray indexedCube = new IndexedQuadArray(8,
    IndexedQuadArray.COORDINATES, 24);
    Point3f[] cubeCoordinates = { new Point3f( 1.0f, 1.0f, 1.0f),
                        new Point3f(-1.0f, 1.0f, 1.0f),
                        new Point3f(-1.0f,-1.0f, 1.0f),
                        new Point3f( 1.0f,-1.0f, 1.0f),
                        new Point3f( 1.0f, 1.0f,-1.0f),
                        new Point3f(-1.0f, 1.0f,-1.0f),
                        new Point3f(-1.0f,-1.0f,-1.0f),
                        new Point3f( 1.0f,-1.0f,-1.0f)};
    int coordIndices[] = {0,1,2,3,7,6,5,4,0,3,7,4,5,6,2,1,0,4,5,1,6,7,3,2};
    indexedCube.setCoordinates(0, cubeCoordinates);
    indexedCube.setCoordinateIndices(0, coordIndices);
    Shape3D cube = new Shape3D(indexedCube, new Appearance());
    return cube;
}
```

If we use this in place of the 'buildShape' procedure in the program from Chapter 2, we get the same output as shown in Figure 3.3. Now let us consider one final one to create the cube, this time using triangles.

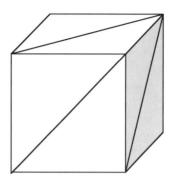

Figure 3.3 *A cube with the faces made from triangles*

Using triangles: the IndexedTriangleArray

Using triangles to create geometry is important because triangles are guaranteed to be coplanar, and we can do this by using the **IndexedTriangleArray** class. The vertices will be the same as for the **IndexedQuadArray**, but we will connect these together to form a total of 12 triangles, as shown in Figure 3.3. We first create the geometry object:

```
IndexedTriangleArray indexedCube = new IndexedTriangleArray(8,
IndexedTriangleArray.COORDINATES, 36);
```

This time the number of vertices is the same but the number of indices has increased to 36 since each face of the six faces is made up of two triangles and each triangle obviously has three vertices. Then the data array that will be used to define the triangles is created:

```
int coordIndices[] = {0,1,2,2,3,0,6,5,4,4,7,6,0,4,1,4,5,1,7,3,2,6,7,2,4,0,3,4,3,7,1,5,6,1,6,2};
```

Finally we use the data arrays to set the vertex and index data exactly as before:

```
indexedCube.setCoordinates(0, cubeCoordinates);
indexedCube.setCoordinateIndices(0, coordIndices);
```

The complete function, that again would replace the original 'buildShape' function in our first program, is:

```
protected Shape3D buildShape() {
    IndexedTriangleArray indexedCube = new IndexedTriangleArray(8
    IndexedTriangleArray.COORDINATES,36);
    Point3f[] cubeCoordinates = { new Point3f( 1.0f, 1.0f, 1.0f),
                                  new Point3f(-1.0f, 1.0f, 1.0f),
                                  new Point3f(-1.0f,-1.0f, 1.0f),
                                  new Point3f( 1.0f,-1.0f, 1.0f),
                                  new Point3f( 1.0f, 1.0f,-1.0f),
                                  new Point3f( 1.0f,-1.0f,-1.0f),
                                  new Point3f(-1.0f,-1.0f,-1.0f),
                                  new Point3f(-1.0f, 1.0f,-1.0f)};
    int coordIndices[] = {0,1,2,2,3,0,6,5,4,4,7,6,0,4,1,4,5,1,7,3,2,6,7,2,4,0,3,4,3,7,1,5,6,1,6,2};
    indexedCube.setCoordinates(0, cubeCoordinates);
    indexedCube.setCoordinateIndices(0, coordIndices);
    return new Shape3D(indexedCube, new Appearance());
}
```

The output of the program should again be as shown in Figure 2.4.

You will by now have realised that, as for any graphics library, creating shapes is a tedious business. Anything other than relatively trivial geometry will be complex and it will be easy to introduce errors into the model. Hence, we need a better way to introduce geometric models into our programs. Fortunately, there are several 'loaders' that allow us to load predefined geometric models from files into our code. We will now look at two examples of such loaders.

Loading pre-made geometric models

There are a number of libraries that enable your Java 3D program to load geometric models, some developed by Sun and included in the Java 3D distribution and some developed by third parties. We'll look at two examples, one for Wavefront Object ('OBJ') files and one for Lightwave3D scenes and objects.

The Wavefront Object (or 'OBJ') loader

The Wavefront Object file format has a relatively simple structure allowing polygon meshes to be defined along with associated material properties. We'll look at how a simple cube like the one we've been using as our basic example is defined in an 'OBJ' file:

```
v  1.0 1.0 1.0
v -1.0 1.0 1.0
v -1.0 -1.0 1.0
v 1.0 -1.0 1.0
v 1.0 1.0 -1.0
v -1.0 1.0 -1.0
v -1.0 -1.0 -1.0
v 1.0 -1.0 -1.0

f 1 2 3 4
f 8 7 6 5
f 1 4 8 5
f 6 7 3 2
f 1 5 6 2
f 7 8 4 3
```

In this, lines starting with a 'v' indicate a vertex definition, the *x*, *y* and *z* coordinates being defined by the following three numbers. The lines starting with an 'f' define the faces and are indices into the list of vertices. This time, the vertices are numbered starting from 1 as opposed from 0 in the Java 3D shape definitions. The data given above should be stored in a simple text file.

To import this into a Java 3D program we need to import the loaders:

```
import com.sun.j3d.loaders.*;
import com.sun.j3d.loaders.objectfile.*;
```

This in fact imports all the classes from the **loader** library, which will suffice even though we will only be using three of the classes in this first example. What we need to do is to replace the code that generates the cube data manually with the code that will read in the 'OBJ' file data. The code to do this is:

```
protected Node buildCube() {
    ObjectFile f = new ObjectFile();
    Scene s = null;
    try {
        s = f.load(filename);
    } catch (Exception e) {
        System.exit(1);
    }

    return s.getSceneGroup();
}
```

Note that this time we are returning a **Node** rather than a **Shape3D**. The first line of the function creates a new **ObjectFile** object. This is the object that actually loads the data. The next line creates a null **Scene** object that will be used to store the information extracted from the file and provide an interface to access the data. The next **try** structure uses the **load** function of the **ObjectFile** object to create the scene object, exiting the program if there is an exception during this process. Assuming the load process is successful, the last line of the function uses the **getSceneGroup** to access the group node that forms the root of the object structure. This is then returned and can be added to the scene hierarchy as before.

If you try and add this to your original code from Chapter 2 as we have with other code fragments in this chapter, you will not see any output when you run the program. This is because the shapes created by the loader have a default appearance and are to be used in scenes with lights in. The programs we have used so far ignored the lighting aspect and used a default flat shaded colour for their surface. We will study the way lights work and interact with surfaces in Chapter 4, so for now we'll create the minimum lighting so we can see our objects. We do this by creating a new function:

```
protected void addLights(BranchGroup b) {
    BoundingSphere bounds = new BoundingSphere(new Point3d(0.0,0.0,0.0), 100.0);
    Color3f ambientColour = new Color3f(1.0f, 1.0f, 1.0f);
    AmbientLight ambLight = new AmbientLight(ambientColour);
    ambientLight1.setInfluencingBounds(bounds);
```

```
    b.addChild(ambLight);
}
```

This basically creates a sphere of influence for the light, creates a colour (in this case white), creates an ambient light and then adds this to the **BranchGroup** passed to the function. To use this in the main program we add the line:

```
addLights(contentBranch);
```

This should be included in the 'buildContentBranch' function. The complete program is therefore:

```
import com.sun.j3d.loaders.*;
import com.sun.j3d.loaders.objectfile.*;
import javax.media.j3d.*;
import javax.vecmath.*;
import java.awt.*;
import java.awt.event.*;

public class ObjectLoader extends Frame implements ActionListener {
    protected Canvas3D myCanvas3D = new Canvas3D(null);
    protected Button myButton = new Button("Exit");
    protected String filename = null;

    protected BranchGroup buildViewBranch(Canvas3D c) {
        BranchGroup viewBranch = new BranchGroup();
        Transform3D viewXfm = new Transform3D();
        viewXfm.set(new Vector3f(0.0f,0.0f,10.0f));
        TransformGroup viewXfmGroup = new TransformGroup(viewXfm);
        ViewPlatform myViewPlatform = new ViewPlatform();
        PhysicalBody myBody = new PhysicalBody();
        PhysicalEnvironment myEnvironment = new PhysicalEnvironment();
        viewXfmGroup.addChild(myViewPlatform);
        viewBranch.addChild(viewXfmGroup);
        View myView = new View();
        myView.addCanvas3D(c);
        myView.attachViewPlatform(myViewPlatform);
        myView.setPhysicalBody(myBody);
        myView.setPhysicalEnvironment(myEnvironment);
        return viewBranch;
    }

    protected void addLights(BranchGroup b) {
        BoundingSphere bounds = new
            BoundingSphere(new Point3d(0.0,0.0,0.0), 100.0);
```

```
            Color3f ambientColour = new Color3f(1.0f, 1.0f, 1.0f);
            AmbientLight ambtLight = new
                            AmbientLight(ambientColour);
            ambLight.setInfluencingBounds(bounds);
            b.addChild(ambLight);
    }

    protected BranchGroup buildContentBranch(Node shape) {
            BranchGroup contentBranch = new BranchGroup();
            Transform3D rotateCube = new Transform3D( );
            rotateCube.set(new AxisAngle4d(1.0,1.0,0.0,Math.PI/4.0));
            TransformGroup rotationGroup = new
                            TransformGroup(rotateCube);
            contentBranch.addChild(rotationGroup);
            rotationGroup.addChild(shape);
            AddLights(contentBranch);
            return contentBranch;
    }

    protected Node buildCube() {
            ObjectFile f = new ObjectFile();
            Scene s = null;
            try {
                    s = f.load(filename);
            } catch (Exception e) {
                    System.exit(1);
            }
            return s.getSceneGroup();
    }

    public void actionPerformed(ActionEvent e) {
            dispose();
            System.exit(0);
    }

    public ObjectLoader(String args[]) {
            if (args.length > 0) {
                    filename = args[0];
                    VirtualUniverse myUniverse = new VirtualUniverse();
                    Locale myLocale = new Locale(myUniverse);
                    myLocale.addBranchGraph(
                                    buildViewBranch(myCanvas3D));
                    myLocale.addBranchGraph(
```

```
                                        buildContentBranch(buildCube()));
            setTitle("ObjectLoader");
            setSize(400,400);
            setLayout(new BorderLayout());
            add("Center", myCanvas3D);
            myButton.addActionListener(this);
            add("South", myButton);
            setVisible(true);
        }
    }


    public static void main(String[] args) {
        ObjectLoader sw = new ObjectLoader(args);
    }
}
```

If you compile and run this you need to supply a command line argument, e.g. to run the program and read in our simple cube file you would type:

`java ObjectLoader cube.obj`

This will give the output shown in Figure 3.4, the default surface assigned to our cube is a mid-grey colour.

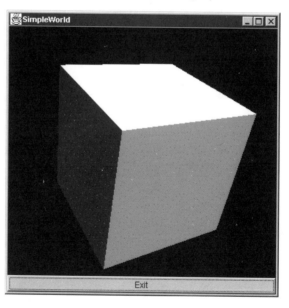

Figure 3.4 A cube loaded from a Wavefront Object file.

Obviously this procedure can be used to load geometry from many different files into the same program. Also, we can create the geometry using 3D design packages such as 3D Studio Max or Lightwave3D and export these to the 'OBJ' file format. Plate 2 shows the program with a more complex model loaded.

The loader actually only supports a subset of the Wavefront Object format, but it does support different materials for different groups of polygons, and even textures. This is an extract from a file that uses different materials:

```
usemtl red
f 1/1/1 2/2/1 3/3/1 4/4/1
f 8/4/2 7/1/2 6/2/2 5/3/2
f 1/2/3 4/3/3 8/4/3 5/1/3
f 6/2/4 7/3/4 3/4/4 2/1/4
f 1/4/5 5/1/5 6/2/5 2/3/5
f 7/2/6 8/3/6 4/4/6 3/1/6
```

The **usemtl** line names a material that will be used for the face definitions that follow until the next **usemtl** statement. Each vertex has three index values, the first is the vertex, the second the texture coordinate and the last is the normal. The material must be defined in a separate material file. This example uses some of the predefined material definitions that are part of the **ObjectFile** class. The full file is given in Appendix A.

Loading entire scenes of objects using the Lightwave3D loader

The **ObjectFile** class allows us to load individual objects, but the **Lw3dLoader** class goes one step further. It allows us to load an entire scene of objects, together with some animation in the Lightwave3D 5.5 format. To do this we import the required classes:

```
import com.sun.j3d.loaders.lw3d.*;
import com.sun.j3d.loaders.*;
```

We then use this to load in the scene data in a similar way as for the 'OBJ' file, except that this time we are loading an entire scene:

```
protected Node buildCube() {
    Lw3dLoader I = new Lw3dLoader();
    Scene s = null;
    try {
        s = I.load(filename);
    }
    catch (Exception e) {
        System.exit(1);
    }
    return s.getSceneGroup();
}
```

The **getSceneGroup** returns the root node of the entire scene, i.e. a group node above the individual objects. If we want to access an individual object, we use the **getObject** function. Here's an extract from a Lightwave3D scene file that loads a particular object:

```
LoadObject heraldbody.lwo
ShowObject 8 7
```

This loads an object and labels it 'heraldbody'. We then access this particular geometry by setting a **TransformGroup** to the root of that particular geometry structure:

```
TransformGroup carXfmNode = new TransformGroup();
carXfmNode = I.getObject("heraldbody");
```

After this, the node 'carXfmNode' will allow us to manipulate the geometry defined in the 'heraldbody.lwo' file. A Lightwave scene loaded into Java 3D is shown in Plate 3.

Another feature of the **Lw3dLoader** is that it will import animations. Only simple key-framed animations can be loaded, and this is incorporated into the Java 3D automatically by adding an interpolator to the objects involved. Plate 4 shows a scene that contains a rotating object running in Java 3D. This is achieved within the loader class, but we will look at how interpolators can be used to add animation on their own in Chapter 6.

Summary

In this chapter we've learnt how to create different geometry types. The basic geometry types in the utility library should allow you to create many of the simple shapes that you need, and the other arrays-type classes enable you to produce any kind of shape that you need, albeit at the expense of some coding complexity. The final option, that of loading in predefined geometry from external files is perhaps the most useful for anything other than trivial systems since it allows you to create very complex shapes using external 3D editing packages for import into your programs.

Up to this point we have ignored the lighting aspect of the scene, only adding lights to show us the geometry and not considering the effect on the scene or the objects' surface properties. The next chapter looks at these issues and allows us to create visually more interesting scenes.

Chapter 4

Lighting and Appearance

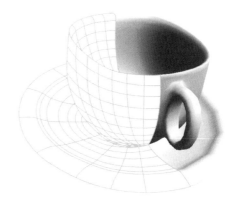

Introduction

To actually see the objects in the scene we need a light source. Up to now we've either ignored this fact or have included simple lights just to allow us to see the shape of the objects that we have created. We are now going to look at how we can define lights and materials to give the objects in the scene a more realistic appearance. We'll start by looking at the way the lighting model works in Java 3D, which like the other features we've looked at so far doesn't stray very far from that used in other existing graphics systems. We'll follow this by looking at material features and then the light types and settings.

The lighting model

The way an object appears in the scene when the lighting model is used depends on two main components: the surface properties and the lights themselves. Both these are under our control, together with a number of other aspects of the rendering process.

Surfaces

There are a number of different components that contribute to the colour of the surface of an object. These are:

- **ambientColor**: This is the light that affects all surfaces equally. It has no real-world equivalent but is useful in modelling the real-world since there are rarely any areas that have no light at all falling in them, i.e. there are rarely completely black areas of shadow.

- **diffuseColor**: This is light that is reflected evenly from the surface independent of the angle that we are looking at the surface from, i.e. it is only dependent on the angle that the surface has to the light source.

- **specularColor**: This component is dependent both on the angle the surface has to the light **and** the viewer. It produces effects like the highlights that appear on shiny surfaces, such as polished pool or snooker balls. The highlights are also affected by another parameter of the surface, its **shininess**. This controls the size of the highlight.

- **emissiveColor**: For most materials this will not be used. It defines the amount of light produced by the surface, for example like that produced by lights themselves. Note that the 'emitted' light does not contribute to the illumination of the rest of the scene, it merely makes the surface itself 'glow'.

These components give us quite a sophisticated surface model. The actual colour that a surface appears to be is the result of these parameters combined with the colour and types of the lights in the scene.

Lights

There are a number of different lights that we have available. All lights have a colour based on the RGB model, and all can be switched on and off. The types of light are:

- **AmbientLight**: This lights all surfaces equally, and so is used with the ambient component of the material.

- **DirectionalLight**: This models a light source that is an infinite distance away, and so the light rays that it contributes to the scene are parallel. This can be used to simulate light from the Sun, since the light from this arrives in (practically) parallel rays.

- **PointLight**: Light from this is emitted equally in all directions from the point that is its position in space. It can be thought of as a perfect light bulb hanging from an invisible light cord.

- **SpotLight:** This models a realistic light that is similar to a real-world spotlight. It has a certain spread and fall-off and so can be closely controlled.

This set of lights gives us extremely good control over how the final scene will appear. We will now look at some of the detail of how the information from the light classes is combined with the surface information to perform the lighting calculations.

The lighting equation

Before we look at the actual equation that combines these elements to produce the final lighting value for a surface we'll look at how the geometry of the model is defined. Figure 4.1   shows the surface, a light source and the viewing position.

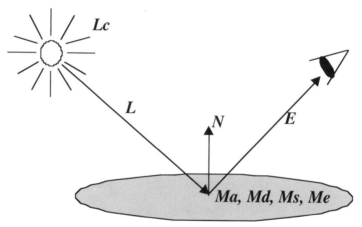

Figure 4.1 The geometry of the lighting model.

In this model, N is the normal vector to the surface (and so defines the way the surface is facing), Lc is the colour of the light, L is the direction of the light relative to the surface, E is the direction of the viewer's position relative to the surface and Ma, Md, Ms and Me are the ambient, diffuse, specular and emissive components of the surface respectively. The actual lighting equation that uses this model is:

$$Me + Ma. \sum_{i}^{NoOfAmbient} (Lc_i) + \sum_{i}^{NoOfLights} (atten_i \, spot_i.(diffuse_i + specular_i))$$

The first element is the emissive surface component and so is independent of any lights in the scene. The second element multiplies together the ambient surface component with the sum of all the ambient lights in the scene, each one contributing according to its colour. The last component is used for all other light types and we will consider each part of this separately.

The '*diff*' component consists of the following:

$$diffuse_i = (L_i \bullet N)Lc_i \, Md$$

The dot product of L_i (the light direction vector) and N (the surface normal) takes into account the angle of the surface to the light, the more the surface is angled towards the light the brighter this component will be. This factor is then merely multiplied by the colour of the light and the colour of the diffuse surface component.

The specular surface component is more complex:

$$specular_i = (S_i \bullet N)^{shininess}.Lc_i \, Ms$$

The dot product in this case takes into account both the direction of the light and the viewer. This is raised to the power of the shininess surface property, and this therefore controls the size of the highlight produced by this component. Finally, as for the diffuse component, the resulting factor is multiplied by the light colour and the surface (in this case, specular) colour.

The '*atten*' component represents the attenuation of the effect of the light. This breaks down into a number of parts:

$$atten_i = \frac{1}{Kc_i + Kl_i.d_i + Kq_i \, d_i^2}$$

There are therefore three components to the attenuation, a constant one (Kc_i), a linear one that increases with the distance of the light from the surface (Kl_i) and a quadratic one that increases with the square of the distance from the surface (Kq_i). The 'K' values are defined for each light as part of the light class itself. Directional lights do not exhibit attenuation so for these the *atten* value is set to 1.

The final component of the lighting equation is the *spot* component which takes into account the features that are unique to spotlights (and so is set to 1 for directional and point lights):

$$spot_i = \max\bigl((-L_i \bullet D_i),0\bigr)^{spotexp_i}$$

This states that the *spot* value is zero when the light is pointing away from the surface, but otherwise depends on the angle between the light and the surface, raised to a power that takes into account the spread of the spotlight, its focus, etc.

So you can see that the lighting model is quite sophisticated and gives control over many different aspects of the scene's final appearance. Fortunately, these are quite easy to control by use of the light and material classes. We'll now change the appearance of our cube by first altering its **Appearance** and then adding and adjusting some light properties.

The Appearance class

In the programs that we have written so far we have only ever created **Appearance** objects with the default settings. We now want to be more specific in our programs, and to do this we need to look at the structure of the **Appearance** class.

The **Appearance** class has a number of attributes which control the way an object appears. These are:

- **ColoringAttributes:** This is used to define the colour used when there is no lighting defined. This is actually the attribute that has been affecting the appearance of our objects so far, which is why they have appeared white (the default setting for this) and very 'flat'. It also defines the *way* in which the colour information is used to shade the object. This is defined in a *shading model*, and can be either **SHADE_FLAT** or **SHADE_GOURAUD**. There are two other settings, **FASTEST** and **NICEST**, which select the quickest and most realistic shading models respectively. These last two options are implementation independent.

- **LineAttributes**: This defines the way lines appear on the object. This has different components, such as the line pattern (e.g. **PATTERN_SOLID**, the default, or PATTERN_DASH), the line width and whether anti-aliasing is used.

- **PointAttributes**: This specifies the way points are drawn. It can be used to set the size of the points and whether they use anti-aliasing or not.

- **PolygonAttributes**: Using this we can define how the polygons in the shape are drawn. This can include **POLYGON_POINT**, **POLYGON_LINE** or **POLYGON_FILL** modes (the latter being the default). It has other components, including a setting that defines whether we ignore or include back-facing polygons which can be set to **CULL_NONE, CULL_BACK** or **CULL_FRONT**.

- **RenderingAttributes**: This controls aspects of the rendering process such as whether an alpha value is tested or whether an object is invisible in the current scene. Invisible objects are useful because they can still be 'picked' or collided with.

- **TransparencyAttributes**: As you would imagine, this controls the transparency of the object! We will not be looking at this feature in depth here.

- **Texture, TextureAttributes, TexCoordGeneration** and **TextureUnitState**: These attributes combined define the texture used when rendering the object. We will be looking at textures in more detail later in this chapter, so we will not consider them here.

- **Material:** This defines the basic material properties for the appearance of the object and represents the easiest way to change the colour of the surface of the object. It will be the main focus of the next section, but is only used when lighting is defined in the scene.

Next we'll go on to define a material, but let us pause briefly to look at how the **PolygonAttributes** class changes the way our shapes are displayed. The default setting for the draw mode is **POLYGON_FILL** and this has resulted in all our objects so far being drawn with filled polygons (i.e. they appear solid). Sometimes it is useful to draw the objects in a wire frame mode to see more easily how they are constructed or how they relate to other objects in the scene. To do this we need to create and use our own **PolygonAttributes** object and insert this into the **Appearance** object for our shape. Consider the code in our simple cube program that used the **Box** utility class:

```
return new Box(1.0f, 1.0f, 1.0f, new Appearance());
```

This used a default **Appearance**. Let's now change this to use a different drawing mode:

```
Appearance app = new Appearance();
PolygonAttributes polyAttr = new PolygonAttributes();
polyAttr.setPolygonMode(PolygonAttributes.POLYGON_LINE);
app.setPolygonAttributes(polyAttr);
return new Box(1.0f, 1.0f, 1.0f, app);
```

If we insert these lines in our first program and then compile and run it, we should get the output shown in Figure 4.2, i.e. only the edges of the polygons are drawn.

This shows that the **Box** utility class uses triangles to create the cube. If we also want to see the backward-facing polygons, we can turn off the back-face culling by inserting this line:

```
PolyAttr.setCullFace(PolygonAttributes.CULL_NONE);
```

This will produce the output given on the left of Figure 4.3, whilst using the value **CULL_FRONT** removes the front faces and produces the output shown on the right of Figure 4.3.

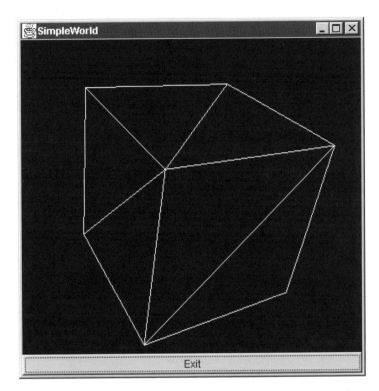

Figure 4.2 *A cube rendered using **POLYGON_LINE** mode.*

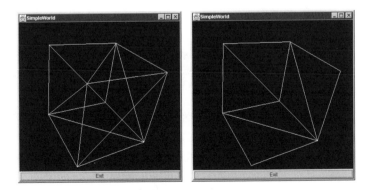

Figure 4.3 *Wireframe rendering with
no culling and front face culling.*

Using the Material class to define the surface

We'll now look at how we define the surface properties through a **Material** class. We first create a set of colours that we'll use in our **Material**. The class **Color3f** is used for this, which uses three floating point values to store the RGB components of the colour, 0.0 being fully off and 1.0 the maximum for each of the red, green and blue values:

```
Color3f ambientColour = new Color3f(1.0f, 1.0f, 1.0f);
Color3f diffuseColour = new Color3f(1.0f, 0.0f, 0.0f);
Color3f specularColor = new Color3f(1.0f, 1.0f, 1.0f);
Color3f emissiveColour= new Color3f(0.0f, 0.0f, 0.0f);
float shininess = 20.0f;
```

This sets the diffuse colour to pure red, the specular colour to pure white and the emissive colour to pure black (i.e. it has no emissive colour). The last line creates a floating point value for the shininess of the surface, which controls the size of the highlight as we discussed earlier. We next create an **Appearance** object and then a **Material** object that uses these colours and add this to the **Appearance**:

```
Appearance app = new Appearance();
Material redShiny = new Material(ambientColour, emissiveColour, diffuseColour,
                                         specularColour, shininess);
app.setMaterial(redShiny);
```

We can now use this in our original cube program in the same way as we did when we changed the draw mode to wireframe:

```
return new Box(1.0f, 1.0f, 1.0f, app);
```

This produces the output shown in Plate 5.

The output exhibits no sense of depth or highlights since there is only an ambient light and this acts on all surfaces evenly. To see the effect of the lighting equation we need to add directional, point or spot lights. Let's first add a directional light, and reduce the amount of ambient light so that we can see the effect of this:

```
protected void AddLights(BranchGroup b) {
    BoundingSphere bounds = new BoundingSphere(new Point3d(0.0,0.0,0.0), 100.0);
    Color3f ambientColour = new Color3f(0.2f, 0.2f, 0.2f);
    AmbientLight ambLight = new AmbientLight(ambientColour);
    ambientLight1.setInfluencingBounds(bounds);
    b.addChild(ambLight);
    Color3f dirColour = new Color3f(1.0f, 1.0f, 1.0f);
    Vector3f lightDir = new Vector3f(-1.0f, -1.0f,-1.0f);
    DirectionalLight dirLight = new DirectionalLight(dirColour,lightDir);
    dirLight.setInfluencingBounds(bounds);
    b.addChild(dirLight);
}
```

This produces the output shown in Plate 6.

We'll now change our basic shape to a sphere instead of a cube to look at how changing the lighting parameters alters the appearance. Replace the line that has the cube construction line with:

```
return new Sphere(2.0f, app);
```

This will give the output shown on the centre of Plate 7, which still has the *shininess* set to 20. The other two images in the same figure are the same sphere with the *shininess* set to 5 (on the left) and 100 (on the right). This shows how the shininess setting controls the size of the highlight.

Obviously, if we alter the other parameters these will have the expected effect on the surface, e.g. changing the specular colour will alter the colour of the highlight. Likewise, changing the colour of the light falling on the surface will have a corresponding result on the final image.

Adding more light types

Using the sphere as our reference object, we'll now go on to add some more lights of different types to see how they affect the scene.

Point lights

We've already discussed the properties of this type of light, so now let's add one to the scene. If we replace the **DirectionalLight** with a **PointLight**, then the effect will be more obvious. Since the point light exhibits attenuation, we need to define the parameters that control this. Recall that it has three attenuation variables, one for constant, one for linear attenuation and one for quadratic. Quadratic is the one that models the real world so we'll use this here. In practice, this is often too strong and you may want to use linear attenuation. Here is how we construct the light:

```
Color3f lightColour2 = new Color3f(1.0f, 1.0f, 1.0f);
Point3f lightPosition2 = new Point3f(1.5f, 1.5f, 1.5f);
Point3f lightAtten2 = new Point3f(0.0f, 0.0f, 1.0f);
Color3f ambientColour = new Color3f(0.2f, 0.2f, 0.2f);
PointLight light2 = new PointLight(lightColour2, lightPosition2,lightAtten2);
light2.setInfluencingBounds(bounds);
```

The two **Point3f** objects define the position of the light and its attenuation. The three components of the attenuation **Point3f** specify the constant, linear and quadratic attenuation respectively. The effect of replacing our directional light with this in our program is shown on the left of Plate 8. The image on the right shows the effect of the same light positioned at (3.0, 3.0, 3.0), i.e. twice as far away and shows how the effect of the light rapidly falls when using quadratic attenuation.

Spot lights

These are the most versatile and realistic light models. We'll replace our point light with one to see how its parameters affect the lighting:

```
Color3f lightColour2 = new Color3f(1.0f, 1.0f, 1.0f);
Point3f lightPosition2 = new Point3f(1.8f, 1.8f, 1.8f);
Point3f lightAtten2 = new Point3f(1.0f, 0.0f, 0.0f);
Vector3f lightDir2 = new Vector3f(-1.0f,-1.0f,-1.0f);
```

```
SpotLight light2 = new SpotLight(lightColour2, lightPosition2,lightAtten2, lightDir2,
                                  (float)(Math.PI/2.0), 0.0f);
light2.setInfluencingBounds(bounds);
```

The **SpotLight** constructor that we are using here takes 6 parameters. The first three are identical to the **PointLight** constructor that we used, i.e. they define the colour, position and attenuation of the light. The fourth parameter defines the direction in which the light is pointing. The fifth specifies the cone angle of the light, the actual angle being twice the value given. The final value represents the concentration of the light within the cone, and so gives a measure of how the light attenuates towards the edge of the cone relative to the centre. Here we have a cone angle of 90° and a concentration value of 0.0, meaning that there is no fall off towards the edge of the cone. The light has also been moved further from the sphere to (1.8, 1.8, 1.8) and the attenuation has been set to a constant value of 1. This is to make the effect more obvious when we alter the **SpotLight** parameters. The top-left image in Plate 9 shows the light with the settings given in the code above. The top-centre image has a cone angle of 30° and the top-right image has a cone angle of 15°. All of the images on the top row have the same concentration value of zero. The bottom row all have a cone angle of 45° but with different concentration values: 5.0 on the left, 20.0 in the centre and 50.0 on the right.

As a final exercise, we'll add a second spotlight in a different position to show how the effects of multiple lights combine. We'll set the properties of our first light back to have a spread of 90° and a concentration value of 0. Then we'll add a second light in front of the sphere pointing back towards it. We'll make the lights different colours, one blue and one green, and so that we can see their effect, change the sphere ambient and diffuse colours to white. The code for our two spotlights is:

```
Color3f blueColour = new Color3f(0.0f, 0.0f, 1.0f);
Point3f bluePosition = new Point3f(1.8f, 1.8f, 1.8f);
Point3f blueAtten = new Point3f(1.0f, 0.0f, 0.0f);
Vector3f blueDir = new Vector3f(-1.0f,-1.0f,-1.0f);
```

```
SpotLight blueLight = new SpotLight(blueColour, bluePosition,
                                    blueAtten, blueDir,
                                    (float)(Math.PI/2.0), 0.0f);
blueLight.setInfluencingBounds(bounds);
Color3f greenColour = new Color3f(0.0f, 1.0f, 0.0f);
Point3f greenPosition = new Point3f(0.0f, 0.0f, 3.0f);
Point3f greenAtten = new Point3f(1.0f, 0.0f, 0.0f);
Vector3f greenDir = new Vector3f(0.0f, 0.0f, -1.0f);
SpotLight greenLight = new SpotLight(greenColour, greenPosition,
                                     greenAtten, greenDir,
                                     (float)(Math.PI/2.0), 0.0f);
greenLight.setInfluencingBounds(bounds);
```

The result is shown in Plate 10.

Lighting geometry array objects

The shapes that we've used so far in this section have had the surface normals generated automatically by the geometry utility class constructors. We're now going to see how we specify normals for surfaces by returning to our cube constructed using the **IndexedQuadArray** class.

Recall how we constructed the cube in Chapter 3:

```
protected Shape3D buildShape() {
    IndexedQuadArray indexedCube = new IndexedQuadArray(8,
    IndexedQuadArray.COORDINATES, 24);
    Point3f[] cubeCoordinates = { new Point3f( 1.0f, 1.0f, 1.0f),
                        new Point3f(-1.0f, 1.0f, 1.0f),
                        new Point3f(-1.0f,-1.0f, 1.0f),
                        new Point3f( 1.0f,-1.0f, 1.0f),
                        new Point3f( 1.0f, 1.0f,-1.0f),
                        new Point3f(-1.0f, 1.0f,-1.0f),
                        new Point3f(-1.0f,-1.0f,-1.0f),
                        new Point3f( 1.0f,-1.0f,-1.0f)};
    int coordIndices[] = {0,1,2,3,7,6,5,4,0,3,7,4,5,6,2,1,0,4,5,1,6,7,3,2};
    indexedCube.setCoordinates(0, cubeCoordinates);
    indexedCube.setCoordinateIndices(0, coordIndices);
    Shape3D cube = new Shape3D(indexedCube, new Appearance());
    return cube;
}
```

In this we only defined the coordinates of each vertex and not the normals. This is indicated by the **IndexedQuadArray.COORDINATE** parameter in the constructor. We're now going to define the normals, so we have to change the constructor call to:

```
IndexedQuadArray indexedCube = new IndexedQuadArray(8,
  IndexedQuadArray.COORDINATES | IndexedQuadArray.NORMALS, 24);
```

We then need to define the data that we'll use to set our normals. We need six normals to create our cube, since each face has only one normal, i.e. it is a flat surface. This is shown in Figure 4.4.

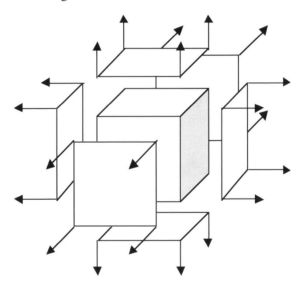

Figure 4.4 *The normals associated with the vertices of each cube face.*

Each normal is defined by a **Vector3f**, so we can create an array of six of these:

```
Vector3f[] normals={ new Vector3f( 0.0f, 0.0f, 1.0f),
                     new Vector3f( 0.0f, 0.0f,-1.0f),
                     new Vector3f( 1.0f, 0.0f, 0.0f),
                     new Vector3f(-1.0f, 0.0f, 0.0f),
                     new Vector3f( 0.0f, 1.0f, 0.0f),
                     new Vector3f( 0.0f,-1.0f, 0.0f)};
```

We then create the array of indices that point into this array, which takes the same form as the coordinate index array. This time, each group of four indices will have the same value since each vertex of each face points the same way:

```
int normalIndices[] = {0,0,0,0,1,1,1,1,2,2,2,2,3,3,3,3,4,4,4,4,5,5,5,5};
```

Finally, we need to use these for the normal data of the cube in a similar way that we do for the coordinate data:

```
indexedCube.setNormals(0,normals);
indexedCube.setNormalIndices(0, normalIndices);
```

As before, we need to set a material for the cube and add the lights to the scene so that the system uses the lighting algorithm. The *buildShape* function in its entirety is:

```
protected Node buildShape() {
    IndexedQuadArray indexedCube = new IndexedQuadArray(8,
            IndexedQuadArray.COORDINATES|IndexedQuadArray.NORMALS, 24);
    Point3f[] cubeCoordinates = { new Point3f( 1.0f, 1.0f, 1.0f),
                        new Point3f(-1.0f, 1.0f, 1.0f),
                        new Point3f(-1.0f,-1.0f, 1.0f),
                        new Point3f( 1.0f,-1.0f, 1.0f),
                        new Point3f( 1.0f, 1.0f,-1.0f),
                        new Point3f(-1.0f, 1.0f,-1.0f),
                        new Point3f(-1.0f,-1.0f,-1.0f),
                        new Point3f( 1.0f,-1.0f,-1.0f)};
    Vector3f[] normals = {new Vector3f( 0.0f, 0.0f, 1.0f),
                        new Vector3f( 0.0f, 0.0f,-1.0f),
                        new Vector3f( 1.0f, 0.0f, 0.0f),
                        new Vector3f(-1.0f, 0.0f, 0.0f),
                        new Vector3f( 0.0f, 1.0f, 0.0f),
                        new Vector3f( 0.0f,-1.0f, 0.0f)};
    int coordIndices[] = {0,1,2,3,7,6,5,4,0,3,7,4,5,6,2,1,0,4,5,1,6,7,3,2};
    int normalIndices[] = {0,0,0,0,1,1,1,1,2,2,2,2,3,3,3,3,4,4,4,4,5,5,5,5};
    indexedCube.setCoordinates(0, cubeCoordinates);
    indexedCube.setCoordinateIndices(0, coordIndices);
    indexedCube.setNormals(0,normals);
    indexedCube.setNormalIndices(0, normalIndices);
    Appearance app = new Appearance();
    Color3f ambientColour = new Color3f(1.0f,0.0f,0.0f);
    Color3f emissiveColour = new Color3f(0.0f,0.0f,0.0f);
    Color3f specularColour = new Color3f(1.0f,1.0f,1.0f);
    Color3f diffuseColour = new Color3f(1.0f,0.0f,0.0f);
```

```
float shininess = 20.0f;
app.setMaterial(new Material(ambientColour,emissiveColour,
                             diffuseColour,specularColour,shininess));
return new Shape3D(indexedCube, app);
}
```

If you insert this in place of the existing *buildShape* function in your program and then compile and run it you should get the output shown in Plate 11, which is the same as the output when we use the **Box** utility class. So why bother? Well, we have specified each normal ourselves to point in the direction of the face, so we can, if we want, define the normals to point in any direction we desire.

Let's demonstrate this by changing the normals of the cube faces so that there is effectively only one normal for each corner of the cube. This means that each face will share its normals with the adjacent faces and so the system will try and shade the cube as if it is a smooth shape with no hard edges. Figure 4.5 shows how we are going to specify the normals.

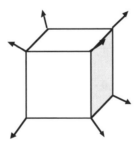

Figure 4.5   Direction of shared cube normals for smooth shading.

To do this, we'll change the vertex normal data and indices to:

```
Vector3f[] normals= {new Vector3f( 1.0f, 1.0f, 1.0f),
                     new Vector3f(-1.0f, 1.0f, 1.0f),
                     new Vector3f(-1.0f,-1.0f, 1.0f),
                     new Vector3f( 1.0f,-1.0f, 1.0f),
                     new Vector3f( 1.0f, 1.0f,-1.0f),
                     new Vector3f(-1.0f, 1.0f,-1.0f),
                     new Vector3f(-1.0f,-1.0f,-1.0f),
```

new **Vector3f**(1.0f,-1.0f,-1.0f)};
int normalIndices[] = {0,1,2,3,7,6,5,4,0,3,7,4,5,6,2,1,0,4,5,1,6,7,3,2};

Note that we have 8 normals now, one for each corner of the cube. If we use this data instead of the original in our program we should get the output shown in Plate 12, showing that the system has shaded the surfaces as if they blended smoothly. The edges are no longer distinct and if it wasn't for the outline it would be difficult to see it was a cube!

Using textures

The use of textures on 3D shapes can add a great deal of realism at little rendering cost when compared to increasing the polygon data. For example, simulating wood grain would involve lots of polygons with different shades of brown to produce a realistic look. If we instead map an image of wood grain onto the surface we immediately have a convincing wood effect with no increase in the number of polygons in the scene. There is an overhead at rendering time since we need to access the texture image when we render the object, but many operations (such as back-face culling or view-volume clipping) are unaffected. Since this is so useful we'll now look at how to implement this in Java 3D.

Textures in Java 3D

Textures are implemented via the **Texture**, **Texture-Attributes**, **TexCoordGeneration** and **TextureUnitState** classes in the **Appearance** node. These classes define the image used, the texture coordinates, the mapping method, etc. Defining the texture mapping for an object in Java 3D is a complex task and so we'll consider the basic requirements here for 2D texture mapping, although Java 3D supports 3D texture mapping as well.

The images used must be a power of 2 in each dimension. This is a common requirement with graphics systems and it allows the system to manipulate the images efficiently. Many different image formats can be used, but for most purposes either GIF or JPG images should be suitable. The texture mapping uses a vertex-based scheme whereby we must define the texture coordinates for each face vertex of a shape. Figure 4.6 shows how this works in practice.

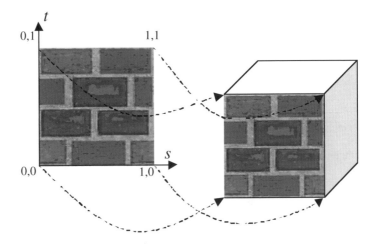

Figure 4.6 Mapping scheme using per-vertex texture coordinates.

Creating and applying a texture

There are a number of operations that we have to perform to achieve this effect. Because of this, we'll move the definition of the **Appearance** to its own procedure. The first thing we have to do is create a **TextureLoader** object that will actually load the texture image:

```
TextureLoader textLoad = new TextureLoader("brick.jpg", this);
```

The constructor has two arguments. The first is the name of the image file that is to be loaded. The second is used to enable the loading process. The **TextureLoader** object uses classes from the Java AWT to perform the actual loading, and this requires an object from the AWT to be involved in the image loading process. When we pass the **this** argument we are saying that the main class (which extends the **Frame** class) is the AWT component that is to be used in the loading process. We needn't bother ourselves any further with this here, as using the main class is sufficient to achieve loading of the image. We next need to create an image component that can be used in the texture process and copy the contents of the loaded image into this:

```
ImageComponent2D textImage = textLoad.getImage();
```

We then create the actual 2D texture class and specify that we want to use the image we have just loaded:

```
Texture2D texture = new Texture2D(Texture2D.BASE_LEVEL,
                    Texture2D.RGB, textImage.getWidth(), textImage.getHeight());
texture.setImage(0, textImage);
```

The first argument of the **Texture2D** constructor states that the texture mapping only uses a base-level image. It is possible to have a multi-level mapping for which multiple images would have to be defined, but we will only consider single level mapping here. The second argument states that the mapping mode will be RGB, i.e. the image will be used to define the RGB values of the surface. Alternatives include **RGBA** (RGB plus an alpha, or transparency, value), **ALPHA** and **LUMINANCE**. The final two arguments define the width and height of the image, and here we access this information directly from the image itself. The next line specifies the image is to be used in the texture as the base level image.

Now we need to create a set of attributes that will be used by the **Appearance** to define the texture:

```
TextureAttributes textAttr = new TextureAttributes();
textAttr.setTextureMode(TextureAttributes.REPLACE);
```

Here we are defining that the texture image will replace the colour of the surface. Alternatives are **BLEND, DECAL** and **MODULATE**. The complete function that creates our appearance is therefore:

```
protected Appearance DefineAppearance() {
    TextureLoader textLoad = new TextureLoader("brick.jpg", this);
    ImageComponent2D textImage = textLoad.getImage();
    Texture2D texture = new Texture2D(Texture2D.BASE_LEVEL,
                                      Texture.RGB,
                                      textImage.getWidth(),
                                      textImage.getHeight());
    texture.setImage(0, textImage);
    Appearance app = new Appearance();
    app.setTexture(texture);
    TextureAttributes textAttr = new TextureAttributes();
    textAttr.setTextureMode(TextureAttributes.REPLACE);
    app.setTextureAttributes(textAttr);
    app.setMaterial(new Material());
    return app;
}
```

To use this, we need to modify the *BuildShape* function to include the texture coordinate data. Before we do that, we need to specify that we will be using texture data in the **IndexedQuadArray** constructor:

```
IndexedQuadArray indexedCube = new IndexedQuadArray(8,
                        IndexedQuadArray.COORDINATES |
                        IndexedQuadArray.NORMALS |
                        IndexedQuadArray.TEXTURE_COORDINATE_2, 24);
```

This is created and used in a similar way to the coordinate and normal data. First we have to define a set of texture coordinates. These are the 2D coordinates that we will use to reference the image data. In this case, we will just use the four corners of the texture image, i.e. ranging from 0,0 to 1,1:

```
TexCoord2f[] textCoord = {new TexCoord2f(1.0f,1.0f),
                new TexCoord2f(0.0f,1.0f),
                new TexCoord2f(0.0f,0.0f),
                new TexCoord2f(1.0f,0.0f)};
```

We then create an array of indices that will map the texture coodinates to the vertices of the shape. In this first program we'll just define the coordinates for one face:

```
int textIndices[] = {0,1,2,3};
```

This says that the first texture coordinate will map onto the first vertex, the second onto the second, etc. Finally, we specify that the shape uses these two arrays for texture coordinates:

```
indexedCube.setTextureCoordinates(0,0,textCoord);
indexedCube.setTextureCoordinateIndices(0,0,textIndices);
```

The first argument in these specifies that the information applies to the first set of texture coordinates, although in this case we are only using one texture and so only need one set of coordinates. The second and third arguments are the same as in the **setCoordinates** and **setCoordinateIndices** methods, i.e. they define the starting position within the array and the array itself. The whole *BuildShape* function is now:

```
protected Shape3D buildShape() {
    IndexedQuadArray indexedCube = new IndexedQuadArray(8,
                        IndexedQuadArray.COORDINATES |
                        IndexedQuadArray.NORMALS |
                        IndexedQuadArray.TEXTURE_COORDINATE_2, 24);
    Point3f[] cubeCoordinates = {new Point3f( 1.0f, 1.0f, 1.0f),
                        new Point3f(-1.0f, 1.0f, 1.0f),
                        new Point3f(-1.0f,-1.0f, 1.0f),
                        new Point3f( 1.0f,-1.0f, 1.0f),
                        new Point3f( 1.0f, 1.0f,-1.0f),
                        new Point3f(-1.0f, 1.0f,-1.0f),
                        new Point3f(-1.0f,-1.0f,-1.0f),
                        new Point3f( 1.0f,-1.0f,-1.0f)};
    int coordIndices[] = {0,1,2,3,7,6,5,4,0,3,7,4,5,6,2,1,0,4,5,1,6,7,3,2};
    Vector3f[] normals= {new Vector3f( 0.0f, 0.0f, 1.0f),
                        new Vector3f( 0.0f, 0.0f,-1.0f),
                        new Vector3f( 1.0f, 0.0f, 0.0f),
                        new Vector3f(-1.0f, 0.0f, 0.0f),
                        new Vector3f( 0.0f, 1.0f, 0.0f),
                        new Vector3f( 0.0f,-1.0f, 0.0f)};
    int normalIndices[] = {0,0,0,0,1,1,1,1,2,2,2,2,3,3,3,3,4,4,4,4,5,5,5,5};
    TexCoord2f[] textCoord = {new TexCoord2f(1.0f,1.0f),
                        new TexCoord2f(0.0f,1.0f),
                        new TexCoord2f(0.0f,0.0f),
                        new TexCoord2f(1.0f,0.0f)};
    int textIndices[] = {0,1,2,3};
    indexedCube.setCoordinates(0, cubeCoordinates);
    indexedCube.setCoordinateIndices(0, coordIndices);
```

```
indexedCube.setNormals(0,normals);
indexedCube.setNormalIndices(0, normalIndices);
indexedCube.setTextureCoordinates(0,0,textCoord);
indexedCube.setTextureCoordinateIndices(0,0,textIndices);
return new Shape3D(indexedCube, DefineAppearance());
}
```

This program (when used with a suitable *brick.jpg* image file), produces the output shown in Plate 13, i.e. the texture only appears on the face for which we have specified the texture coordinates.

This texture is a little large for the face; we would like the bricks to appear smaller. We can do this by changing the texture coordinates. If we want the texture to be tiled twice in each direction, resulting in four copies of the texture image to be applied to the face, we merely change the texture coodinates so that they will be larger than the actual image. This will cause the pattern to be repeated in each direction:

```
TexCoord2f[] textCoord = {new TexCoord2f(2.0f, 2.0f),new TexCoord2f(0.0f, 2.0f),
                          new TexCoord2f(0.0f, 0.0f),new TexCoord2f(2.0f, 0.0f)};
```

We'd also like the texture to be on all the faces, so we need to add the correct coordinates to the texture index array:

```
int textIndices[] = {0,1,2,3,3,0,1,2,1,2,3,0,1,2,3,0,3,0,1,2,1,2,3,0};
```

If we change these lines and recompile and run the program we get the output shown in Plate 14.

Generating texture coordinates

In this example it was easy to generate the texture coordinates for each vertex since each face only had four vertices and it was obvious how the texture should map to these. With more complex geometry this is more difficult and time consuming to the point where it is impractical. In this case there are two options open to us. Either we can create the object with its texture mapping data in an external 3D authoring package and import it using a loader that supports textures (such as the **ObjectFile** loader we looked at earlier), or we can try and generate the textures automatically from the geometry in some way. Luckily, Java 3D provides a class to help us create automatic texture coordinates — the **TexCoordGeneration** class.

This class generates coordinates as best it can from the geometric data of the object using a linear mapping. To use this class in our program, we first create the necessary object:

```
TexCoordGeneration textCoorder = new TexCoordGeneration(
    TexCoordGeneration.OBJECT_LINEAR,
    TexCoordGeneration.TEXTURE_COORDINATE_2);
```

The first parameter states that we are going to use linear mapping in object space, which is what we would normally use. This means that the texture is fixed on the object, so that when we move the object the texture moves with it. The alternative is to use **EYE_LINEAR**, which uses the view coordinate system to perform the mapping. This means that the texture will be aligned relative to the viewer. The second parameter defines that we will be generating 2D coordinates, the option being **TEXTURE_COORDINATE_3** for 3D textures.

We then create our **Appearance** *app* as before, but add the line:

```
app.setTexCoordGeneration(textCoorder);
```

This tells the **Appearance** that we will be using the texture coordinate generator to create our texture coordinates. To use this in our *BuildShape* function, we must remove all references to texture coordinates since our **TexCoordGeneration** object will do this for us. We can also remove the normal data if we like, as the object will also generate these. Plate 15 shows three variations of using this. The left image shows the use of **OBJECT_LINEAR** mapping on a cube, the centre is **EYE_LINEAR** applied to a cube and the right is **OBJECT_LINEAR** applied to a sphere. As you can see, the texture mapping treats the whole object as one surface, so in the case of the cube the mapping is only correct for one of the sides. This is not always what you want, and the **TexCoordGeneration** object should be used with care.

There are many other options that you can use with textures in Java 3D, we have already mentioned the possibility of 3D textures, but you can also have different resolutions of textures on the same object. This is useful if you are going to view the object from a large distance *and* close up. Anybody who has played the computer game DOOM will know that if you get very close to some textures they look very pixelated and blocky. Conversely if you view a very detailed texture from a long distance you are at best wasting a large image file on a small screen area or at worst the texture exhibits aliasing. Java 3D allows you to combat this by using multiple texture resolutions. For now though, we'll content ourselves with being able to increase visual realism with 2D textures.

Summary

In this chapter, we have covered a lot of ground, looking at lighting equations, light models, basic materials and texture mapping. You should now be in a position to create realistic looking geometric objects, either from primitives in the utility library, from hard-coded geometry arrays or by loading in data created in external applications. You've seen how to surface them using basic colours and then apply textures mapped in various ways. We've also seen how to add different types of light to illuminate the surfaces. What nearly all the scenes we've looked at so far have in common is that they only had one geometric object in the scene. We're now going to look at some classes that allow us to group objects together in various ways.

Chapter

5

Groups and Transformations

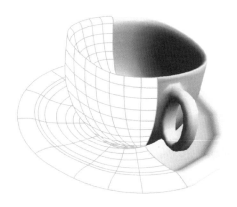

Introduction

To effectively construct and manipulate geometry, we need to be able to create hierarchies of object and form parent-child relationships. There are various ways that we can do this. We have already used the **TransformGroup** node in most of our programs so that we could rotate our objects slightly to give a better sense of perspective. In the programs we have written, the **TransformGroup** had only one child but they can of course have multiple children. There are other types of group that we'll look at in this chapter, including the **BranchGroup** (which we have also used) and the **Switch** class. We'll start by considering the **BranchGroup** since it has a number of special features.

The BranchGroup

We've already seen how the **BranchGroup** is used to add the scene content and the view definition parts of the scene graph hierarchy. This is one of the special uses of the **BranchGroup**; only an instance of this class can be inserted into **Locale**. It has some other useful properties though. When it is inserted in the scene graph anywhere other than attached to the **Locale** it can be detached from its parent. This can only occur when the field **ALLOW_DETACH** is set to true, and it is achieved by calling the method **detach**. The other important feature is that a **BranchGroup** can be *compiled*. Once a branch is compiled it is no longer possible to alter the contents of the branch, but there may be efficiency gains, for example by combining transformations in the branch. This is achieved by calling the **compile** function of the **BranchGroup**. We'll not consider this any further here, but bear in mind that if you are having performance problems, grouping static parts of the geometry together and compiling that part of the scene graph can be worthwhile.

The TransformGroup

We have already used this extensively, but now we'll look at it in detail. Table 5.1 shows the important methods of this class.

Table 5.1 A selection of the **TransformGroup** methods.

Method	Purpose
TransformGroup()	Constructs a **TransformGroup** with the identity transform
TransformGroup(Transform3D)	Constructs a **TransformGroup** with the given **Transform3D**
void addChild(Node)	Adds a child node at the end of the current children
void getChild(int)	Returns the child node at the position specified in the list of children
void insertChild(Node, int)	Inserts the node on the child list at the given position
void numChildren()	Returns the number of children
void removeChild(int)	Removes the child at the given position
void setChild(Node, int)	Replaces the child at the given index
void getTransform(Transform3D)	Sets the argument to the **Transform3D** of this group
void setTransform(Transform3D)	Sets the **Transform3D** of this group to the given parameter

Now we'll build up a hierarchy of shapes to form the scene to get a feel for the **TransformGroup** node. The hierarchy for this is shown in Plate 1. We'll start by creating the circular building in the centre of the scene, together with the 'ground' on which it stands:

```
BranchGroup theScene = new BranchGroup();

Appearance groundApp = new Appearance();
Color3f groundColour = new Color3f(0.0f, 0.5f, 0.0f);
groundApp.setMaterial(new Material(groundColour,emissiveColour,
                    groundColour, specularColour, shininess));
Transform3D grndXfm = new Transform3D();
grndXfm.set(new Vector3f(0.0f, -1.0f, 0.0f));
TransformGroup grndXfmGrp = new TransformGroup(grndXfm);
Box ground = new Box(100.0f, 0.1f, 100.0f, groundApp);
grndXfmGrp.addChild(ground);
```

```
theScene.addChild(grndXfmGrp);

Appearance wallApp = new Appearance();
Color3f emissiveColour = new Color3f(0.0f, 0.0f, 0.0f);
Color3f specularColour = new Color3f(0.5f, 0.5f, 0.5f);
Color3f wallColour = new Color3f(0.5f, 0.5f, 0.5f);
float shininess = 10.0f;
wallApp.setMaterial(new Material(wallColour, emissiveColour,
                                 wallColour, specularColour, shininess));
TransformGroup house = new TransformGroup();
Cylinder walls = new Cylinder(1.0f, 1.0f,Cylinder.GENERATE_NORMALS, wallApp);
house.addChild(walls);

Appearance roofApp = new Appearance();
Color3f roofColour = new Color3f(0.5f,0.0f,0.0f);
roofApp.setMaterial(new Material(roofColour, emissiveColour,
                                 roofColour, specularColour, shininess));
Transform3D roofXfm = new Transform3D();
roofXfm.set(new Vector3f(0.0f,1.0f,0.0f));
TransformGroup roofXfmGrp = new TransformGroup(roofXfm);
Cone myRoof = new Cone(1.0f, 1.0f, Cone.GENERATE_NORMALS, roofApp);
roofXfmGrp.addChild(myRoof);
house.addChild(roofXfmGrp);
```

We can then go on to create the rest of the scene, the full program for which is given in Appendix A.

The obvious advantage to this is that we can move whole groups of objects without major changes to the program structure.

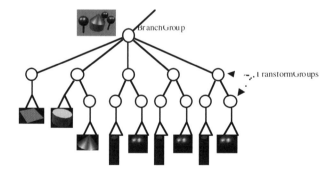

Figure 5.1 Content branch of scene graph of simple primitives.

If we change the contents of the **TransformGroup** *house* we move the walls and the house at the same time. This will prove useful later when we look at behaviours and interaction since it will allow us to move groups of objects around relative to each other from another part of the program.

The component of the **TransformGroup** that defines the actual Transformation is an instance of the class **Transform3D**. This is a very flexible representation of a 3D transformation and can be set to many different values in a fairly intuitive way. In the example above, we have just used it to define translations by using the version of the **set** function that takes 3 floating point values representing the *x*, *y* and *z* components. Table 5.2 shows that there are many different versions of the **Transform3D** constructor to define different types of transformations. Once an instance has been created, the data in the **Transform3D** can also be altered in a number of ways, either by setting the data or by performing a number of mathematical operations. Table 5.2 also shows some of these functions.

To see how we can use some of these methods we'll construct a simple application to rotate a cube when we click on a button. We start by declaring our class as in our previous examples:

```
public class SimpleTransform extends Frame implements ActionListener {
    protected Canvas3D myCanvas3D = new Canvas3D(null);
    protected Button exitButton = new Button("Exit");
    protected Button leftButton = new Button("<-");
    protected Button rightButton = new Button("->");
    protected TransformGroup rotationGroup;
```

In addition to our previous declarations, we also declare two other buttons which we'll use to rotate our object. We also declare the **TransformGroup** here that we'll be using later to define the rotation. The next bit we need to adapt is our *buildContentBranch*:

Table 5.2 Some of the more useful **Transform3D** methods.

Method	Purpose
Transform3D()	Creates an identity transform
Transform3D(float[])	Creates a transform from 16 values. Data fills the matrix from top left, row by row
Transform3D(Matrix3f, Vector3f, float)	Creates a transform from a matrix representing a rotation, a vector representing a translation and a number representing a scale factor
Transform3D(Quat4f, Vector3f, float)	The data represents a quaternion, a translation and a scale
Transform3D(Transform3D)	Creates a duplicate of a transform
void invert()	Inverts the transform
void transpose()	Transposes the transform matrix
void add(Transform3D)	Adds the argument to the transform
void sub(Transform3D)	Subtracts the argument from the transform
void mul(double)	Multiplies each element by the scalar
void mul(Transform3D)	Multiplies the transform by the given transform
void rotX(double) void rotY(double) void rotZ(double)	Sets the transform to a counter-clockwise rotation in radians about the appropriate axis
void set(AxisAngle4f)	Sets the transform to the rotation equivalent to the argument
void set(double)	Sets the transform to the equivalent of a matrix scaling of the argument
void set(float[])	Fills the transform matrix with the array values
void set(float, Vector3f)	Sets the transform to represent a scale and a translation
void set(Matrix3f, Vector3f, float)	The arguments represent a rotation, a translation and a scale
void set(Quat4f)	Sets the transform to the quaternion
void set(Vector3f)	The argument represents a translation
void setRotation(AxisAngle4f) void setRotation(Matrix3f) void setRotation(Quat4f)	Sets the rotation element of the transform to the rotation represented by the argument leaving the rest of the matrix unchanged
void setScale(Vector3d) void setScale(double)	Sets the scale elements of the transform to the value represented by the argument
void setTranslation(Vector3f)	Redefines the translation element of the transform matrix

```
protected BranchGroup buildContentBranch(Node shape) {
    BranchGroup contentBranch = new BranchGroup();
    Transform3D rotateCube = new Transform3D( );
    rotateCube.set(new AxisAngle4d(1.0,1.0,0.0,Math.PI/4.0));
```

```
rotationGroup = new TransformGroup(rotateCube);
rotationGroup.setCapability(
                TransformGroup.ALLOW_TRANSFORM_READ);
rotationGroup.setCapability(
                TransformGroup.ALLOW_TRANSFORM_WRITE);
contentBranch.addChild(rotationGroup);
rotationGroup.addChild(shape);
AddLights(contentBranch);
return contentBranch;
}
```

This creates the **TransformGroup** and sets the capabilities such that we can both read the current value of the **Transform3D** associated with it and write the transform. The correct action now has to be defined for each of the buttons so that the shape rotates. This is done by 'getting' the current value of the transform, creating a new **Transform3D** that stores the additional rotation, multiplying the current value by the additional transform and then 'setting' it back to the **TransformGroup** node:

```
public void actionPerformed(ActionEvent e) {
    if (e.getSource() == exitButton) {
        dispose();
        System.exit(0);
    } else if (e.getSource() == leftButton) {
        Transform3D temp = new Transform3D();
        rotationGroup.getTransform(temp);
        Transform3D tempDelta = new Transform3D();
        tempDelta.rotY(-0.3);
        temp.mul(tempDelta);
        rotationGroup.setTransform(temp);
    } else if (e.getSource() == rightButton) {
        Transform3D temp = new Transform3D();
        rotationGroup.getTransform(temp);
        Transform3D tempDelta = new Transform3D();
        tempDelta.rotY(0.3);
        temp.mul(tempDelta);
        rotationGroup.setTransform(temp);
    }
}
```

Finally, we modify the constructor for the class to include the buttons:

```
public SimpleTransform() {
    VirtualUniverse myUniverse = new VirtualUniverse();
    Locale myLocale = new Locale(myUniverse);
    myLocale.addBranchGraph(buildViewBranch(myCanvas3D));
    myLocale.addBranchGraph(buildContentBranch(buildShape()));
    setTitle("SimpleWorld");
    setSize(400,400);
    setLayout(new BorderLayout());
    Panel bottom = new Panel();
    bottom.add(leftButton);
    bottom.add(rightButton);
    bottom.add(exitButton);
    add(BorderLayout.CENTER, myCanvas3D);
    add(BorderLayout.SOUTH, bottom);
    exitButton.addActionListener(this);
    leftButton.addActionListener(this);
    rightButton.addActionListener(this);
    setVisible(true);
}
```

The other functions, such as *addLights*, *buildViewBranch* and *buildShape* can be left as in our other programs. The output of this running, with a cube as the shape, is given in Figure 5.2.

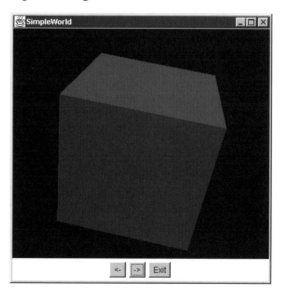

*Figure 5.2 Using the **TransformGroup** to rotate an object.*

The Switch class

This class has some of the properties of the other group nodes, such as the ability to add and remove children. What makes it unique is that only some of its children are rendered at any time, and which child or children is rendered can be selected. Let's create a shape that will switch between a cylinder and a cone:

```
Switch firstSwitch = new Switch(0);
firstSwitch.setCapability(Switch.ALLOW_SWITCH_WRITE);
firstSwitch.addChild(new Cylinder());
firstSwitch.addChild(new Cone());
```

This creates a switch with two children of different shapes. The zero argument to the **Switch** constructor states that we initially want the first child to be rendered. We also have to use the **setCapability** method with the parameter shown so that we can alter which node is rendered by writing the selection value into the **Switch**. There are two methods to access the values that define which child is rendered: **getWhichChild**, which returns an integer defining which child is currently displayed and **setWhichChild** which takes an integer parameter to set the rendered child. Figure 5.3 shows a simple application that allows switching between geometric shapes by clicking on the appropriate buttons; the source code for this is given in Appendix A.

We can also define that several children are rendered at once.

We will meet the **Switch** node again when we look at behaviours in Chapter 7.

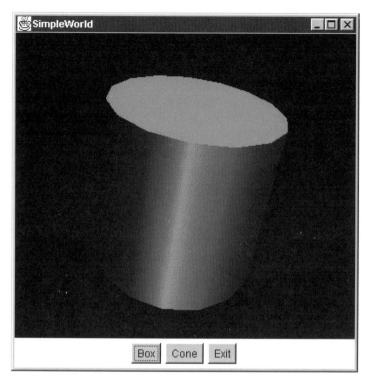

Figure 5.3 *Simple application that uses the* **Switch** *node.*

Summary

This chapter has introduced classes that allow us to group objects of our scene graph to create a hierarchy, position them and swap between different parts of the hierarchy. We'll use some of these classes in most of our programs.

Chapter

6

Animation

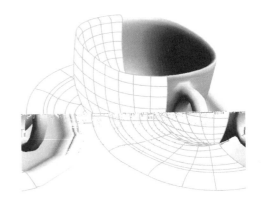

Introduction

The applications that we've created so far have been static. Programs of this type are of minimal interest and severely limit the type of applications that we can produce. To create more interesting programs we're going to need some kind of dynamic content, and the two primary ways to do this are through *animation* and *interaction*. We'll look at animation now and at interaction in Chapter 7.

The easiest way to perform animation is through a family of classes called *interpolators*. These allow you to change certain non-geometric aspects of shapes, such as their position or colour. They work by taking two or more given states, e.g. two colours, and interpolating the parameter defined between the given values. The way in which the interpolation is carried out can be specified by a number of simple parameters, and the result is similar to that achieved in animation systems that use 'key-framing'.

Another way to animate a shape is to cause it to 'morph' into another shape. This is possible in Java 3D through the use of the **Morph** class, which takes multiple **GeometryArrays** and interpolates between them. We'll look at this later in the chapter, but we'll start by looking at some interpolators.

Interpolators and their features

One of the simplest types of behaviour that you'll come across is one that moves an object between two positions or states. This is achieved by instances of subclasses of the **Interpolator** class. There are many types of interpolator, including:

- **PositionInterpolator**: interpolates between two positions in a similar way to key-framing in animation systems.
- **RotationInterpolator**: interpolates between two orientations, again like key-framing.
- **ScaleInterpolator**: the same for scaling of an object.
- **ColorInterpolator**: interpolates between two colours.

So far, we've looked at types of interpolators, but we next need to consider how we control the interpolation process. This is through *Alpha values*.

Alpha values

Interpolators use two mappings to control the interpolation process. The first maps time to an intermediate *alpha* value, whilst the second maps the *alpha* value to a value corresponding to the type of interpolator, e.g. a transform or a colour. The *alpha* value varies from 0.0 to 1.0 over a given time interval. The way the *alpha* value is generated is controlled by a number of parameters:

- Trigger time: the time at which the whole process begins.
- Phase delay: the time before the initial *alpha* change (attack).
- Increasing ramp time: the time for the increasing alpha value.
- At-one time: the time for the constant high alpha value.
- Decreasing ramp time: the time for the decreasing alpha value.
- At-zero time: the time for the constant low alpha value.

This is shown diagrammatically in Figure 6.1. The change in *alpha* can occur once or can be made to loop.

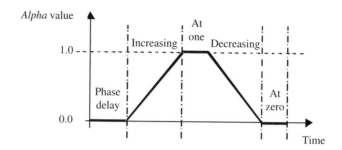

Figure 6.1 *Variation of the alpha value with time.*

A rotation interpolator example

Let's now look at a simple example that will cause a shape to rotate. First, we create the *alpha* generator. This is an instance of the class **Alpha**:

```
Alpha rotationAlpha = new Alpha(-1, Alpha.INCREASING_ENABLE,0, 0, 4000, 0, 0, 0, 0, 0 );
```

The first parameter defines the number of times that the generator will loop. A value of -1 means that it will loop forever. The second parameter defines the mode. This can be one of:

- **INCREASING_ENABLE.** This changes the meaning of the other parameters to be active or non-active. Those active for this mode are:
  - ➢ **increasingAlphaDuration**: defines the period of time during which alpha goes from zero to one.
  - ➢ **increasingAlphaRampDuration**: defines the period of time during which the alpha step size increases at the beginning of the **increasingAlphaDuration**.
  - ➢ **alphaAtOneDuration**: defines the period of time that alpha stays at one.
- **DECREASING_ENABLE.** The active parameters for this mode are:

> ➢ **decreasingAlphaDuration**: defines the period of time during which alpha goes from one to zero.
> ➢ **decreasingAlphaRampDuration**: defines the period of time during which the alpha step size decreases at the end of the decreasingAlphaDuration.
> ➢ **alphaAtZeroDuration**: the period of time that alpha stays at zero.
- The OR'ed value of both the above: all the parameters are active.

The next parameter is the trigger time. This is in milliseconds and represents the time since the system start time that this object first triggers. The fourth parameter is the phase delay duration, and represents the number of milliseconds that are waited after trigger time before starting the generation of alpha values. The final parameters are those discussed in the description of the modes, and they are in order: **increasingAlphaDuration**, **increasingAlphaRampDuration**, **alphaAtOneDuration**, **decreasingAlphaDuration**, **decreasingAlphaRampDuration** and **alphaAtZeroDuration**.

All this is difficult to comprehend without looking at some examples! In the example above, we have the following values:

- **loopCount** = -1: generator will loop indefinitely
- **mode** = INCREASING_ENABLE: parameters enabled as above
- **triggerTime** = 0: generator will be triggered immediately
- **phaseDelayDuration** = 0: no delay between trigger occurring and generator starting
- **increasingAlphaDuration** = 4000: time taken for *alpha* to go from 0.0 to 1.0 - enabled in this mode
- **increasingAlphaRampDuration** = 0: this means that the *alpha* step size remains the same during the process – enabled in this mode

- **alphaAtOneDuration** = 0: *alpha* doesn't hold at 1.0 for any period
- **decreasingAlphaDuration** = 0: time taken for *alpha* to go from one to zero – not enabled in this mode
- **decreasingAlphaRampDuration** = 0: constant step process for the change from 1.0 to 0.0 – not enabled in this mode
- **alphaAtZeroDuration** = 0: *alpha* doesn't hold at zero for any period

This means that alpha will change from 0.0 to 1.0 at a constant rate over a period of 4000 milliseconds, starting immediately and repeating indefinitely. The next thing we have to do is create the interpolator itself:

```
RotationInterpolator rotator = new RotationInterpolator(rotationAlpha,
                                    objTrans, yAxis,0.0f, (float)Math.PI*2.0f );
```

This creates a rotation interpolator that uses the alpha generator we defined above in the first parameter. The second parameter is the **TransformGroup** that is affected by the output of this *alpha* generator. The third parameter defines the axis about which the rotation will occur, expressed as a rotation relative to the *y*-axis. The fourth parameter is the minimum angle of rotation, zero, and the final parameter is the maximum angle, in this case the radian equivalent of 360 degrees.

The next thing to do is to create the bounding volume. We want the behaviour to be active all the time, so we create a spherical bounding volume that contains all the components of our scene:

```
BoundingSphere bounds =      new BoundingSphere(new Point3d( 0.0, 0.0, 0.0 ), 100.0 );
```

This creates a spherical volume of radius 100 centred on the origin. We then use this to set the scheduling bounds of the interpolator:

```
rotator.setSchedulingBounds( bounds );
```

Finally, we add the interpolator into our scene graph in the same branch of the scene as our objects that are being affected by the behaviour:

```
objTrans.addChild( rotator );
```

We should now put all this together with our previous example of the simple cube.

Full example

```
import javax.media.j3d.*;
import javax.media.j3d.*;
import javax.vecmath.*;
import java.awt.*;
import java.awt.event.*;
import com.sun.j3d.utils.geometry.*;

public class SimpleRotator extends Frame implements ActionListener {
    protected Canvas3D myCanvas3D = new Canvas3D(null);
    protected Button exitButton = new Button("Exit");

    protected BranchGroup buildViewBranch(Canvas3D c) {
        BranchGroup viewBranch = new BranchGroup();
        Transform3D viewXfm = new Transform3D();
        viewXfm.set(new Vector3f(0.0f,0.0f,10.0f));
        TransformGroup viewXfmGroup = new TransformGroup(viewXfm);
        ViewPlatform myViewPlatform = new ViewPlatform();
        PhysicalBody myBody = new PhysicalBody();
        PhysicalEnvironment myEnvironment = new PhysicalEnvironment();
        viewXfmGroup.addChild(myViewPlatform);
        viewBranch.addChild(viewXfmGroup);
        View myView = new View();
        myView.addCanvas3D(c);
        myView.attachViewPlatform(myViewPlatform);
        myView.setPhysicalBody(myBody);
        myView.setPhysicalEnvironment(myEnvironment);
        return viewBranch;
    }

    protected void addLights(BranchGroup b) {
        BoundingSphere bounds = new BoundingSphere(new
                                Point3d(0.0,0.0,0.0), 100.0);
        Color3f ambLightColour = new Color3f(0.5f, 0.5f, 0.5f);
        AmbientLight ambLight = new AmbientLight(ambLightColour);
        ambLight.setInfluencingBounds(bounds);
        Color3f dirLightColour = new Color3f(1.0f, 1.0f, 1.0f);
```

```java
        Vector3f dirLightDir = new Vector3f(-1.0f, -1.0f, -1.0f);
        DirectionalLight dirLight = new DirectionalLight(dirLightColour, dirLightDir);
        dirLight.setInfluencingBounds(bounds);
        b.addChild(ambLight);
        b.addChild(dirLight);
    }


    protected BranchGroup buildContentBranch(Node shape) {
        BranchGroup contentBranch = new BranchGroup();
        Transform3D rotateCube = new Transform3D( );
        TransformGroup rotationGroup = new TransformGroup(rotateCube);
        rotationGroup.setCapability(TransformGroup.ALLOW_TRANSFORM_WRITE);
        Alpha rotationAlpha = new Alpha(
        -1,Alpha.INCREASING_ENABLE,0,0,4000,0,0,0,0,0);
        Transform3D yAxis = new Transform3D();
        RotationInterpolator rotator = new
            RotationInterpolator(rotationAlpha, rotationGroup,
                    yAxis, 0.0f, (float) Math.PI*2.0f);
        BoundingSphere bounds = new BoundingSphere(new
                    Point3d(0.0,0.0,0.0), 100.0);
        rotator.setSchedulingBounds(bounds);
        contentBranch.addChild(rotationGroup);
        rotationGroup.addChild(shape);
        rotationGroup.addChild(rotator);
        addLights(contentBranch);
        return contentBranch;
    }
    protected Node buildShape() {
        Appearance app = new Appearance();
        Color3f ambientColour = new Color3f(1.0f,0.0f,0.0f);
        Color3f emissiveColour = new Color3f(0.0f,0.0f,0.0f);
        Color3f specularColour = new Color3f(1.0f,1.0f,1.0f);
        Color3f diffuseColour = new Color3f(1.0f,0.0f,0.0f);
        float shininess = 20.0f;
        app.setMaterial(new Material(ambientColour,emissiveColour,
                                    diffuseColour,specularColour,shininess));
        return new Box(2.0f, 2.0f, 2.0f, app);
    }


    public void actionPerformed(ActionEvent e) {
        if (e.getSource() == exitButton) {
            dispose();
            System.exit(0);
        }
```

```
        }

    public SimpleRotator() {
        VirtualUniverse myUniverse = new VirtualUniverse();
        Locale myLocale = new Locale(myUniverse);
        myLocale.addBranchGraph(buildViewBranch(myCanvas3D));
        myLocale.addBranchGraph(buildContentBranch(buildShape()));
        setTitle("SimpleRotator");
        setSize(400,400);
        setLayout(new BorderLayout());
        Panel bottom = new Panel();
        bottom.add(exitButton);
        add(BorderLayout.CENTER, myCanvas3D);
        add(BorderLayout.SOUTH, bottom);
        exitButton.addActionListener(this);
        setVisible(true);
    }

    public static void main(String[] args) {
        SimpleRotator sw = new SimpleRotator();
    }
}
```

If this is compiled and run, you should see a rotating cube spinning about the *y*-axis.

The other interpolators that operate in a similar way are the **ColorInterpolator**, **TransparencyInterpolator**, **PositionInterpolator**, and the **ScaleInterpolator**. These take a start and an end value for a transparency, a colour, a position and a scale respectively and produce an interpolation between those values according to a given *alpha* value. More complex types of interpolator are derivatives of the **PathInterpolator** class.

PathInterpolator classes

These classes take a set of values and interpolate between these values. Each of these varies one or more components of an associated **TransformGroup**, and the way that the variation happens is defined by a series of 'knot' values and

Essential Java 3D *fast*

an *alpha* generator. The *alpha* value (which as before varies from 0.0 to 1.0) is mapped to the interpolation key transforms (i.e. the translation, rotation, scale, etc.) by associated key values for each transform. Figure 6.2 shows how a path interpolator can be used to vary the position (given by the T values) of an object.

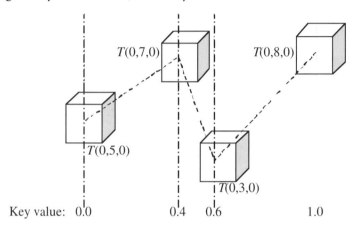

Figure 6.2 *Varying the object translation using a PositionPathInterpolator.*

The classes are:

- **PositionPathInterpolator.** Takes a series of translations and modifies its associated **TransformGroup.**
- **RotationPathInterpolator.** Takes a set of rotations and modifies the **TransformGroup** appropriately.
- **RotPosPathInterpolator.** Changes both the translation and the rotation according to the given set of transforms.
- **RotPosScalePathInterpolator.** Changes the translation, rotation and scale.

To see how these work, we'll write a program using the most complex class, the **RotPosScalePathInterpolator.**

We need to construct a set of rotation, position and scale values to use with the interpolator, an *alpha* generator and the interpolator. When we create the **RotPosScale-**

PathInterpolator, we associate it with the **Transform-Group** of the object and set the scheduling bounds. Here's the code for a function we can add to our code:

```
/** Create an interpolator that affects the position, scale and rotation of a transform group */
protected RotPosScalePathInterpolator createInterpolator(TransformGroup TG) {
    //Create the alpha generator as before
    Alpha RPSAlpha = new Alpha(-1, Alpha.INCREASING_ENABLE, 0,0,4000,0,0,0,0,0);
    //The knot values specify how the transforms map to the alpha values
    float[] knots = {0.0f,0.1f,0.8f,1.0f};
    //The scale values
    float[] scales = {1.0f,0.5f,2.0f,1.0f};
    //Rotations defined as quaternions
    Quat4f[] rotations = {new Quat4f(0.0f,0.0f,0.0f,0.0f),new Quat4f(0.0f,1.0f,0.0f,0.0f),
                          new Quat4f(0.0f,2.0f,0.0f,0.0f),
                          new Quat4f(1.0f,0.0f,1.0f,0.0f)};
    //Positions expressed as points in 3D space
    Point3f[] positions = {new Point3f(0.0f,0.0f,0.0f),new Point3f(-1.0f,0.0f,0.0f),
                           new Point3f(0.0f,1.0f,0.0f),
                           new Point3f(0.0f,0.0f,0.0f)};
    //The axis that the transformations are relative to
    Transform3D yAxis = new Transform3D();
    RotPosScalePathInterpolator RPSInterpolator =
                new RotPosScalePathInterpolator(RPSAlpha,TG,yAxis,knots,
                                                rotations,positions,scales);
    //Now we create the bounding region within which the interpolator
    //works, in this case a sphere big enough to enclose the entire scene
    BoundingSphere bounds = new BoundingSphere(new Point3d(0.0,0.0,0.0), 100.0);
    RPSInterpolator.setSchedulingBounds(bounds);
    return RPSInterpolator;
}
```

This function takes a **TransformGroup** and applies the interpolator to it before returning the new **RotPosScalePathInterpolator**. This must be added as a child of the content branch **BranchGroup**. If you compile and run this you should see that your chosen shape moves, changes size and rotates in a repetitive way.

What you should notice from this is that the motion isn't very smooth. This is because the *alpha* value has step changes, i.e. it suddenly starts changing after the phase delay, increases linearly and then suddenly stops changing and remains at one, as shown in Figure 6.1. We can make things change more smoothly by using the ramp duration values. We can set **increasingAlphaRampDuration** to any value up to half of the **increasingAlphaDuration** value and the change will be smoothed during this period. For example, if we change the declaration of our **Alpha** object:

Alpha RPSAlpha = **new Alpha**(-1, **Alpha.INCREASING_ENABLE**,0,2000,4000,0,0,0,0,0);

then the graph of the *alpha* value will be as shown in Figure 6.3.

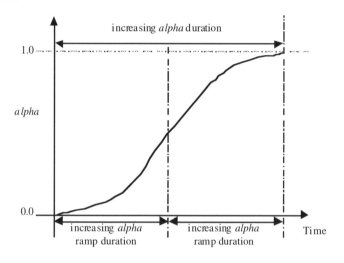

Figure 6.3 *Change of alpha value using a non-zero increasing ramp duration value.*

This gives a 'slow-in-slow-out' type motion that is common in animation.

As we've already stated, interpolators allow you to change non-geometric features of a shape. If we want to change the actual shape of the object we need to use the **Morph** class, which we'll look at now.

Performing 3D morphing

Morphing in 3D is now a common feature in computer animation. Anyone who has seen *Terminator 2: Judgement*

Day will remember the way in which the main villain changed shape at will, metamorphosizing between various shapes. This morphing process is also used in less obvious areas, such as character animation to change the facial expression of a character. As such, it would be nice to be able to do this in Java 3D, and fortunately there is a class designed to allow you to do just this: the **Morph** class.

The **Morph** class doesn't actually perform any animation. What it does do is to create a shape that is the result of the weighted combination of a number of key shapes. Each key shape must be a **GeometryArray** and must contain the same number of vertices. A floating point weight value for each key shape is used to specify how strongly the shape affects the final result, with weights adding up to 1.0. An example of how this works is shown in Figure 6.4.

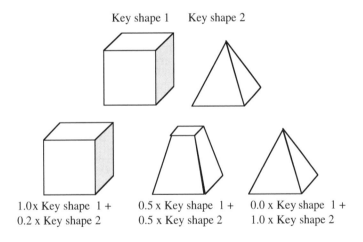

Key shape 1   Key shape 2

1.0x Key shape 1 +   0.5 x Key shape 1 +   0.0 x Key shape 1 +
0.2 x Key shape 2   0.5 x Key shape 2   1.0 x Key shape 2

Figure 6.4 *How the key shapes and weight values define a shape.*

To use this we need to change the weight values. In the next chapter we'll see how we can do this automatically, but for our first morph example we'll change the values manually in a similar way to how we demonstrated the switch node.

To start with we need to make two shapes, the cube and the pyramid. We already know how to make the cube, and the pyramid is the same but with the four vertices of the top face coincident. We need to build it this way so that it has six vertices like the cube. Here's the code to create the pyramid:

```
IndexedQuadArray indexedPyramid = new IndexedQuadArray(8,
    IndexedQuadArray.COORDINATES|IndexedQuadArray.NORMALS,24);
    Point3f[] pyramidCoordinates = {new Point3f( 0.0f, 1.0f, 0.0f),
                        new Point3f(0.0f, 1.0f, 0.0f),
                        new Point3f(-1.0f,-1.0f, 1.0f),
                        new Point3f( 1.0f,-1.0f, 1.0f),
                        new Point3f( 0.0f, 1.0f,0.0f),
                        new Point3f(0.0f, 1.0f,0.0f),
                        new Point3f(-1.0f,-1.0f,-1.0f),
                        new Point3f( 1.0f,-1.0f,-1.0f)};
Vector3f[] pyramidNormals= {new Vector3f( 0.0f, 0.0f, 1.0f),
                        new Vector3f( 0.0f, 0.0f,-1.0f),
                        new Vector3f( 1.0f, 0.0f, 0.0f),
                        new Vector3f(-1.0f, 0.0f, 0.0f),
                        new Vector3f( 0.0f, 1.0f, 0.0f),
                        new Vector3f( 0.0f,-1.0f, 0.0f)};
int pyramidCoordIndices[] = {0,1,2,3,7,6,5,4,0,3,7,4,5,6,2,1,0,4,5,1,6,7,3,2};
int pyramidNormalIndices[] = {0,0,0,0,1,1,1,1,2,2,2,2,3,3,3,3,4,4,4,4,5,5,5,5};
indexedPyramid.setCoordinates(0, pyramidCoordinates);
indexedPyramid.setNormals(0,pyramidNormals);
indexedPyramid.setCoordinateIndices(0, pyramidCoordIndices);
indexedPyramid.setNormalIndices(0, pyramidNormalIndices);
```

We then create an array of our shapes to use with our **Morph** object:

```
GeometryArray[] theShapes = new GeometryArray[2];
theShapes[0] = indexedCube;
theShapes[1] = indexedPyramid;
```

Next we need to actually create the **Morph** object. We'll do this in a separate function:

```
protected Morph createMorph(GeometryArray[] theShapes, Appearance app) {
    myMorph = new Morph(theShapes,app);
    myMorph.setWeights(weights);
    myMorph.setCapability(Morph.ALLOW_WEIGHTS_READ);
    myMorph.setCapability(Morph.ALLOW_WEIGHTS_WRITE);
```

```
        return myMorph;
}
```

We then add the **Morph** created by this function to the scene graph. Finally, we need to add two buttons that will allow us to change the weight values:

```
public void actionPerformed(ActionEvent e) {
    if (e.getSource() == exitButton) {
        dispose();
        System.exit(0);
    } else if (e.getSource() == cubeButton) {
        if (weights[0] <= 0.9) {
            weights[0] += 0.1;
            weights[1] -= 0.1;
            myMorph.setWeights(weights);
        }
    } else if (e.getSource() == pyraButton) {
        if (weights[1] <= 0.9) {
            weights[0] -= 0.1;
            weights[1] += 0.1;
            myMorph.setWeights(weights);
        }
    }
}
```

This then changes the weights in increments of 0.1, keeping the total weighting at 1.0, according to the button pressed. The whole program is given here:

```
import javax.media.j3d.*;
import javax.media.j3d.*;
import javax.vecmath.*;
import java.awt.*;
import java.awt.event.*;

public class SimpleMorph extends Frame implements ActionListener {
    protected Canvas3D myCanvas3D = new Canvas3D(null);
    protected Button cubeButton = new Button("Cube");
    protected Button pyraButton = new Button("Pyramid");
    protected Button exitButton = new Button("Exit");
    protected Morph myMorph;
    protected double[] weights = {0.5,0.5};

    protected BranchGroup buildViewBranch(Canvas3D c) {
```

```java
        BranchGroup viewBranch = new BranchGroup();
        Transform3D viewXfm = new Transform3D();
        viewXfm.set(new Vector3f(0.0f,0.0f,5.0f));
        TransformGroup viewXfmGroup = new TransformGroup(viewXfm);
        ViewPlatform myViewPlatform = new ViewPlatform();
        PhysicalBody myBody = new PhysicalBody();
        PhysicalEnvironment myEnvironment = new PhysicalEnvironment();
        viewXfmGroup.addChild(myViewPlatform);
        viewBranch.addChild(viewXfmGroup);
        View myView = new View();
        myView.addCanvas3D(c);
        myView.attachViewPlatform(myViewPlatform);
        myView.setPhysicalBody(myBody);
        myView.setPhysicalEnvironment(myEnvironment);
        return viewBranch;
    }


    protected void addLights(BranchGroup b) {
        BoundingSphere bounds =
                            new BoundingSphere(new Point3d(0.0,0.0,0.0), 100.0);
        Color3f ambLightColour = new Color3f(0.5f, 0.5f, 0.5f);
        AmbientLight ambLight = new AmbientLight(ambLightColour);
        ambLight.setInfluencingBounds(bounds);
        Color3f dirLightColour = new Color3f(1.0f, 1.0f, 1.0f);
        Vector3f dirLightDir = new Vector3f(-1.0f, -1.0f, -1.0f);
        DirectionalLight dirLight =
            new DirectionalLight(dirLightColour, dirLightDir);
        dirLight.setInfluencingBounds(bounds);
        b.addChild(ambLight);
        b.addChild(dirLight);
    }


    protected Morph createMorph(GeometryArray[] theShapes, Appearance app) {
        myMorph = new Morph(theShapes,app);
        myMorph.setWeights(weights);
        myMorph.setCapability(Morph.ALLOW_WEIGHTS_READ);
        myMorph.setCapability(Morph.ALLOW_WEIGHTS_WRITE);
        return myMorph;
    }


    protected BranchGroup buildContentBranch() {
        Appearance app = new Appearance();
        Color3f ambientColour = new Color3f(1.0f,0.0f,0.0f);
        Color3f emissiveColour = new Color3f(0.0f,0.0f,0.0f);
```

```
Color3f specularColour = new Color3f(1.0f,1.0f,1.0f);
Color3f diffuseColour = new Color3f(1.0f,0.0f,0.0f);
float shininess = 20.0f;
app.setMaterial(new Material(ambientColour,emissiveColour,
                            diffuseColour,specularColour,shininess));
IndexedQuadArray indexedCube = new IndexedQuadArray(8,
    IndexedQuadArray.COORDINATES | IndexedQuadArray.NORMALS, 24);
Point3f[] cubeCoordinates = {new Point3f( 1.0f, 1.0f, 1.0f),
                    new Point3f(-1.0f, 1.0f, 1.0f),
                    new Point3f(-1.0f,-1.0f, 1.0f),
                    new Point3f( 1.0f,-1.0f, 1.0f),
                    new Point3f( 1.0f, 1.0f,-1.0f),
                    new Point3f(-1.0f, 1.0f,-1.0f),
                    new Point3f(-1.0f,-1.0f,-1.0f),
                    new Point3f( 1.0f,-1.0f,-1.0f)};
Vector3f[] cubeNormals = { new Vector3f( 0.0f, 0.0f, 1.0f),
                    new Vector3f( 0.0f, 0.0f,-1.0f),
                    new Vector3f( 1.0f, 0.0f, 0.0f),
                    new Vector3f(-1.0f, 0.0f, 0.0f),
                    new Vector3f( 0.0f, 1.0f, 0.0f),
                    new Vector3f( 0.0f,-1.0f, 0.0f)};
int cubeCoordIndices[] = {0,1,2,3,7,6,5,4,0,3,7,4,5,6,2,1,0,4,5,1,6,7,3,2};
int cubeNormalIndices[] = {0,0,0,0,1,1,1,1,2,2,2,2,3,3,3,3,4,4,4,4,5,5,5,5};
indexedCube.setCoordinates(0, cubeCoordinates);
indexedCube.setNormals(0, cubeNormals);
indexedCube.setCoordinateIndices(0, cubeCoordIndices);
indexedCube.setNormalIndices(0, cubeNormalIndices);
IndexedQuadArray indexedPyramid = new IndexedQuadArray(8,
                        IndexedQuadArray.COORDINATES |
                        IndexedQuadArray.NORMALS, 24);
Point3f[] pyramidCoordinates = {new Point3f( 0.0f, 1.0f, 0.0f),
                        new Point3f(0.0f, 1.0f, 0.0f),
                        new Point3f(-1.0f,-1.0f, 1.0f),
                        new Point3f( 1.0f,-1.0f, 1.0f),
                        new Point3f( 0.0f, 1.0f,0.0f),
                        new Point3f(0.0f, 1.0f,0.0f),
                        new Point3f(-1.0f,-1.0f,-1.0f),
                        new Point3f( 1.0f,-1.0f,-1.0f)};
Vector3f[] pyramidNormals= {new Vector3f( 0.0f, 0.0f, 1.0f),
                        new Vector3f( 0.0f, 0.0f,-1.0f),
                        new Vector3f( 1.0f, 0.0f, 0.0f),
                        new Vector3f(-1.0f, 0.0f, 0.0f),
                        new Vector3f( 0.0f, 1.0f, 0.0f),
```

```
                                        new Vector3f( 0.0f,-1.0f, 0.0f)};
        int pyramidCoordIndices[] =
                {0,1,2,3,7,6,5,4,0,3,7,4,5,6,2,1,0,4,5,1,6,7,3,2};
        int pyramidNormalIndices[] = {0,0,0,0,1,1,1,1,2,2,2,2,3,3,3,3,4,4,4,4,5,5,5,5};
        indexedPyramid.setCoordinates(0, pyramidCoordinates);
        indexedPyramid.setNormals(0,pyramidNormals);
        indexedPyramid.setCoordinateIndices(0, pyramidCoordIndices);
        indexedPyramid.setNormalIndices(0, pyramidNormalIndices);
        GeometryArray[] theShapes = new GeometryArray[2];
        theShapes[0] = indexedCube;
        theShapes[1] = indexedPyramid;
        BranchGroup contentBranch = new BranchGroup();
        Transform3D rotateCube = new Transform3D( );
        rotateCube.set(new AxisAngle4d(1.0,1.0,0.0,Math.PI/4.0));
        TransformGroup rotationGroup =
                        new TransformGroup(rotateCube);
        contentBranch.addChild(rotationGroup);
        addLights(contentBranch);
        rotationGroup.addChild(createMorph(theShapes,app));
        return contentBranch;
    }

    public void actionPerformed(ActionEvent e) {
        if (e.getSource() == exitButton) {
            dispose();
            System.exit(0);
        } else if (e.getSource() == cubeButton) {
            if (weights[0] <= 0.9) {
                weights[0] += 0.1;
                weights[1] -= 0.1;
                myMorph.setWeights(weights);
            }
        } else if (e.getSource() == pyraButton) {
            if (weights[1] <= 0.9) {
                weights[0] -= 0.1;
                weights[1] += 0.1;
                myMorph.setWeights(weights);
            }
        }
    }

    public SimpleMorph() {
        VirtualUniverse myUniverse = new VirtualUniverse();
        Locale myLocale = new Locale(myUniverse);
```

```
        myLocale.addBranchGraph(buildViewBranch(myCanvas3D));
        myLocale.addBranchGraph(buildContentBranch());
        setTitle("SimpleMorph");
        setSize(400,400);
        setLayout(new BorderLayout());
        Panel bottom = new Panel();
        bottom.add(pyraButton);
        bottom.add(cubeButton);
        bottom.add(exitButton);
        add(BorderLayout.CENTER, myCanvas3D);
        add(BorderLayout.SOUTH, bottom);
        pyraButton.addActionListener(this);
        cubeButton.addActionListener(this);
        exitButton.addActionListener(this);
        setVisible(true);
    }

    public static void main(String[] args) {
        SimpleMorph sw = new SimpleMorph();
    }
}
```

Summary

We now know how to add simple animations to our applications using interpolators. This allows us to do many different types of animation, but each type is relatively simple. We have also seen how to vary the animation using different *alpha* generators. Finally we saw how to create morphs between shapes, but only by driving the morph process from user input. In the next chapter we'll look at how we can use *behaviours* to provide more advanced functionality, including the ability to drive morphing operations.

Chapter

7

Interaction and Behaviour

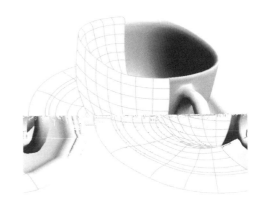

Introduction

In the previous chapter we learnt how to perform simple animation, but the programs we have written have supported no direct interaction with the 3D environment. We've created programs where we can change certain aspects of the objects by using buttons whose actions affect some of the scene graph, but by using the features of Java 3D we can support much richer animation and interaction.

Most dynamic elements that you'll want to incorporate in a scene will come through *behaviours*. There are a number of different classes that we will look at, all derived from the parent class **Behavior**. We'll first look at some features common to all behaviours before moving on to look at some examples.

Use of behaviours and their features

Behaviours can be used for many things. A behaviour can perform any kind of processing that you can do in Java, including modifying the scene graph (e.g. adding and deleting objects). Each behaviour has the following features:

- An **initialize** method. This is used to set up the data to be used in the behaviour.
- A **processStimulus** function. This carries out the actual processing of the behaviour, i.e. it's where the work is done.
- Scheduling bounds. This defines the region within which the behaviour is active in the same way that lights have an influence bounds. It is usually either a spherical or cubic region, and the behaviour becomes active when the user enters the bounding

volume. This allows you to define complex behaviours that only process data when the user is in the vicinity. If you need a behaviour that is active all the time, create a large spherical bounding volume that encloses the whole scene.

- Wake up criteria. These define when the behaviour starts. Even if the scheduling bounds cause the behaviour to be active, the wake up criteria specify whether the behaviour is active or not. Typical criteria would be:
  - A number of frames or milliseconds have elapsed.
  - An AWT component posts an event. An example of this would be the use of a mouse to move about an environment: the mouse event would trigger the behaviour and this would process the mouse data to change the position of the viewpoint.
  - A transform changes in a **TransformGroup**.
  - A shape collides with another shape. This can trigger a behaviour when a shape comes into collision or exits from a collision with another object, or moves whilst in collision with another object. The collision can either be based on object bounding volumes or the actual object geometry.
  - A view platform or sensor gets close. This can trigger a behaviour when either the viewer or a sensor enters into a region.

These are defined by using an instance of a subclass of **WakeupCriterion**. You can also combine wake up criteria using Boolean AND and OR operations to produce conditions. For example, in a game application a user may have to press two buttons within a set time limit. This would be implemented by having the trigger criterion as being near the first button. When this is satisfied, the condition becomes either the user being near the second button or a certain time elapsing. If the time elapses before the second button is pressed the condition reverts to the initial state. If the user comes into close proximity of the second button before the time elapses then the door is opened.

Behavior: the base behaviour class

This is an abstract class that defines the essential functions for all behaviours. The important functions that you'll use or override when you create your own behaviours are given in Table 7.1

Table 7.1 Important functions of the **Behavior** class.

Function	Purpose
initialize()	Called automatically when the behaviour is created.
void processStimulus(Enumeration)	Called when the wake up conditions are satisfied. This is where the processing for the behaviour is implemented.
void WakeupOn(WakeupCondition)	Sets the condition that triggers the **processStimulus** function.
void setEnable(boolean), boolean getEnable()	Access the boolean that defines whether the behaviour is active.
void setSchedulingBounds(Bounds), bounds getSchedulingBounds()	Access the bounds in which the behaviour is active.
void postId(int)	Use to signify through a unique integer that this behaviour has been triggered. Other behaviours can act on this.

When we create a behaviour we redefine the **initialize** method to set up any data and to specify the initial condition that triggers the behaviour using the **wakeupOn** method. We then redefine the **processStimulus** method to do the actual work required in our behaviour.

The wake up criteria

There are a number of different wake up conditions that can be used to trigger the behaviour to run. The constructors for these are given in Table 7.2.

Table 7.2 Some wake up criteria constructors.

Criterion	Trigger condition
WakeupOnElapsedTime(long)	Elapsed time is reached
WakeupOnElapsedFrames(int)	A number of frames has passed
WakeupOnAWTEvent(int)	An AWT event occurs
WakeupOnTransformChange(TransformGroup)	The transform of the given **TransformGroup** occurs
WakeupOnViewPlatformEntry(Bounds)	The **ViewPlatform** intersects with the given **Bounds**
WakeupOnViewPlatformExit	The **ViewPlatform** leaves the given **Bounds**
WakeupOnCollisionEntry(Node, int)	Given **Node** geometry collides with another object. The second parameter is either **USE_BOUNDS** or **USE_GEOMETRY**
WakeupOnCollisionExit(Node, int)	As above but when the geometry no longer collides
WakeupOnCollisionMovement(Node, int)	As above, but the geometry moves whilst still colliding
WakeupOnBehaviorPost(Behavior, int)	Another behaviour 'posts' the ID value
WakeupOnActivation()	The view volume enters the behaviour's scheduling bounds
WakeupOnDeactivation()	As above but when it leaves the bounds

As you can see there are a lot of options for triggering the behaviour. But we can do better than this as we have already mentioned, by AND'ing or OR'ing the criteria together. There are a number of classes to do this, as shown in Table 7.3.

Table 7.3 Classes that combine conditions.

Class	Condition generated
WakeupAnd(WakeupCriterion[ ])	The AND of all the given criteria
WakeupOr(WakupCriterion[ ])	The OR of all the given crieria
WakeupAndOfOrs(WakeupOr[ ])	The AND of the given OR's
WakeupOrOfAnds(WakeupAnd[ ])	The OR of the given AND's

We'll now look at an example of a simple behaviour class.

A first behaviour: simple morph

For our first behaviour, we'll create a class to drive the morphing operation that we developed in the previous chapter. We're going to create a class *SimpleMorphBehaviour* that is derived from the base behaviour class **Behavior**. This will take an *alpha* value and generate two weight values for our **Morph** object.

First we construct a new class that extends the **Behavior** class:

```
public class SimpleMorphBehaviour extends Behavior {
    ...
}
```

Then we define the data that we'll be using in this class to generate the weights from the *alpha* value:

```
protected Alpha theAlpha;
protected Morph theMorph;
protected double theWeights[] = new double[2]; //Weights for the Morph
protected boolean running = false; //Defines whether animation is running
protected WakeupCriterion[] wakeConditions;
protected WakeupOr oredConditions; //Used to combine the conditions
```

Next we'll define the **initialize** method to set up the data and necessary conditions:

```
public void initialize() {
    wakeConditions = new WakeupCriterion[2];
    wakeConditions[0] = new WakeupOnAWTEvent(KeyEvent.KEY_PRESSED);
    wakeConditions[1] = new WakeupOnElapsedTime(0);
    oredConditions = new WakeupOr(wakeConditions);
```

```
    wakeupOn (wakeConditions[0]);
}
```

This creates an array of two criteria. It then creates an AWT criterion that will trigger when any key is pressed and set this as the first element in the array. Then it creates a time-based criterion that will trigger immediately. These are then OR'ed together to create one new criterion. Finally we then set the initial trigger criterion to be the AWT one.

The **processStimulus** method must now be redefined to peform our processing:

```
public void processStimulus(Enumeration criteria) {
    WakeupCriterion theCriteria;
    theCriteria = (WakeupCriterion) criteria.nextElement();
    if (theCriteria instanceof WakeupOnAWTEvent) {
        running = !running;
    }
    if (running) {
        double alphaValue = theAlpha.value();
        theWeights[0] = 1.0 - alphaValue;
        theWeights[1] = alphaValue;
        theMorph.setWeights(theWeights);
    }
    wakeupOn(oredConditions);
}
```

This is the process that is triggered by the conditions specified. The first criterion is accessed from the **Enumeration**, and then this is checked to see if it is an instance of the **WakeupOnAWTEvent**. If it is, then a key must have been pressed, so we change the value of the *running* variable, starting the animation if it was stopped or *vice-versa*. If the running variable is true, then we perform the processing that changes the morph weights. This takes the *alpha* value and sets the first weight to that value, sets the second to one minus the *alpha* value and then writes these weights back to the **Morph** class. Finally, we set the new trigger condition to be the OR'ed criterion, so it will next perform processing when either another key is pressed, or when 'no time' has elapsed (i.e. all the time).

Finally we create the constructor:

```
public SimpleMorphBehaviour(Alpha a, Morph m) {
    theAlpha = a;
    theMorph = m;
}
```

This merely copies the given parameters into the data for the class. We put all this together in one file. What we need to do then is to modify our original morph program so that it uses this to drive the animation. Our *createMorph* function becomes:

```
protected void createMorph(GeometryArray[] theShapes, Appearance a) {
    double[] weights = {0.0,1.0};
    Alpha morphAlpha = new Alpha(-1,
        Alpha.INCREASING_ENABLE|Alpha.DECREASING_ENABLE,
                                0,0,4000,2000,0,4000,2000,0);
    myMorph = new Morph(theShapes,a);
    myMorph.setWeights(weights);
    myMorph.setCapability(Morph.ALLOW_WEIGHTS_WRITE);
    myBehave = new SimpleMorphBehaviour(morphAlpha,myMorph);
    myBehave.setSchedulingBounds(bounds);
}
```

This creates the necessary *SimpleMorphBehaviour* class. We then call this function from the *buildContentBranch* function, adding these lines:

```
createMorph(theShapes, app);
rotationGroup.addChild(myBehave);
```

We also of course have to remove all the references to the buttons from our previous morph program. The full listing for the new version of this is given in Appendix A and running the program will initially produce a static view of a cube. When a key is pressed (if the graphics frame has focus), the cube should begin morphing into a pyramid and then back to a cube. This should repeat until a key is pressed again. You will notice that the animation doesn't start from the place where it stops, i.e. it 'jumps' to a new shape before continuing. This is because when we stop and start the animation, all we do is start and stop the calculation of the weight values from the *alpha* value. The *alpha* value itself is always changing value, even when the animation is disabled.

User input utilities

There are a number of utility classes that are supplied with the standard distribution that make developing applications with user input easier. These extend the basic **Behavior** class and include classes for key and mouse interaction. Some of these and their constructors are given in Table 7.4.

Table 7.4 Constructors for some of utility behaviours.

Class	Functionality
KeyNavigatorBehavior(TransformGroup)	Used to modify the given **TransformGroup**as the result of keys pressed
MouseRotate(TransformGroup), MouseTranslate(TransformGroup), MouseZoom(TransformGroup)	Modifies the given **TransformGroup**according to the mouse input
PickRotateBehavior(BranchGroup, Canvas3D, Bounds, int), PickTranslateBehavior(BranchGroup, Canvas3D, Bounds, int), PickZoomBehavior(BranchGroup, Canvas3D, Bounds, int),	Allows us to pick an object and modify an associated transformation

To see how to use these we'll start by using one of these classes to add some interaction to a scene.

Using the MouseRotate behaviour

The mouse classes allow us to change the transformation of a **TransformGroup**. In our first example we'll just add a rotation behaviour that will allow us to rotate an object by clicking and dragging in the graphics window. To do this we would add some code to our *buildContentBranch* function:

```
TransformGroup spinGroup = new TransformGroup();
spinGroup.setCapability(TransformGroup.ALLOW_TRANSFORM_WRITE);
```

```
spinGroup.setCapability(TransformGroup.ALLOW_TRANSFORM_READ);
MouseRotate mouseSpin = new MouseRotate()
mouseSpin.setTransformGroup(spinGroup);
contentBranch.addChild(mouseSpin);
mouseSpin.setSchedulingBounds(bounds);
```

This creates a new **TransformGroup**, sets up the ability to read and write its transformation, creates a **MouseRotate** object and then associates the **TransformGroup** with the **MouseRotate** object. Clicking and dragging the mouse then changes the rotation part of the specified trans-formation, so any objects that are children of this will be affected. We also need to add:

import com.sun.j3d.utils.behaviors.mouse.*;

to our import statements. Adding this to one of our previous programs will result in the shape being rotated when we click and drag in the graphics window. If we want to add translation and zooming behaviours, we would need to create a **TransformGroup** for each of these behaviours.

Using the pick utility behaviours

The **MouseRotate** behaviour allows us to affect one transformation in the scene. If we want to select an object then we would need to change the relevant **TransformGroup** in our code. We can, however, use one of the pick utility classes to select and manipulate a shape. Before we look at an example, we need to consider how the picking mechanism works.

In any graphics picking mechanism, a way is needed that associates a screen coordinate selected by the user with a 3D object in the scene graph. In Java 3D (as in most systems) this is achieved by ray casting: a ray is projected into the scene from the screen coordinate and the intersections of this ray with the objects in the scene are calculated. The object that is intersected by the ray is then the object picked. There are, however, some complications to this, especially when the object is part of a hierarchy.

If the object that we 'pick' through the ray casting operation is part of a hierarchy, do we 'pick' the leaf node or its parent? For example, if we click on a screen coordinate that corresponds to the wheel of a 3D model of a car, are we trying to pick the wheel or the entire car? The answer to this question is application and situation specific; most CAD or animation systems allow you to select whether you wish to pick the child node or its parent. So if the answer to our picking dilemma is open to debate, how do we create a program that ensures that the correct node is selected in the scene graph?

Java 3D allows us to define which nodes are returned when we pick an object. This means that when a node is found to intersect a pick ray, there is a 'path' from the intersected node to the root of the scene graph. Any node along that path may be the one that we want the user to pick, so we need to set the capability 'EN-ABLE_PICK_REPORTING' for each node that we wish to be 'pickable'. If there is more than one node in the path, the node further down the hierarchy (i.e. nearer the node that is intersected by the ray) is returned.

To make a group node 'pickable' we use the **setCapability** method:

```
pickableGroup.setCapability(TransformGroup.ENABLE_PICK_REPORTING);
```

To use the **PickRotateBehavior** class, we also need to set up the **TransformGroup** so that we can modify the transformation:

```
pickableGroup.setCapability(TransformGroup.ALLOW_TRANSFORM_WRITE);
pickableGroup.setCapability(TransformGroup.ALLOW_TRANSFORM_READ);
```

We then need to create and add the behaviour class to the scene graph:

```
PickRotateBehavior pickRotate =
                new PickRotateBehavior(contentBranch, myCanvas3D, bounds);
contentBranch.addChild(pickRotate);
```

As you can see, the constructor takes three parameters: a **BranchGroup** that is the root of all nodes that the behaviour applies to, a **Canvas3D** that defines the pick coordinates and a **Bounds** object that specifies where the behaviour is active. There are similar classes for other object manipulation operations, i.e. **PickZoomBehavior** and **PickTranslateBehavior**.

Extending the PickMouseBehaviour

We can also extend the **PickMouseBehavior** utility class to create our own behaviours. Let's create a simple application that will print out the name of an object when we pick it. We need to first associate a 'name' with each object that we might pick. We can do this by adding some user data to the objects using the **setUserData** method of the **Object** class:

```
leftCube.setUserData(new String("left cube"));
rightCube.setUserData(new String("right cube"));
```

We then create a new behaviour to print out this string when we pick the object:

```
import javax.media.j3d.*;
import com.sun.j3d.utils.picking.*;
import com.sun.j3d.utils.picking.behaviors.*;

public class SimplePickBehaviour extends PickMouseBehavior {
    public SimplePickBehaviour(Canvas3D pickCanvas, BranchGroup pickRoot,
                            Bounds pickBounds) {
        super(pickCanvas, pickRoot, pickBounds);
        setSchedulingBounds(pickBounds);
    }
    public void updateScene(int xpos, int ypos) {
        Primitive pickedShape = null;
        pickCanvas.setShapeLocation(xpos,ypos);
        pickResult = pickCanvas.pickClosest();
        if (pickResult != null)
            pickedShape = (Primitive) pickResult.getNode(PickResult.PRIMITIVE);
        if (pickedShape != null)
            System.out.println("Picked the " + pickedShape.getUserData());
        else
            System.out.println("Picked nothing");
}
```

The output of this program is shown in Figure 7.1.

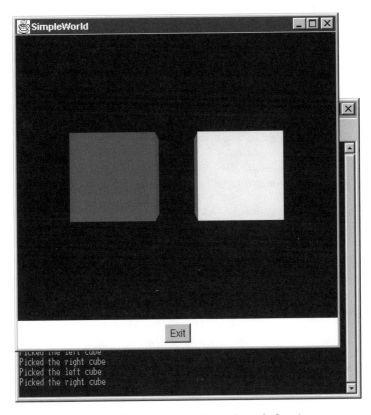

Figure 7.1 Using the simple picking behaviour.

You'll notice that the cubes are selected when either mouse button is pressed. This is not what you'd normally expect as it's conventional to use the left mouse button for selection and the right mouse button for other functions. If we want to implement this, we need to only activate the behaviour when the appropriate button is pressed. We do this by redefining the wake up criteria and performing processing on the event that triggers the behaviour. Our more sophisticated behaviour is given here:

```
import javax.media.j3d.*;
import com.sun.j3d.utils.picking.*;
import com.sun.j3d.utils. picking.behaviors. *;
import java.util.*;
import java.awt.AWTEvent;
import java.awt.event.MouseEvent;
```

```java
public class SimplePickBehaviour extends PickMouseBehavior {
    WakeupOnAWTEvent buttonPressed =
      new WakeupOnAWTEvent(MouseEvent.MOUSE_EVENT_MASK);

    public SimplePickBehaviour(BranchGroup pickRoot,
                               Canvas3D pickCanvas, Bounds pickBounds) {
        super(pickCanvas, pickRoot, pickBounds);
        setSchedulingBounds(pickBounds);
    }

    public void initialize() {
        wakeupOn(buttonPressed);
    }

    public void processStimulus(Enumeration criteria) {
        WakeupOnAWTEvent theCriterion =
                (WakeupOnAWTEvent) criteria.nextElement();
        AWTEvent theEvents[] = theCriterion.getAWTEvent();
        if (theEvents[0].getID() == MouseEvent.RELEASED) {
            MouseEvent theMouseEvent = (MouseEvent) theEvents[0];
            if ((theMouseEvent.getModifiers()
                & MouseEvent.BUTTON1_MASK) != 0) {
                int xpos = theMouseEvent.getX();
                int ypos = theMouseEvent.getY();
                Primitive pickedShape = null;
                PickResult pickResult = null;
                pickCanvas.setShapeLocation(xpos,ypos);
                pickResult = pickCanvas.pickClosest();
                if (pickResult != null)
                    pickedShape =
                        (Primitive) pickResult.getNode(PickResult.PRIMITIVE);
                if (pickedShape != null)
                    System.out.println("Picked the " + pickedShape.getUserData());
                else
                    System.out.println("Picked nothing");
            }
            wakeupOn(buttonPressed);
        }
    }

    public void updateScene(int xpos, int ypos) {}
}
```

As you can see, this is more complex, but more flexible. We start by creating a criterion that specifies when the behaviour is triggered.

In this case the **MOUSE_EVENT_MASK** means that the behaviour will be triggered whenever a mouse event occurs. We have moved the processing part from the **updateScene** method to the **processStimulus** method. This is because we need access to the event that caused the behaviour to be triggered.

In the **processStimulus** function we first obtain the actual AWT events from the **WakeupOnAWTEvent** object. We check that this is an instance of a **MouseEvent** and then proceed to process this by checking that it was the left mouse button (using the **BUTTON1_MASK**) followed by obtaining and using the mouse coordinates. The **updateScene** method is now empty.

If you compile this and use it with our previous code you'll find that it operates as before except only the left mouse button can be used to pick an object.

Using the keyboard utilities

The other primary input method is via the keyboard. In many applications the keyboard would be used to navigate around the scene, as in many computer games and virtual reality applications. The **KeyNavigatorBehavior** utility class is designed to make this easy to implement.

Let's add some keyboard navigation to our code. We can do this by adding the following lines to our familiar *buildViewBranch* function:

```
TransformGroup viewXfmGroup = new TransformGroup(viewXfm);
viewXfmGroup.setCapability(TransformGroup.ALLOW_TRANSFORM_READ);
viewXfmGroup.setCapability(TransformGroup.ALLOW_TRANSFORM_WRITE);
ViewPlatform myViewPlatform = new ViewPlatform();
KeyNavigatorBehavior keyNav = new KeyNavigatorBehavior(viewXfmGroup);
keyNav.setSchedulingBounds(bounds);
viewBranch.addChild(keyNav);
```

You should now be able to move around your scene using the keyboard cursor keys. If you try this you might find one disadvantage. Since this behaviour is only active when the view platform is within the scheduling bounds it is possible to use the key navigation to move outside these bounds. This means that the behaviour will no longer be active, and therefore there's no way to move back into the active region. We're stranded! Luckily there is a way round this as there is a way to define behaviours as being active everywhere.

To do this, we need to create an instance of a **BoundingLeaf**. This class is used to store references to bounds, such as bounding spheres or bounding boxes. In this case, we create a bounding leaf with spherical bounds and then add this to the below the view transform. If we use this object as the bounds for a behaviour, the behaviour will always be active since the bound is moving with the view platform. Our code then becomes:

```
TransformGroup viewXfmGroup = new TransformGroup(viewXfm);
viewXfmGroup.setCapability(TransformGroup.ALLOW_TRANSFORM_READ);
viewXfmGroup.setCapability(TransformGroup.ALLOW_TRANSFORM_WRITE);
BoundingSphere movingBounds = new BoundingSphere(new Point3d(0.0,0.0,0.0), 100.0);
BoundingLeaf boundLeaf = new BoundingLeaf(movingBounds);
viewXfmGroup.addChild(boundLeaf);
KeyNavigatorBehavior keyNav = new KeyNavigatorBehavior(viewXfmGroup);
keyNav.setSchedulingBounds(movingBounds);
viewBranch.addChild(keyNav);
```

Now the behaviour will always be active and we won't get stranded no matter how far we move.

Collision detection and response

Another important aspect of a dynamic 3D environment is the detection of collisions. This can be an extremely complex and processor intensive task in real-time environments, but (again) the Java 3D designers have included classes that assist in this.

Table 7.5 Some of the collision criteria constructors.

Constructor	Functionality
WakeupOnCollisionEntry(Node) WakeupOnCollisionEntry(Bounds) WakeupOnCollisionEntry(SceneGraphPath) WakeupOnCollisionEntry(Node, int) WakeupOnCollisionEntry(Bounds, int) WakeupOnCollisionEntry(SceneGraphPath, int)	Triggers on the specified node colliding with another object. The two argument form's integer parameter can be either **USE_BOUNDS**or **USE_GEOMETRY**
WakeupOnCollisionExit(Node) WakeupOnCollisionExit(Bounds) WakeupOnCollisionExit(SceneGraphPath) WakeupOnCollisionExit(Node, int) WakeupOnCollisionExit(Bounds, int) WakeupOnCollisionExit(SceneGraphPath, int)	As above but triggers on the object no longer colliding with another object
WakeupOnCollisionMovement(Node) WakeupOnCollisionMovement(Bounds) WakeupOnCollisionMovement(SceneGraphPath) WakeupOnCollisionMovement(Node, int) WakeupOnCollisionMovement(Bounds, int) WakeupOnCollisionMovement(SceneGraphPath, int)	As above but triggers when one or more of the colliding objects moves

These classes, given in Table 7.5, are in the form of wake up criteria that can be used to trigger a behaviour when an object collides with another object.

Creating our own collision detector

We'll create our own collision behaviour using these to criteria detect when a collision event occurs. First, we create the class that extends the **Behavior** class:

```
public class CollisionDetector extends Behavior {
    ...
}
```

Within this we define the data that we'll be using. We're going to use all three of the wake up criteria, so we need a **WakeupOr** to combine these. We also need to store the **Shape3D** object that we are checking for a collision:

```
protected WakeupCriterion[] theCriteria;
protected WakeupOr oredCriteria;
protected Shape3D collidingShape;
```

Next we create the constructor which merely stores the shape node and sets the scheduling bounds:

```
public CollisionDetector(Shape3D theShape, Bounds theBounds) {
    collidingShape = theShape;
    setSchedulingBounds(theBounds);
}
```

The **initialize** method is used to create the criteria and set up the initial trigger conditions. We create one of each criterion and OR them together:

```
public void initialize() {
    theCriteria = new WakeupCriterion[3];
    theCriteria[0] = new WakeupOnCollisionEntry(collidingShape);
    theCriteria[1] = new WakeupOnCollisionExit(collidingShape);
    theCriteria[2] = new WakeupOnCollisionMovement(collidingShape);
    oredCriteria = new WakeupOr(theCriteria);
    wakeupOn(oredCriteria);
}
```

Finally we define the **processStimulus** method to do the actual processing. We obtain the criterion from the **Enumeration** passed to the function and then check which type of criterion it is by using the **instanceof** function. This defines what text will be written to the screen. For each case we use the **getTriggeringPath** method to obtain the **SceneGraphPath** and the **getObject** method of the result to obtain the actual colliding node. We then use the **getUserData** to print out the name of the node (which we must have set previously in the main program class).

```
public void processStimulus(Enumeration criteria) {
    WakeupCriterion theCriterion =
                    (WakeupCriterion) criteria.nextElement();
    if (theCriterion instanceof WakeupOnCollisionEntry) {
        Node theLeaf = ((WakeupOnCollisionEntry)
                            theCriterion).getTriggeringPath().getObject();
        System.out.println("Collided with " + theLeaf.getUserData());
    } else if (theCriterion instanceof WakeupOnCollisionExit) {
        Node theLeaf = ((WakeupOnCollisionExit)
                            theCriterion).getTriggeringPath().getObject();
```

```
        System.out.println("Stopped colliding with  " + theLeaf.getUserData());
    } else {
        Node theLeaf = ((WakeupOnCollisionMovement)
                        theCriterion).getTriggeringPath().getObject();
        System.out.println("Moved whilst colliding with " + theLeaf.getUserData());
    }
    wakeupOn(oredCriteria);
}
```

To use this class we merely create an instance with the desired parameters and insert this in the scene graph:

```
CollisionDetector myColDet = new CollisionDetector(moveCube, bounds);
contentBranch.addChild(myColDet);
```

A program that uses this to detect the collisions between a movable cube and two stationary cubes is given in Appendix A, the output of which is shown in Figure 7.2.

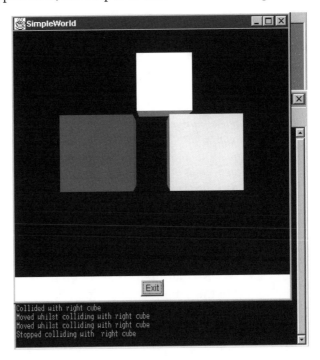

Figure 7.2 *The simple collisionDetector class in a simple application.*

If you run this program, you will notice one of the problems of using the collision wake up criteria. Only one collision can be handled at a time. If you move the white cube between the two stationary cubes (i.e. so it comes into contact with the second cube whilst still in contact with the first), you'll see that the events generated still just say that the cube is in collision with only one cube. We never get the collision entry trigger from the second collision. This could be a problem in many systems. We can usually work around this by some careful programming.

If we create a collision detector object for the two static cubes, then these will generate events when the moving cube comes in contact with them. Each cube will generate an event when the moving cube collides with them, regardless of whether the other cube is currently in collision. The code for the collision behaviour is almost identical, but we change the **processStimulus** function so that it prints out the name of the static cube:

```
public void processStimulus(Enumeration criteria) {
    WakeupCriterion theCriterion = (WakeupCriterion) criteria.nextElement();
    if (theCriterion instanceof WakeupOnCollisionEntry) {
        System.out.println("Collided with " + collidingShape.getUserData());
    }
    else if (theCriterion instanceof WakeupOnCollisionExit) {
        System.out.println("Stopped colliding with  " +
                            collidingShape.getUserData());
    } else {
        System.out.println("Moved whilst colliding with " +
                            collidingShape.getUserData());
    }
    wakeupOn(oredCriteria);
}
```

We'll rename this class *CollisionDetector2*, and then use this in the main program with each of the static cubes:

```
CollisionDetector2 myColDetLeft = new CollisionDetector2(leftCube, bounds);
contentBranch.addChild(myColDetLeft);
CollisionDetector2 myColDetRight = new CollisionDetector2(rightCube, bounds);
contentBranch.addChild(myColDetRight);
```

Summary

This chapter has looked at how to add dynamic elements and interaction into our programs. We've looked at behaviours that drive animation, behaviours that support user input and behaviours that detect collisions between objects. These are just a small subset of the kind of effects you can achieve through behaviours. In fact you will probably find that much of the code of your 3D environments is implemented using behaviours.

Chapter

8

Advanced Topics

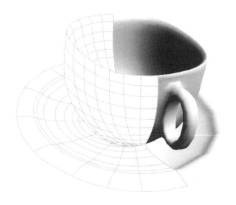

Introduction

In this chapter we'll look at some topics that don't fit elsewhere. These include features that have been included that are generally associated with Virtual Reality applications. Java 3D is very much aimed at these kinds of real-time applications, as we have already seen from the early chapters that looked at how the view model supported information about the physical dimensions of the user and their environment.

Compiling scene graph content

During the development of our programs, we've seen that the scene graph is quite flexible. We can change many aspects of it: through switch nodes we can change which branch is used for rendering, we can change shapes through morph nodes, we can change the transformations associated with groups of objects, etc. We can also add and remove nodes, although we haven't studied this explicitly. We pay a price for all this flexibility in respect of efficiency. Because the scene graph is dynamic, we need to store the contents in such a way that any changes can be incorporated immediately into the scene graph. If we were sure that certain elements in our scene would never change, we could store the scene graph in a more compact and efficient way and so improve the performance of our system. Java 3D supports such compiling, but obviously this should be used with care.

The **BranchGroup** has the method **compile**:

```
contentBranch.compile();
```

This compiles everything below the **BranchGroup** in the scene graph. The precise effect that this has is not defined in the Java 3D specification, but it is likely to at least combine the transformations in **TransformGroups** in each branch. It might also combine geometric elements to improve efficiency, possibly producing one geometry node from many different nodes.

It is still possible to specify some nodes that are to be accessed after the branch has been compiled. This is by setting the capabilities, such as the **ALLOW_TRANS-FORM_READ** and **ALLOW_TRANSFORM_WRITE** capabilities of the **TransformGroup**. Obviously this will reduce the amount of compilation that will take place and the result will be less efficient. This does mean that you will be able to compile all the programs presented in this book. Try this and compare the speed of execution to that without compilation. In general, you should compile all your branches that are actually used in your scene. When a branch is added to a locale, it is said to become 'live'. This means that the content is rendered, and that unless the appropriate capabilities have been set, we can no longer alter the content. This means that you might as well compile all nodes that are used in locales.

If you do need to alter some aspect of a node or branch, you'll need to check whether it has been compiled or is live. There are methods to do this in the **SceneGraphObject** class, and these methods are inherited by virtually all the classes that you'll be using in a scene graph. The two methods are **isCompiled** and **isLive**, both of which have no parameters and return booleans indicating the current state of the object.

Billboards

In any real-time graphics system there is a certain 'polygon budget'. This is the number of polygons per frame or per second that the system can render and still maintain the desired update rate and will vary according to the system hardware and software used. We must always use this efficiently, and so we'll always try to cut corners where we can. One way we can do this is through 'billboards'.

Billboards are elements in the scene that automatically rotate so that the same face is always facing the user. In this way we can create the illusion that an object is 3D when in fact it is a 2D flat object.

To use a billboard in a scene we need to create an instance of the class **Billboard**. The constructors for this class are shown in Table 8.1. The are also a number of functions that allow us to set the data of this billboard after we have constructed it. These are also given in Table 8.1.

Table 8.1 The **Billboard** methods.

Method	Functionality
Billboard()	Default constructor
Billboard(TransformGroup)	Constructor that sets the transform that is affected by the billboard action
Billboard(TransformGroup, int, Vector3f)	As above, but also sets the mode (which can be either ROTATE_ABOUT_AXIS or ROTATE_ABOUT_POINT), and the axis about which the rotation occurs
Billboard(TransformGroup, int, Point3f)	As above but sets the point about which the rotation occurs
void setAlignmentAxis(Vector3f) void setAlignmentAxis(float, float, float)	Sets the alignment axis
void setRotationPoint(Point3f) void setRotationPoint(float, float, float)	Sets the rotation point
void setAlignmentMode(int)	Sets the alignment mode to ROTATE_ABOUT_AXIS or ROTATE_ABOUT_POINT
void setTarget(TransformGroup)	Sets the transform that is to be affected

Let's create a single polygon and associate a billboard with it. We need to create a **TransformGroup**, our geometry and then put this together with the **Billboard** object:

```
TransformGroup billBoardGroup = new TransformGroup();
billBoardGroup.setCapability(TransformGroup.ALLOW_TRANSFORM_WRITE);
ColorCube colouredCube = new ColorCube();
billBoardGroup.addChild(colouredCube);
Billboard myBillboard = new Billboard(billBoardGroup, ROTATE_ABOUT_AXIS,
                              new Vector3f(0.0f,1.0f,0.0f));
```

We then have to add the object and the **Billboard** to the content branch of our scene graph. To see this in action you'll need to be able to navigate around the scene, so you'll need to add something like the **KeyNavigatorBehavior** that we used in Chapter 7. The full program is given in Appendix A. Figure 8.1 shows the output from the program. The viewpoint has been moved to show that the multi-coloured cube has rotated to keep the red face towards the user. You can also see the underside of the cube since we are using axis rotation. If we had used point rotation then the cube would have tilted towards the viewer as well so the underside would not visible.

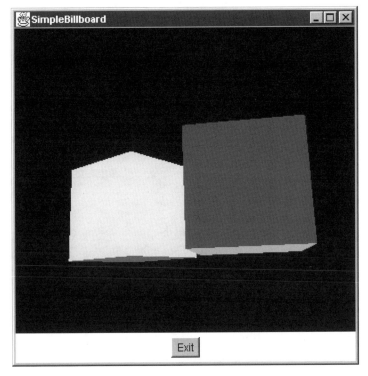

Figure 8.1 The output from the billboard program.

Level of detail

Like the **Billboard** class, the use of levels of detail is to improve the efficiency of our system. It allows us to use different complexities of model according to how near we are to the object, i.e. we use a simple less accurate model for when we are a long distance from the object and more and more complex (and accurate) models as we move nearer to the object.

There are two aspects to this: the actual switching between the models and the detection of the distance between the viewpoint and the object. The switching is performed by the **Switch** node that we used in Chapter 5, whilst the detection and actual driving of the switch is performed by a **DistanceLOD** object. The **DistanceLOD** class has a switch node and a set of distances associated with it. The important methods of the class are given in Table 8.2.

Table 8.2 Some of the DistanceLOD methods.

Method	Functionality
DistanceLOD()	Default constructor.
DistanceLOD(float[])	Constructor that sets switching distances.
DistanceLOD(float[], Point3f)	As above, but also sets point from which the distances are measured.
setPosition(Point3f)	Sets the position from which the distances are measured.
addSwitch(Switch)	Adds a Switch node to the list of switches that are driven by this class.

Here's an example of how we put it all together:

```
Switch LODswitch = new Switch();
LODswitch.setCapability(Switch.ALLOW_SWITCH_WRITE);
LODswitch.addChild(new Cylinder(1.0f,1.0f,Cylinder.GENERATE_NORMALS,10,10,app));
LODswitch.addChild(new Cylinder(1.0f,1.0f,Cylinder.GENERATE_NORMALS,5,5,app));
LODswitch.addChild(new Cylinder(1.0f,1.0f,Cylinder.GENERATE_NORMALS,3,3,app));
float[] LODdistances = {5.0f,10.0f,15.0f};
DistanceLOD myLOD = new DistanceLOD(LODdistances, new Point3f(0.0f,0.0f,0.0f));
myLOD.setSchedulingBounds(bounds);
myLOD.addSwitch(LODswitch);
```

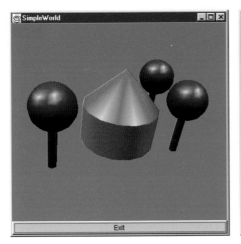

Plate 1: A simple scene constructed from primitives.

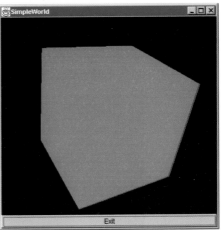

Plate 3: Simple red material with ambient only lighting.

Plate 2: A complex geometry loaded into Java3D.

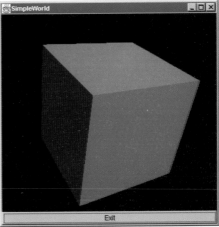

Plate 4: Simple red surface with directional light.

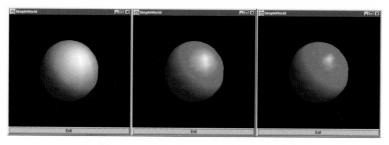

Plate 5: Shininess settings of 5, 20 and 100 respectively.

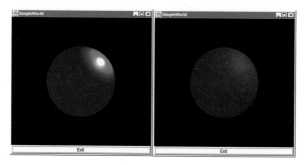

Plate 6: Doubling the distance of a point light from a sphere.

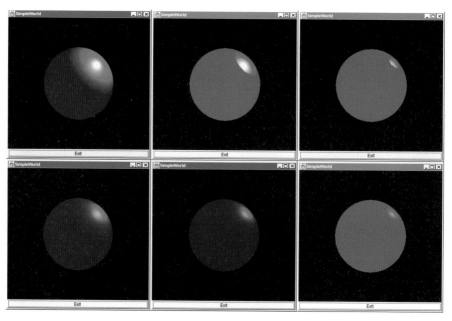

Plate 7: Spot lights with different spreads and concentrations.

Plate 8: The effect of green and blue spotlights on a white sphere.

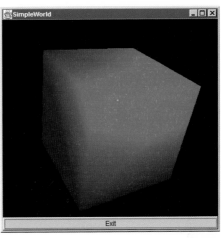

Plate 10: Cube created with shared surface normals.

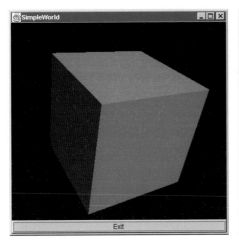

Plate 9: Created from an IndexedQuadArray with normals defined.

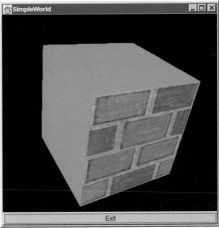

Plate 11: Texture applied to one face of the cube.

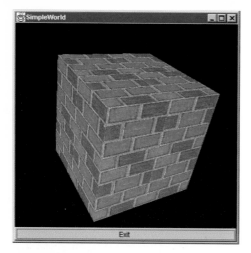

Plate 12: Texture mapping on all faces.

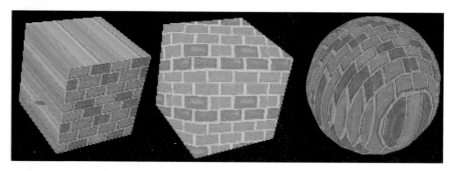

Plate 13: Effects generated by automatic texture coordinate generation.

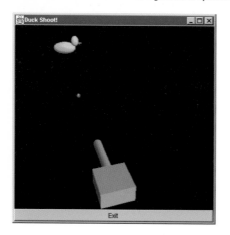

Plate 14: The duck shoot program.

```
BranchGroup contentBranch = new BranchGroup();
contentBranch.addChild(myLOD);
```

This creates three different resolution cylinders and adds them to the switch node. It then creates an array of floating point values that represent the distances at which we want to switch between the different models. The **DistanceLOD** object is then created using these distances and the switch node added to it. We could, if we wanted, add more switch nodes to the object, and each of these will be switched simultaneously. When this is used in a program that we can navigate round (e.g. using the **KeyNavigatorBehavior**), the switch node will swap between the different resolutions accordingly. Figure 8.2 shows the three different cylinders displayed as we move away from the cylinder.

Figure 8.2 *The different versions of the object displayed using the LOD feature.*

Obviously this example would not be used in a real application because the final resolution is so coarse and the switch is noticeable. If you use this in your own programs you want the switching to occur at a distance such that the viewer doesn't notice that the shape has changed.

Sound

It might seem odd to include a section on sound in a book about graphics, but sound can add much more realism to a graphical scene. In an interactive environment there is an important relationship between sound and graphics. And even if you don't agree with this, Sun have included some classes for including sound, so it's sensible to take a look at them here.

There are a number of classes that we need to consider when we add sound to our scene. First, we need to create an instance of an object that provides an interface to the audio devices of our hardware. In many cases this will be a special class that is written to work with our particular sound architecture. Second, we need to create the objects that actually represent our sounds and then add these to the scene.

The classes that provide the interface to our sound hardware will generally extend the class **AudioEngine3D**. An example that comes with the utility libraries is the **JavaSoundMixer**. Here's how we would add code to our previous *buildContentBranch* method:

```
JavaSoundMixer myMixer = new JavaSoundMixer(myEnvironment);
myMixer.initialize();
```

This creates an object associated with the physical environment and initialises it. Once we have done this, we can add sounds to the scene. There are a number of different sounds that we can create. The simplest of these is the **BackgroundSound**. This plays a sound that is of constant volume throughout the scene. This means that it doesn't have a position associated with it. Here's a method that will add a background sound to our scene:

```
protected void addBackgroundSound (BranchGroup b, String soundFile) {
    MediaContainer droneContainer = new MediaContainer(soundFile);
    BackgroundSound drone =      new BackgroundSound(droneContainer, 1.0f);
    drone.setSchedulingBounds(bounds);
    drone.setEnable(true);
    drone.setLoop(BackgroundSound.INFINITE_LOOPS);
    b.addChild(drone);
}
```

This creates a **MediaContainer** to load the sound file and then creates an instance of **BackgroundSound** with the sound file container and an initial gain of one. The gain value is used as a multiplier for the sound volume. We then set the active bounding volume, the sound is switched on by setting the 'enable' value to true and the loop value is set to repeat forever. Finally the sound is added to the scene graph.

We next want to add some **PointSound** objects. These are sounds that appear to emanate from a single point in space. Besides having a location associated with them, they also have a definable fall-off rate. This is how much the sound reduces in volume with increasing distance and is defined as a series of linear segments. Here's the code for a function that will add a sound file to a **TransformGroup**:

```
protected void addObjectSound(TransformGroup tg, PointSound sound,
                                        String soundFile, float edge) {
    Transform3D objXfm = new Transform3D();
    Vector3f objPosition = new Vector3f();
    tg.getTransform(objXfm);
    objXfm.get(objPosition);
    MediaContainer soundContainer = new MediaContainer(soundFile);
    PointSound sound = new PointSound();
    sound.setSoundData(soundContainer);
    sound.setInitialGain(1.0f);
    sound.setPosition(new Point3f(objPosition));
    sound.setSchedulingBounds(bounds);
    sound.setEnable(true);
    sound.setLoop(BackgroundSound.INFINITE_LOOPS);
    Point2f[] attenuation = {new Point2f(1.0f,1.0f), new Point2f(edge,0.0f)};
    sound.setDistanceGain(attenuation);
    Point3f temp = new Point3f();
    sound.getPosition(temp);
    System.out.println(temp);
    tg.addChild(sound);
}
```

This first accesses the translation component of the given **TransformGroup** so that we can use this to set the position of the sound. Next we create the **PointSound** object and set the various data elements to initialise the sound. The **setDistanceGain** method takes an array of **Point2f** objects that represent distance-gain pairs. Each pair is used to define the gain at a given distance to produce a volume change as we approach the position of the sound. In this example we have only defined two values, one at the position of the sound set to 1.0 and one at a distance of 'edge' units which is set to 0.0. This means that if we move further than 'edge' units from the sound we will hear nothing, with the sound rising linearly until we reach the position of the sound. This is shown in Figure 8.3. We can use as many distance-gain pairs as we want to create more complex fall-off characteristics than the simple linear model used here.

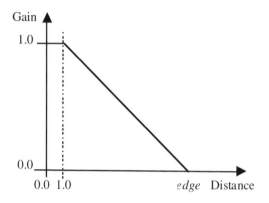

Figure 8.3 *The relationship of sound gain to distance in our simple example.*

The full example given in Appendix A adds two **PointSound** objects to our scene and allows you to switch these on and off using some AWT buttons. It uses the **KeyNavigatorBehavior** so that you can move through the scene to hear the affect of the fall off.

There is another type of sound we create: a **ConeSound**. This is much like an audio version of the **SpotLight** in that it is directed in a particular direction and has a conical sound spread. An array of values can be used to define how the sound falls off as you move away from the focus of the cone. There is also an **AuralAttributes** class. This defines a whole set of parameters about the audio environment, including the implementation of the Doppler effect and the reverberation model for the environment. We will not study these here as they are documented in the document distribution that accompanies Java 3D and would only be used in complex aural environments.

Summary

This chapter has looked at some advanced features that can increase the realism and performance of your Java 3D applications. The compilation of scene components is useful to increase the efficiency of your code and has very little penalty as long as you are aware of its implications. We've seen how some techniques that come from the virtual reality area are supported in Java 3D to increase the performance and we've also looked at how we can add sound to our scenes to increase the realism. These latter areas can be used as final touches to your programs to produce more convincing and faster responding programs.

Putting this together with what you've learnt in the rest of the book, you should now be able to use Java 3D to produce dynamic, interactive 3D worlds. This is only the beginning, and Java 3D is still young in the computing world. You can be sure though that it will go from strength to strength, and you should now be in a position to exploit this.

Chapter 9

Duck Shoot!

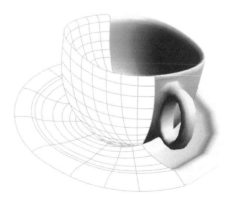

Introduction

This final chapter will use some of the techniques from the previous chapters to build a simple game. This will involve building shapes from primitives, loading shapes from external files, animation, user interaction and collision detection. We're going to build a simple game that involves shooting a 'duck' that moves across the screen from left to right. When we hit the duck, we want it to flip over to show that we have killed it.

The game has two main elements: the duck itself and the gun and projectile (which in our case is a simple ball). Each of these components has a definite behaviour, and we'll look at how we build the program by describing the desired behaviour of each element.

The program elements

Each element will have a behaviour associated with it that extends the base **Behavior** class. We also need different geometry for each element.

The duck

The duck is required to move constantly from left to right and detect when it is hit by the ball fired from the gun. We could build the duck's shape from simple primitives from the utility classes, but in this case we're going to load the duck's geometry from an external file. The two duck shapes, one representing the 'live' duck and one the 'dead' one are shown in Figure 9.1.

To load the duck we need to use a loader class from the utility classes. The movement of the duck is a classic case for an **Interpolator**. For the behaviour that implements the 'dying' we need soomething that will detect collisions. To change the duck's shape, we'll use a **Switch** node to swap between the two shapes. Let's put all this togther in a function that will build the duck part of the scene graph.

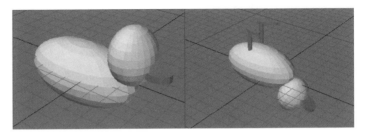

Figure 9.1 The two duck shapes

The code for the duck function is:

```
protected BranchGroup buildDuck() {
BranchGroup theDuck = new BranchGroup();
duckSwitch = new Switch(0);
duckSwitch.setCapability(Switch.ALLOW_SWITCH_WRITE);
ObjectFile liveDuckFile = new ObjectFile();
ObjectFile deadDuckFile = new ObjectFile();
Scene liveDuckScene = null;
Scene deadDuckScene = null;
try {
     liveDuckScene =liveDuckFile.load("duck.obj");
     deadDuckScene =deadDuckFile.load("deadduck.obj");
} catch (Exception e) {
     System.exit(1);
}
TransformGroup duckRotXfmGrp = new TransformGroup();
Transform3D duckRotXfm = new Transform3D();
Matrix3d duckRotMat = new Matrix3d();
duckRotMat.rotY(Math.PI/2);
duckRotXfm.set(duckRotMat,new Vector3d(0.0,0.0,-30.0),1.0);
duckRotXfmGrp.setTransform(duckRotXfm);
duckRotXfmGrp.addChild(duckSwitch);
duckSwitch.addChild(liveDuckScene.getSceneGroup());
duckSwitch.addChild(deadDuckScene.getSceneGroup());
TransformGroup duckMovXfmGrp = new TransformGroup();
duckMovXfmGrp.setCapability(TransformGroup.ALLOW_TRANSFORM_READ);
duckMovXfmGrp.setCapability(TransformGroup.ALLOW_TRANSFORM_WRITE);
duckMovXfmGrp.addChild(duckRotXfmGrp);
```

```
duckAlpha = new Alpha(-1,0,0,3000,0,0);
Transform3D axis = new Transform3D();
PositionInterpolator moveDuck =
    new PositionInterpolator(duckAlpha,duckMovXfmGrp,axis,-30.0f,30.0f);
    moveDuck.setSchedulingBounds(bounds);
    theDuck.addChild(moveDuck);
    theDuck.addChild(duckMovXfmGrp);
    return theDuck;
}
```

This creates a root for the duck object and then creates a
Switch that will allow the swapping of the two shapes. We
then use two **ObjectFile** objects to load the two geometries
and create a transform that positions the duck 30 units
along the *z*-axis. We also create another **TransformGroup**
that is used in the **PositionInterpolator**. The capabilties are
set on this so that we can write the translation of the duck.
We create the **PositionInterpolator** and associated **Alpha**
so that the duck will move from the left of the screen to the
right in 3 seconds. Notice that we have set the **Alpha**
parameters so that the motion will loop forever but only
with an increasing value, i.e. it will 'jump' back to the start
after finishing it. We then put all this together and return
the root of the branch.

Notice that at this stage we haven't created the
behaviour. We're going to create the behaviour in a
separate class. The code for this is given here:

```
public class DuckBehaviour extends Behavior {
 protected Node collidingShape;
 protected WakeupCriterion[] theCriteria;
 protected WakeupOr oredCriteria;
 protected Switch theSwitch;
 protected Alpha theTargetAlpha;
 protected boolean dead = false;
 public DuckBehaviour(Node theShape, Switch sw, Alpha a1,Bounds theBounds) {
     collidingShape = theShape;
     theSwitch = sw;
     theTargetAlpha = a1;
     setSchedulingBounds(theBounds);
 }
 public void initialize() {
     theCriteria = new WakeupCriterion[2];
     theCriteria[0] = new WakeupOnCollisionEntry(collidingShape);
```

```
            theCriteria[1] = new WakeupOnElapsedTime(1);
            oredCriteria = new WakeupOr(theCriteria);
            wakeupOn(oredCriteria);
    }
    public void processStimulus(Enumeration criteria) {
            while (criteria.hasMoreElements()) {
                WakeupCriterion theCriterion = (WakeupCriterion)
                                             criteria.nextElement();
                if (theCriterion instanceof WakeupOnCollisionEntry) {
                    if (dead == false) {
                        theSwitch.setWhichChild(1);
                        dead = true;
                    }
                }
                else if (theCriterion instanceof WakeupOnElapsedTime) {
                    if (theTargetAlpha.value() < 0.1) {
                        theSwitch.setWhichChild(0);
                        dead = false;
                    }
                }
            }
            wakeupOn(oredCriteria);
    }
}
```

The local variables represent the shape that we'll be checking for collisions (the duck), the criteria that we'll use to trigger this behaviour, the switch that we're using to swap between the two shapes, the **Alpha** being used to drive the duck position and a boolean to store whether the duck is alive or dead. The constructor is used to set up this data so that we can pass to the behaviour the actual objects used for our duck.

The **initialize** function creates the trigger conditions. In this case we want to perform the shape swap when the ball collides with the duck, so we create a **WakeupOn-CollisionEntry** criterion. We also want to change back to the live duck before it starts its pass across the screen. To do this we create a **WakeupOnElapsedTime** criterion with a time of 1 millisecond. This will therefore always trigger, and we can use this to check the *alpha* value so that when it is zero we set the duck shape to the live duck.

The **processStimulus** function performs a different process depending on the type of criterion. For a collision process we check to see if the duck is 'live', and if it is we swap the duck shape for the dead one using the **Switch** (we check if it's 'live' we don't want to shoot it twice!). For a time elapsed criterion we check the current *alpha* value and if it is less that 0.1 we set the duck geometry back to the live one ready for its next journey.

There are a couple of things worth noting here. First, we're not checking what object has collided with the duck. We don't need to verify that it's the ball because we know that no other object could collide with the duck. Secondly, we could use the collision process to keep score of the number of ducks we've killed. Finally, we are checking that the *alpha* value is less than 0.1 rather than equal to zero since we cannot guarantee that the behaviour will be triggered when the value is zero.

The gun and ball

Again we'll use a function to build both these components. We're looking at them togther since the behaviour links the two. The first function we'll look at is one that builds the gun:

```
protected BranchGroup buildGun() {
    BranchGroup theGun = new BranchGroup();
    Appearance gunApp = new Appearance();
    Color3f ambientColour = new Color3f(0.5f,0.5f,0.5f);
    Color3f emissiveColour = new Color3f(0.0f,0.0f,0.0f);
    Color3f specularColour = new Color3f(1.0f,1.0f,1.0f);
    Color3f diffuseColour = new Color3f(0.5f,0.5f,0.5f);
    float shininess = 20.0f;
    gunApp.setMaterial(new Material(ambientColour,emissiveColour,
                            diffuseColour,specularColour,shininess));
    TransformGroup init = new TransformGroup();
    TransformGroup barrel = new TransformGroup();
    Transform3D gunXfm = new Transform3D();
    Transform3D barrelXfm = new Transform3D();
    barrelXfm.set(new Vector3d(0.0,-2.0,0.0));
    barrel.setTransform(barrelXfm);
```

```
Matrix3d gunXfmMat = new Matrix3d();
gunXfmMat.rotX(Math.PI/2);
gunXfm.set(gunXfmMat,new Vector3d(0.0,0.0,0.0),1.0);
init.setTransform(gunXfm);
gunXfmGrp.setCapability(
        TransformGroup.ALLOW_TRANSFORM_WRITE);
gunXfmGrp.addChild(new Box(1.0f,1.0f,0.5f,gunApp));
barrel.addChild(new Cylinder(0.3f,4.0f,gunApp));
gunXfmGrp.addChild(barrel);
theGun.addChild(init);
init.addChild(gunXfmGrp);
return theGun;
}
```

This first creates a grey coloured material for our gun and then builds the gun and its turret from a cylinder and box. These are positioned so that they form the desired shape. We also create a **TransformGroup** with its write capability set so that the user can rotate the turret.

The next function that we'll look at is that which builds the ball. This is similar to the *buildGun* function but just uses a **Sphere** object to build the ball. We again create a **TransformGroup** with the capability to change the transformation, and in this case we also create a **PositionInterpolator** to allow us to 'shoot' the ball. This is different to the duck interpolator because it only runs once (i.e. it doesn't loop). We now need to look at the gun's behaviour.

The gun's behaviour is again declared in a different class:

```
public class GunBehaviour extends Behavior {
    protected WakeupOr oredCriteria;
    protected Alpha theGunAlpha;
    protected PositionInterpolator theInterpolator;
    protected int aim = 0;
    protected TransformGroup aimXfmGrp;
    protected Matrix3d aimShotMat = new Matrix3d();
    protected Matrix3d aimGunMat = new Matrix3d();
    protected Transform3D aimShotXfm = new Transform3D();
    protected Transform3D aimGunXfm = new Transform3D();
    public GunBehaviour(Alpha a1,PositionInterpolator pi,
                    TransformGroup gunRotGrp,Bounds theBounds) {
```

```java
        theGunAlpha = a1;
        theInterpolator = pi;
        setSchedulingBounds(theBounds);
        aimXfmGrp = gunRotGrp;
}
public void initialize() {
        theCriteria = new WakeupCriterion[2];
        theCriteria[0] = new WakeupOnElapsedTime(1);
        theCriteria[1] = new WakeupOnAWTEvent(KeyEvent.KEY_PRESSED);
        oredCriteria = new WakeupOr(theCriteria);
        wakeupOn(oredCriteria);
}
public void processStimulus(Enumeration criteria) {
        while (criteria.hasMoreElements()) {
                WakeupCriterion theCriterion = (WakeupCriterion)
                                        criteria.nextElement();
                if (theCriterion  instanceof WakeupOnAWTEvent) {
                        AWTEvent[] triggers =
                        ((WakeupOnAWTEvent)theCriterion).getAWTEvent();
                        if (triggers[0] instanceof KeyEvent) {
                                int keyPressed = ((KeyEvent)triggers[0]).getKeyCode();
                                if (keyPressed == KeyEvent.VK_LEFT) {
                                        if (aim < 8)
                                        aim += 1;
                                        aimShotMat.rotY(((aim/32.0) + 0.5)*Math.PI);
                                        aimGunMat.rotZ(((aim/-32.0))*Math.PI);
                                        aimShotXfm.setRotation(aimShotMat);
                                        aimGunXfm.setRotation(aimGunMat);
                                        aimXfmGrp.setTransform(aimGunXfm);
                                        theInterpolator.setAxisOfTranslation(aimShotXfm);
                                } else if (keyPressed == KeyEvent.VK_RIGHT) {
                                        if (aim > -8)
                                                aim -= 1;
                                        aimShotMat.rotY(((aim/32.0) + 0.5)*Math.PI);
                                        aimGunMat.rotZ(((aim/-32.0))*Math.PI);
                                        aimGunXfm.setRotation(aimGunMat);
                                        aimShotXfm.setRotation(aimShotMat);
                                        aimXfmGrp.setTransform(aimGunXfm);
                                        theInterpolator.setAxisOfTranslation(aimShotXfm);
                                } else if (keyPressed == KeyEvent.VK_SPACE) {
                                        theGunAlpha.setStartTime(System.currentTimeMillis());
                                }
                        }
                }
        }
```

```
          }
          wakeupOn(oredCriteria);
      }
}
```

This creates some data that we need in the behaviour: the trigger criterion, the *alpha* and the interpolator used for moving the ball, the **TransformGroup** used to rotate the gun and some transforms and matrices used to create the data used to rotate the gun turret and fire the ball. The constructor is used to set up this data with the correct values.

The **initialize** function creates a criterion that causes the behaviour to be triggered when a key is pressed and sets this to be used by this behaviour.

The **processStimulus** function is (as usual) where the work in this behaviour occurs. We check to see which key has been pressed by getting the key code of the AWT event that triggered this behaviour. If it is a left or a right cursor key we rotate the turret and the coordinate system of the interpolator appropriately. We only rotate the turret up to a predefined limit. If the spacebar has been pressed we want to 'fire' the ball. This involves setting the start time of the ball interpolator to the current system time, i.e. the interpolator will start the ball moving when the spacebar is pressed.

Putting it all together

We now define the process that puts it all together:

```
protected BranchGroup buildContentBranch() {
    BranchGroup contentBranch = new BranchGroup();
    Node theDuck = buildDuck();
    contentBranch.addChild(theDuck);
    Node theBall = buildBall();
    contentBranch.addChild(theBall);
    DuckBehaviour hitTheDuck =
        newDuckBehaviour(theDuck,duckSwitch,duckAlpha,bounds);
    GunBehaviour shootTheGun =
```

```
        new GunBehaviour(ballAlpha,moveBall,gunXfmGrp,bounds);
    contentBranch.addChild(hitTheDuck);
    contentBranch.addChild(shootTheGun);
    contentBranch.addChild(buildGun());
    addLights(contentBranch);
    return contentBranch;
}
```

This uses the functions and behaviours that we've defined together with an *addLights* function similar to that used in our previous examples. If we put all this together in one program and compile and run it, we should get a simple game in which we can shoot ducks. A screen shot from the program is shown in Plate 14, and the full code listing is given in Appendix A.

You'll probably be able to think of many ways that we could improve on this. We could randomize the time at which the duck starts to move across the screen, we could add an AWT component to keep score of the number of ducks hit, we could add more ducks, etc. You could also use a **Morph** object to make the duck 'explode' when we hit it, and use other interpolators to give the duck flapping wings or running feet.

Summary

This final chapter has not introduced anything new. What it has done is used elements from previous chapters to build a useful (if trivial) game. Hopefully this should demonstrate how you would use both predefined and primitive geometries and interpolators to add animation and show how to give certain objects behaviours to produce a dynamic, interactive application.

Appendix

A

Source Code

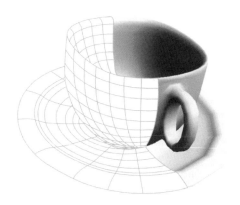

Introduction

This appendix contains code examples from all the chapters. Each application is presented in its entirety, although if only small modifications are made to programs in the text these are not generally presented here. The examples are organised into the chapters in which they appeared. The code here includes more comments than the extracts that are in the main text, so hopefully they are self-explanatory.

Chapter 2

SimpleWorld application

```java
//Import the Java3D classes
import javax.media.j3d.*;
//Import the vector classes so we can perform simple maths
import javax.vecmath.*;
//Import the AWT classes so we can create window etc.
import java.awt.*;
//Import the AWT events so we can use a button to exit the program
import java.awt.event.*;
/**
 * This is our first simple program that creates a cube.  We have
 * no lighting defined so the object appears a bright white colour.
 * The cube is tilted slightly so that we can see its shape by
 * creating a transform group.
 * @author I.J.Palmer
 * @version 1.0
 */
public class SimpleWorld extends Frame implements ActionListener {
    /** The canvas 3D used to display the scene. */
    protected Canvas3D myCanvas3D = new Canvas3D(null);
    /** The AWT button used to exit the application. */
    protected Button myButton = new Button("Exit");
    /**
     * This function builds the view branch of the scene
     * graph.  It creates a branch group and then creates the
     * necessary view elements to give a useful view of our
     * content.
     * @param c Canvas3D that will display the view
     * @return BranchGroup that is the root of the view elements
     */
    protected BranchGroup buildViewBranch(Canvas3D c) {
        //This is the root of our view branch
        BranchGroup viewBranch = new BranchGroup();
        //The transform that will move our view
```

```
        //back 5 units along the z-axis
        Transform3D viewXfm = new Transform3D();
        viewXfm.set(new Vector3f(0.0f,0.0f,5.0f));
        //The transform group that will be the parent
        //of our view platform elements
        TransformGroup viewXfmGroup = new TransformGroup(viewXfm);
        ViewPlatform myViewPlatform = new ViewPlatform();
        //Next the physical elements are created
        PhysicalBody myBody = new PhysicalBody();
        PhysicalEnvironment myEnvironment = new PhysicalEnvironment();
        //Then we put it all together
        viewXfmGroup.addChild(myViewPlatform);
        viewBranch.addChild(viewXfmGroup);
        View myView = new View();
        myView.addCanvas3D(c);
        myView.attachViewPlatform(myViewPlatform);
        myView.setPhysicalBody(myBody);
        myView.setPhysicalEnvironment(myEnvironment);
        return viewBranch;
}
/**
 * This builds the content branch of our scene graph.
 * It uses the buildCube function to create the actual shape,
 * adding to to the transform group so that the shape
 * is slightly tilted to reveal its 3D shape.
 * @param shape Node that represents the geometry for the content
 * @return BranchGroup that is the root of the content branch
 */
protected BranchGroup buildContentBranch(Node shape) {
        //Create the branch group that will be the root of the content branch
        BranchGroup contentBranch = new BranchGroup();
        //Create the transform that will cause the shape to appear tilted
        Transform3D rotateCube = new Transform3D( );
        rotateCube.set(new AxisAngle4d(1.0,1.0,0.0,Math.PI/4.0));
        TransformGroup rotationGroup = new TransformGroup(rotateCube);
        //Put the branch together
        contentBranch.addChild(rotationGroup);
        rotationGroup.addChild(shape);
        return contentBranch;
}
/**
 * This constructs a cube as an array of quadrilateral polygons.
 * There are six faces, each with four vertices (obviously!).
 * The cube extends 1 unit along each axis in the positive
```

```
* and negative directions and is centred on the origin.
* @return Node that is the cube
*/
protected Node buildCube() {
        //Create the array of numbers that will form the
        //vertex information.
        float[] cubeFaces = {
                1.0f, -1.0f,  1.0f, 1.0f, 1.0f,  1.0f, -1.0f,  1.0f, 1.0f, -1.0f, -1.0f,  1.0f,
                -1.0f, -1.0f, -1.0f, -1.0f, 1.0f, -1.0f, 1.0f,  1.0f, -1.0f, 1.0f, -1.0f, -1.0f,
                1.0f, -1.0f, -1.0f, 1.0f,  1.0f, -1.0f, 1.0f,  1.0f,  1.0f, 1.0f, -1.0f,  1.0f,
                -1.0f, -1.0f,  1.0f, -1.0f,  1.0f,  1.0f, -1.0f,  1.0f, -1.0f, -1.0f, -1.0f, -1.0f,
                1.0f,  1.0f,  1.0f,   1.0f,  1.0f, -1.0f, -1.0f,  1.0f, -1.0f, -1.0f,  1.0f,  1.0f,
                -1.0f, -1.0f,  1.0f, -1.0f, -1.0f, -1.0f, 1.0f, -1.0f, -1.0f, 1.0f, -1.0f,  1.0f
        };
        //Create the array of quadrilaterals from the vertices
        QuadArray cubeData = new QuadArray(24, QuadArray.COORDINATES);
        cubeData.setCoordinates(0, cubeFaces);
        //Create a default appearance
        Appearance app = new Appearance();
        //Create and return the cube
        return new Shape3D(cubeData, app);
}
/**
* Handles the exit button action to quit the program.
*/
public void actionPerformed(ActionEvent e) {
        dispose();
        System.exit(0);
}
/**
* This creates a default universe and locale, creates a window
* and uses the functions defined in this class to build the
* view and content branches of the scene graph.
*/
public SimpleWorld() {
        //Create a default universe and locale
        VirtualUniverse myUniverse = new VirtualUniverse();
        Locale myLocale = new Locale(myUniverse);
        //Use the functions to build the scene graph
        myLocale.addBranchGraph(buildViewBranch(myCanvas3D));
        myLocale.addBranchGraph(buildContentBranch(buildCube()));
        //Do some AWT stuff to set up the window
        setTitle("SimpleWorld");
```

```
            setSize(400,400);
            setLayout(new BorderLayout());
            add(BorderLayout.CENTER, myCanvas3D);
            myButton.addActionListener(this);
            add(BorderLayout.SOUTH, myButton);
            setVisible(true);
    }
    /**
     * Just create the class and run!
     */
    public static void main(String[] args) {
            SimpleWorld sw = new SimpleWorld();
    }
}
```

Chapter 3

SimpleCone application

```
import javax.media.j3d.*;
import javax.vecmath.*;
import java.awt.*;
import java.awt.event.*;
import com.sun.j3d.utils.geometry.*;
/**
 * This program uses the geometric primitive library to build a shape.
 * @author I.J.Palmer
 * @version 1.0
 */
public class SimpleCone extends Frame implements ActionListener {
    /** The canvas 3D used to display the scene. */
    protected Canvas3D myCanvas3D = new Canvas3D(null);
    /** The AWT button used to exit the application. */
    protected Button myButton = new Button("Exit");
    /**
     * This function builds the view branch of the scene
     * graph.  It creates a branch group and then creates the
     * necessary view elements to give a useful view of our
     * content.
     * @param c Canvas3D that will display the view
     * @return BranchGroup that is the root of the view elements
     */
    protected BranchGroup buildViewBranch(Canvas3D c) {
        BranchGroup viewBranch = new BranchGroup();
        Transform3D viewXfm = new Transform3D();
        viewXfm.set(new Vector3f(0.0f,0.0f,5.0f));
        TransformGroup viewXfmGroup = new TransformGroup(viewXfm);
        ViewPlatform myViewPlatform = new ViewPlatform();
        PhysicalBody myBody = new PhysicalBody();
        PhysicalEnvironment myEnvironment = new PhysicalEnvironment();
        viewXfmGroup.addChild(myViewPlatform);
        viewBranch.addChild(viewXfmGroup);
```

```java
        View myView = new View();
        myView.addCanvas3D(c);
        myView.attachViewPlatform(myViewPlatform);
        myView.setPhysicalBody(myBody);
        myView.setPhysicalEnvironment(myEnvironment);
        return viewBranch;
}
/**
 * This builds the content branch of our scene graph.
 * It takes the given shape,
 * adding to the transform group so that the shape
 * is slightly tilted to reveal its 3D shape.
 * @param shape Node that represents the geometry for the content
 * @return BranchGroup that is the root of the content branch
 */
protected BranchGroup buildContentBranch(Node shape) {
        BranchGroup contentBranch = new BranchGroup();
        Transform3D rotateCube = new Transform3D( );
        rotateCube.set(new AxisAngle4d(1.0,1.0,0.0,Math.PI/4.0));
        TransformGroup rotationGroup = new TransformGroup(rotateCube);
        contentBranch.addChild(rotationGroup);
        rotationGroup.addChild(shape);
        return contentBranch;
}
/**
 * This uses the Cone utility class to create a simple cone.
 * @return Node that is the cone
 */
protected Node buildCone() {
        return new Cone(1.0f,2.0f,
                                Cone.GENERATE_NORMALS, new Appearance());
}
/**
 * Handles the exit button action to quit the program.
 */
public void actionPerformed(ActionEvent e) {
        dispose();
        System.exit(0);
}
/**
 * This creates a default universe and locale, creates a window
 * and uses the functions defined in this class to build the
 * view and content branches of the scene graph.
 */
```

```java
public SimpleCone() {
    VirtualUniverse myUniverse = new VirtualUniverse();
    Locale myLocale = new Locale(myUniverse);
    myLocale.addBranchGraph(buildViewBranch(myCanvas3D));
    myLocale.addBranchGraph(buildContentBranch(buildCone()));
    setTitle("SimpleCone");
    setSize(400,400);
    setLayout(new BorderLayout());
    add(BorderLayout.CENTER, myCanvas3D);
    myButton.addActionListener(this);
    add(BorderLayout.SOUTH, myButton);
    setVisible(true);
}
/**
 * Just create the class and run!
 */
public static void main(String[] args) {
    SimpleCone sc = new SimpleCone();
}
}
```

SimpleIndexedQuadArray

This builds a cube from an indexed array of quadrilaterals.

```java
import javax.media.j3d.*;
import javax.vecmath.*;
import java.awt.*;
import java.awt.event.*;
import com.sun.j3d.utils.geometry.*;
/**
 * This builds a simple class using the an indexed quadrilateral
 * array.  This demonstrates the use of the IndexedQuadArray class.
 * It defines both the vertices and the normals of the cube such
 * that the shape is shaded with flat faces.
 * @author I.J.Palmer
 * @version 1.0
 */
public class SimpleIndexedQuad extends Frame implements ActionListener {
    protected Canvas3D myCanvas3D = new Canvas3D(null);
    protected Button myButton = new Button("Exit");
```

```java
/**
 * This function builds the view branch of the scene
 * graph.  It creates a branch group and then creates the
 * necessary view elements to give a useful view of our
 * content.
 * @param c Canvas3D that will display the view
 * @return BranchGroup that is the root of the view elements
 */
protected BranchGroup buildViewBranch(Canvas3D c) {
    BranchGroup viewBranch = new BranchGroup();
    Transform3D viewXfm = new Transform3D();
    viewXfm.set(new Vector3f(0.0f,0.0f,5.0f));
    TransformGroup viewXfmGroup = new TransformGroup(viewXfm);
    ViewPlatform myViewPlatform = new ViewPlatform();
    PhysicalBody myBody = new PhysicalBody();
    PhysicalEnvironment myEnvironment = new PhysicalEnvironment();
    viewXfmGroup.addChild(myViewPlatform);
    viewBranch.addChild(viewXfmGroup);
    View myView = new View();
    myView.addCanvas3D(c);
    myView.attachViewPlatform(myViewPlatform);
    myView.setPhysicalBody(myBody);
    myView.setPhysicalEnvironment(myEnvironment);
    return viewBranch;
}
/**
 * This builds the content branch of our scene graph.
 * It uses the buildShape function to create the actual shape,
 * adding to to the transform group so that the shape
 * is slightly tilted to reveal its 3D shape. It also uses
 * the addLights function to add some lights to the scene.
 * @param shape Node that represents the geometry for the content
 * @return BranchGroup that is the root of the content branch
 */
protected BranchGroup buildContentBranch(Node shape) {
    BranchGroup contentBranch = new BranchGroup();
    Transform3D rotateCube = new Transform3D( );
    rotateCube.set(new AxisAngle4d(1.0,1.0,0.0,Math.PI/4.0));
    TransformGroup rotationGroup = new TransformGroup(rotateCube);
    contentBranch.addChild(rotationGroup);
    rotationGroup.addChild(shape);
    return contentBranch;
}
/**
```

```
 * Build a cube from an IndexedQuadArray.  This method creates
 * the vertices as a set of eight points and the normals as a set of
 * six vectors (one for each face).  The data is then defined such
 * that each vertex has a different normal associated with it when
 * it is being used for a different face.
 * @return Node that is the shape.
 */
protected Node buildShape() {
        //The shape.  The constructor specifies 8 vertices, that both
        //vertices and normals are to be defined and that there are
        //24 normals to be specified (4 for each of the 6 faces).
        IndexedQuadArray indexedCube = new IndexedQuadArray(8
                                        IndexedQuadArray.COORDINATES 24);
         //The vertex coordinates defined as an array of points.
        Point3f[] cubeCoordinates = { new Point3f( 1.0f, 1.0f, 1.0f),
                                        new Point3f(-1.0f, 1.0f, 1.0f),
                                        new Point3f(-1.0f,-1.0f, 1.0f),
                                        new Point3f( 1.0f,-1.0f, 1.0f),
                                        new Point3f( 1.0f, 1.0f,-1.0f),
                                        new Point3f(-1.0f, 1.0f,-1.0f),
                                        new Point3f(-1.0f,-1.0f,-1.0f),
                                        new Point3f( 1.0f,-1.0f,-1.0f)};
        //Define the indices used to reference vertex array
        int coordIndices[] = {0,1,2,3,7,6,5,4,0,3,7,4,5,6,2,1,0,4,5,1,6,7,3,2};
        //Set the data
        indexedCube.setCoordinates(0, cubeCoordinates);
        indexedCube.setCoordinateIndices(0, coordIndices);
        //Create and return the shape
        return new Shape3D(indexedCube, new Appearance());
}
/**
 * Handles the exit button action to quit the program.
 */
public void actionPerformed(ActionEvent e) {
        dispose();
        System.exit(0);
}
public SimpleIndexedQuad() {
        VirtualUniverse myUniverse = new VirtualUniverse();
        Locale myLocale = new Locale(myUniverse);
        myLocale.addBranchGraph(buildViewBranch(myCanvas3D));
        myLocale.addBranchGraph(buildContentBranch(buildShape()));
        setTitle("SimpleIndexedQuad");
```

```
            setSize(400,400);
            setLayout(new BorderLayout());
            add(BorderLayout.CENTER, myCanvas3D);
            add(BorderLayout.SOUTH,myButton);
            myButton.addActionListener(this);
            setVisible(true);
        }
        public static void main(String[] args) {
            SimpleIndexedQuad siq = new SimpleIndexedQuad();
        }
    }
}
```

SimpleIndexTriangleArray

Build a cube from an indexed triangle array.

```
import javax.media.j3d.*;
import javax.vecmath.*;
import java.awt.*;
import java.awt.event.*;
/**
 * This builds a simple class using the an indexed triangle
 * array.  This demonstrates the use of the IndexedTriangleArray class.
 * @author I.J.Palmer
 * @version 1.0
 */
public class SimpleIndexedTriangles extends Frame implements ActionListener {
    protected Canvas3D myCanvas3D = new Canvas3D(null);
    protected Button myButton = new Button("Exit");
    /**
     * This function builds the view branch of the scene
     * graph.  It creates a branch group and then creates the
     * necessary view elements to give a useful view of our
     * content.
     * @param c Canvas3D that will display the view
     * @return BranchGroup that is the root of the view elements
     */
    protected BranchGroup buildViewBranch(Canvas3D c) {
        BranchGroup viewBranch = new BranchGroup();
        Transform3D viewXfm = new Transform3D();
        viewXfm.set(new Vector3f(0.0f,0.0f,10.0f));
        TransformGroup viewXfmGroup = new TransformGroup(viewXfm);
        ViewPlatform myViewPlatform = new ViewPlatform();
```

```java
        PhysicalBody myBody = new PhysicalBody();
        PhysicalEnvironment myEnvironment = new PhysicalEnvironment();
        viewXfmGroup.addChild(myViewPlatform);
        viewBranch.addChild(viewXfmGroup);
        View myView = new View();
        myView.addCanvas3D(c);
        myView.attachViewPlatform(myViewPlatform);
        myView.setPhysicalBody(myBody);
        myView.setPhysicalEnvironment(myEnvironment);
        return viewBranch;
}
/**
 * This builds the content branch of our scene graph.
 * It uses the buildShape function to create the actual shape,
 * adding to to the transform group so that the shape
 * is slightly tilted to reveal its 3D shape. It also uses
 * the addLights function to add some lights to the scene.
 * @param shape Node that represents the geometry for the content
 * @return BranchGroup that is the root of the content branch
 */
protected BranchGroup buildContentBranch(Shape3D shape) {
        BranchGroup contentBranch = new BranchGroup();
        Transform3D rotateCube = new Transform3D( );
        rotateCube.set(new AxisAngle4d(1.0,1.0,0.0,Math.PI/4.0));
        TransformGroup rotationGroup = new TransformGroup(rotateCube);
        contentBranch.addChild(rotationGroup);
        rotationGroup.addChild(shape);
        addLights(contentBranch);
        return contentBranch;
}
/**
 * Build a cube from an IndexedTriangleArray.  This method creates
 * the vertices as a set of eight points and the normals as a set of
 * six vectors (one for each face).  The data is then defined such
 * that each vertex has a different normal associated with it when
 * it is being used for a different face.
 * @return Node that is the shape.
 */
protected Node buildShape() {
        //Create a triangle array with 8 vertices and 36 indices
        //into this, i.e. 12 triangles, 2 for each face
        IndexedTriangleArray indexedCube =
        new IndexedTriangleArray(8,IndexedTriangleArray.COORDINATES,36);
```

```
                  Point3f[] cubeCoordinates = { new Point3f( 1.0f, 1.0f, 1.0f),
                                                new Point3f(-1.0f, 1.0f, 1.0f),
                                                new Point3f(-1.0f,-1.0f, 1.0f),
                                                new Point3f( 1.0f,-1.0f, 1.0f),
                                                new Point3f( 1.0f, 1.0f,-1.0f),
                                                new Point3f( 1.0f,-1.0f,-1.0f),
                                                new Point3f(-1.0f,-1.0f,-1.0f),
                                                new Point3f(-1.0f, 1.0f,-1.0f)};
              int coordIndices[] =
                  {0,1,2,2,3,0,6,5,4,4,7,6,0,4,1,4,5,1,7,3,2,6,7,2,4,0,3,4,3,7,1,5,6,1,6,2};
              indexedCube.setCoordinates(0, cubeCoordinates);
              indexedCube.setCoordinateIndices(0, coordIndices);
              return new Shape3D(indexedCube, new Appearance());
          }
          public void actionPerformed(ActionEvent e) {
              dispose();
              System.exit(0);
          }
          public SimpleIndexedTriangles() {
              VirtualUniverse myUniverse = new VirtualUniverse();
              Locale myLocale = new Locale(myUniverse);
              myLocale.addBranchGraph(buildViewBranch(myCanvas3D));
            myLocale.addBranchGraph(buildContentBranch(buildShape()));
              setTitle("SimpleIndexedTriangles");
              setSize(400,400);
              setLayout(new BorderLayout());
            add(BorderLayout.CENTER, myCanvas3D);
            add(BorderLayout.SOUTH,myButton);
            myButton.addActionListener(this);
            setVisible(true);
          }
          public static void main(String[] args) {
              SimpleIndexedTriangles sit = new SimpleIndexedTriangles();
          }
      }
}
```

ObjectLoader

This uses the **ObjectFile** to load a Wavefront object geometry from an external file.

```java
import javax.media.j3d.*;
import javax.vecmath.*;
import java.awt.*;
import java.awt.event.*;
import com.sun.j3d.loaders.*;
import com.sun.j3d.loaders.objectfile.*;
/**
 * This is a simple application that uses the ObjectLoader
 * class to load a geometric shape from a Wavefront object file.
 * @author I.J.Palmer
 * @version 1.0
 */
public class ObjectLoader extends Frame implements ActionListener {
    protected Canvas3D myCanvas3D = new Canvas3D(null);
    protected Button myButton = new Button("Exit");
    //String used to store the filename of the shape
    private String filename = null;
    /**
     * This function builds the view branch of the scene
     * graph.  It creates a branch group and then creates the
     * necessary view elements to give a useful view of our
     * content.
     * @param c Canvas3D that will display the view
     * @return BranchGroup that is the root of the view elements
     */
    protected BranchGroup buildViewBranch(Canvas3D c) {
        BranchGroup viewBranch = new BranchGroup();
        Transform3D viewXfm = new Transform3D();
        viewXfm.set(new Vector3f(0.0f,0.0f,10.0f));
        TransformGroup viewXfmGroup = new TransformGroup(viewXfm);
        ViewPlatform myViewPlatform = new ViewPlatform();
        PhysicalBody myBody = new PhysicalBody();
        PhysicalEnvironment myEnvironment = new PhysicalEnvironment();
        viewXfmGroup.addChild(myViewPlatform);
        viewBranch.addChild(viewXfmGroup);
        View myView = new View();
        myView.addCanvas3D(c);
        myView.attachViewPlatform(myViewPlatform);
        myView.setPhysicalBody(myBody);
        myView.setPhysicalEnvironment(myEnvironment);
        return viewBranch;
    }
    /**
```

```
* Add some lights so that we can illuminate the scene.
* This adds one ambient light to bring up the overall
* lighting level and one directional shape to show
* the shape of the objects in the scene.
* @param b BranchGroup that the lights are to be added to.
*/
protected void addLights(BranchGroup b) {
    BoundingSphere bounds =
                    new BoundingSphere(new Point3d(0.0,0.0,0.0), 100.0);
    Color3f ambientColour = new Color3f(1.0f, 1.0f, 1.0f);
    AmbientLight ambientLight = new AmbientLight(ambientColour);
    ambientLight.setInfluencingBounds(bounds);
    light.setInfluencingBounds(bounds);
    b.addChild(ambientLight);
}
/**
* This builds the content branch of our scene graph.
* It uses the buildShape function to create the actual shape,
* adding to to the transform group so that the shape
* is slightly tilted to reveal its 3D shape. It also uses
* the addLights function to add some lights to the scene.
* @param shape Node that represents the geometry for the content
* @return BranchGroup that is the root of the content branch
*/
protected BranchGroup buildContentBranch(Node shape) {
    BranchGroup contentBranch = new BranchGroup();
    Transform3D rotateCube = new Transform3D( );
    rotateCube.set(new AxisAngle4d(1.0,1.0,0.0,Math.PI/4.0));
    TransformGroup rotationGroup = new TransformGroup(rotateCube);
    contentBranch.addChild(rotationGroup);
    rotationGroup.addChild(shape);
    addLights(contentBranch);
    return contentBranch;
}
/**
* This builds a shape by loading the geometry from a file.
* This is achieved by creating an instance of an ObjectFile
* from the utility classes.  The name of the file that is loaded
* is defined by the argument passed to the program when it is run.
*/
protected Node buildShape() {
    //Create the object that will load and process the file
    ObjectFile f = new ObjectFile();
    //Create the scene that will store the data loaded and
```

```java
        //set it to null
        Scene s = null;
        //Try and load the data from the file.  Exit if there
        //is an error.
        try {
            s = f.load(filename);
        } catch (Exception e) {
            System.exit(1);
        }
        //Return the root of the scene that we have loaded.
        return s.getSceneGroup();
    }
    public void actionPerformed(ActionEvent e) {
        dispose();
        System.exit(0);
    }
    /**
     * This stores the first string argument to be used in the
     * object loader function.
     */
    public ObjectLoader(String args[]) {
        if (args.length > 0) {
            filename = args[0];
            VirtualUniverse myUniverse = new VirtualUniverse();
            Locale myLocale = new Locale(myUniverse);
            myLocale.addBranchGraph(buildViewBranch(myCanvas3D));
            myLocale.addBranchGraph(buildContentBranch(buildShape()));
            setTitle("ObjectLoader");
            setSize(400,400);
            setLayout(new BorderLayout());
            add(BorderLayout.CENTER, myCanvas3D);
            myButton.addActionListener(this);
            add(BorderLayout.SOUTH, myButton);
            setVisible(true);
        }
    }
    public static void main(String[] args) {
        ObjectLoader ol = new ObjectLoader(args);
    }
}
```

LightwaveLoader

This uses the **Lw3dLoader** class to load an entire Lightwave scene.

```java
import javax.media.j3d.*;
import javax.vecmath.*;
import java.awt.*;
import java.awt.event.*;
import com.sun.j3d.loaders.*;
import com.sun.j3d.loaders.objectfile.*;
/**
* This is a simple application that uses the ObjectLoader
* class to load a geometric shape from a Wavefront object file.
* @author I.J.Palmer
* @version 1.0
*/
public class ObjectLoader extends Frame implements ActionListener {
    protected Canvas3D myCanvas3D = new Canvas3D(null);
    protected Button myButton = new Button("Exit");
    //String used to store the filename of the shape
    private String filename = null;
    /**
     * This function builds the view branch of the scene
     * graph.  It creates a branch group and then creates the
     * necessary view elements to give a useful view of our
     * content.
     * @param c Canvas3D that will display the view
     * @return BranchGroup that is the root of the view elements
     */
    protected BranchGroup buildViewBranch(Canvas3D c) {
        BranchGroup viewBranch = new BranchGroup();
        Transform3D viewXfm = new Transform3D();
        viewXfm.set(new Vector3f(0.0f,0.0f,10.0f));
        TransformGroup viewXfmGroup = new TransformGroup(viewXfm);
        ViewPlatform myViewPlatform = new ViewPlatform();
        PhysicalBody myBody = new PhysicalBody();
        PhysicalEnvironment myEnvironment = new PhysicalEnvironment();
        viewXfmGroup.addChild(myViewPlatform);
        viewBranch.addChild(viewXfmGroup);
        View myView = new View();
        myView.addCanvas3D(c);
        myView.attachViewPlatform(myViewPlatform);
```

```
            myView. setPhysicalBody(myBody);
            myView.setPhysicalEnvironment(myEnvironment);
            return viewBranch;
    }
    /**
     * Add some lights so that we can illuminate the scene.
     * This adds one ambient light to bring up the overall
     * lighting level and one directional shape to show
     * the shape of the objects in the scene.
     * @param b BranchGroup that the lights are to be added to.
     */
    protected void addLights(BranchGroup b) {
        BoundingSphere bounds =
                        new BoundingSphere(new Point3d(0.0,0.0,0.0), 100.0);
        Color3f ambientColour = new Color3f(1.0f, 1.0f, 1.0f);
        AmbientLight ambientLight = new AmbientLight(ambientColour);
        ambientLight.setInfluencingBounds(bounds);
        light.setInfluencingBounds(bounds);
        b.addChild(ambientLight);
    }
    /**
     * This builds the content branch of our scene graph.
     * It uses the buildShape function to create the actual shape,
     * adding to to the transform group so that the shape
     * is slightly tilted to reveal its 3D shape. It also uses
     * the addLights function to add some lights to the scene.
     * @param shape Node that represents the geometry for the content
     * @return BranchGroup that is the root of the content branch
     */
    protected BranchGroup buildContentBranch(Node shape) {
        BranchGroup contentBranch = new BranchGroup();
        Transform3D rotateCube = new Transform3D( );
        rotateCube.set(new AxisAngle4d(1.0,1.0,0.0,Math.PI/4.0));
        TransformGroup rotationGroup = new TransformGroup(rotateCube);
        contentBranch.addChild(rotationGroup);
        rotationGroup.addChild(shape);
        addLights(contentBranch);
        return contentBranch;
    }
    /**
     * This builds a shape by loading the geometry from a file.
     * This is achieved by creating an instance of a Lw3dLoader
     * from the utility classes.  The name of the file that is loaded
```

```java
 * is defined by the argument passed to the program when it is run.
 */
protected Node buildCube() {
    Lw3dLoader l = new Lw3dLoader();
    Scene s = null;
    try {
        s = l.load(filename);
    }
    catch (Exception e) {
        System.exit(1);
    }
    return s.getSceneGroup();
}
public void actionPerformed(ActionEvent e) {
    dispose();
    System.exit(0);
}
/**
 * This stores the first string argument to be used in the
 * loader function.
 */
public LightwaveLoader(String args[]) {
    if (args.length > 0) {
        filename = args[0];
        VirtualUniverse myUniverse = new VirtualUniverse();
        Locale myLocale = new Locale(myUniverse);
        myLocale.addBranchGraph(buildViewBranch(myCanvas3D));
        myLocale.addBranchGraph(buildContentBranch(buildShape()));
        setTitle("LightwaveLoader");
        setSize(400,400);
        setLayout(new BorderLayout());
        add(BorderLayout.CENTER, myCanvas3D);
        myButton.addActionListener(this);
        add(BorderLayout.SOUTH, myButton);
        setVisible(true);
    }
}
public static void main(String[] args) {
    LightwaveLoader lwl = new LightwaveLoader(args);
}
}
```

Chapter 4

SimpleWireFrame

Build a cube but this time render only the polygon edges.

```
import javax.media.j3d.*;
import javax.vecmath.*;
import java.awt.*;
import java.awt.event.*;
/**
* This builds a simple class using the Box utility class but only
* renders the edges of the polygons.
* @author I.J.Palmer
* @version 1.0
*/
public class SimpleWireFrame extends Frame implements ActionListener {
       protected Canvas3D myCanvas3D = new Canvas3D(null);
       protected Button myButton = new Button("Exit");
      /**
       * This function builds the view branch of the scene
       * graph.  It creates a branch group and then creates the
       * necessary view elements to give a useful view of our
       * content.
       * @param c Canvas3D that will display the view
       * @return BranchGroup that is the root of the view elements
       */
       protected BranchGroup buildViewBranch(Canvas3D c) {
             BranchGroup viewBranch = new BranchGroup();
             Transform3D viewXfm = new Transform3D();
             viewXfm.set(new Vector3f(0.0f,0.0f,10.0f));
             TransformGroup viewXfmGroup = new TransformGroup(viewXfm);
             ViewPlatform myViewPlatform = new ViewPlatform();
             PhysicalBody myBody = new PhysicalBody();
             PhysicalEnvironment myEnvironment = new PhysicalEnvironment();
             viewXfmGroup.addChild(myViewPlatform);
             viewBranch.addChild(viewXfmGroup);
```

```
            View myView = new View();
            myView.addCanvas3D(c);
            myView.attachViewPlatform(myViewPlatform);
            myView.setPhysicalBody(myBody);
            myView.setPhysicalEnvironment(myEnvironment);
            return viewBranch;
    }
    /**
     * Add some lights so that we can illuminate the scene.
     * This adds one ambient light to bring up the overall
     * lighting level and one directional shape to show
     * the shape of the objects in the scene.
     * @param b BranchGroup that the lights are to be added to.
     */
    protected void addLights(BranchGroup b) {
            BoundingSphere bounds =
                    new BoundingSphere(new Point3d(0.0,0.0,0.0), 100.0);
            Color3f lightColour = new Color3f(1.0f, 1.0f, 1.0f);
            Vector3f lightDir  = new Vector3f(-1.0f,-1.0f,-1.0f);
            Color3f ambientColour = new Color3f(1.0f,1.0f,1.0f);
            AmbientLight ambientLight = new AmbientLight(ambientColour);
            ambientLight.setInfluencingBounds(bounds);
            DirectionalLight light = new DirectionalLight(lightColour, lightDir);
            light.setInfluencingBounds(bounds);
            b.addChild(light);
            b.addChild(ambientLight);
    }
    /**
     * This builds the content branch of our scene graph.
     * It uses the buildShape function to create the actual shape,
     * adding to to the transform group so that the shape
     * is slightly tilted to reveal its 3D shape. It also uses
     * the addLights function to add some lights to the scene.
     * @param shape Node that represents the geometry for the content
     * @return BranchGroup that is the root of the content branch
     */
    protected BranchGroup buildContentBranch(Shape3D shape) {
            BranchGroup contentBranch = new BranchGroup();
            Transform3D rotateCube = new Transform3D( );
            rotateCube.set(new AxisAngle4d(1.0,1.0,0.0,Math.PI/4.0));
            TransformGroup rotationGroup = new TransformGroup(rotateCube);
            contentBranch.addChild(rotationGroup);
            rotationGroup.addChild(shape);
            addLights(contentBranch);
```

```java
        return contentBranch;
    }
    /**
     * Build a cube from the Box utility class.  This time we only
     * render the edges of the polygons by creating an appearance
     * which the appropriate attributes.
     * @return Node that is the shape.
     */
    protected Node buildShape() {
        Appearance app = new Appearance();
        PolygonAttributes polyAttr = new PolygonAttributes();
        polyAttr.setPolygonMode(PolygonAttributes.POLYGON_LINE);
        //Uncomment the next line to show all edges
        //polyAttr.setCullFace(PolygonAttributes.CULL_NONE);
        //Uncomment the next line to show the rear facing polygons only
        //polyAttr.setCullFace(PolygonAttributes.CULL_FRONT);
        app.setPolygonAttributes(polyAttr);
        return new Box(1.0f, 1.0f, 1.0f, app);
    }
    public void actionPerformed(ActionEvent e) {
        dispose();
        System.exit(0);
    }
    public SimpleWireFrame() {
        VirtualUniverse myUniverse = new VirtualUniverse();
        Locale myLocale = new Locale(myUniverse);
        myLocale.addBranchGraph(buildViewBranch(myCanvas3D));
        myLocale.addBranchGraph(buildContentBranch(buildShape()));
        setTitle("SimpleWireFrame");
        setSize(400,400);
        setLayout(new BorderLayout());
        add(BorderLayout.CENTER, myCanvas3D);
        add(BorderLayout.SOUTH,myButton);
        myButton.addActionListener(this);
        setVisible(true);
    }
    public static void main(String[] args) {
        SimpleWireFrame swf = new SimpleWireFrame();
    }
}
```

SimpleDirLight

This creates a sphere, an ambient light and a directional light to show the effect of the illumination model.

```java
import javax.media.j3d.*;
import javax.vecmath.*;
import java.awt.*;
import java.awt.event.*;
import com.sun.j3d.utils.geometry.*;
/**
* This builds a red sphere using the Sphere utility class and
* adds lights so that you can see it shape.  It creates a
* material for the sphere, creates an ambient light and a
* one directional light.
* @author I.J.Palmer
* @version 1.0
*/
public class SimpleDirLight extends Frame implements ActionListener {
    protected Canvas3D myCanvas3D = new Canvas3D(null);
    protected Button myButton = new Button("Exit");
    /**
     * This function builds the view branch of the scene
     * graph.  It creates a branch group and then creates the
     * necessary view elements to give a useful view of our
     * content.
     * @param c Canvas3D that will display the view
     * @return BranchGroup that is the root of the view elements
     */
    protected BranchGroup buildViewBranch(Canvas3D c) {
        BranchGroup viewBranch = new BranchGroup();
        Transform3D viewXfm = new Transform3D();
        viewXfm.set(new Vector3f(0.0f,0.0f,10.0f));
        TransformGroup viewXfmGroup = new TransformGroup(viewXfm);
        ViewPlatform myViewPlatform = new ViewPlatform();
        PhysicalBody myBody = new PhysicalBody();
        PhysicalEnvironment myEnvironment = new PhysicalEnvironment();
        viewXfmGroup.addChild(myViewPlatform);
        viewBranch.addChild(viewXfmGroup);
        View myView = new View();
        myView.addCanvas3D(c);
        myView.attachViewPlatform(myViewPlatform);
        myView.setPhysicalBody(myBody);
```

```
        myView.setPhysicalEnvironment(myEnvironment);
        return viewBranch;
}
/**
 * This creates some lights and adds them to the BranchGroup.
 * @param b BranchGroup that the lights are added to.
 */
protected void addLights(BranchGroup b) {
        // Create a bounds for the lights
        BoundingSphere bounds =
                new BoundingSphere(new Point3d(0.0,0.0,0.0),100.0);
        //Set up the ambient light
        Color3f ambientColour = new Color3f(0.2f,0.2f,0.2f);
        AmbientLight ambientLight = new AmbientLight(ambientColour);
        ambientLight.setInfluencingBounds(bounds);
        //Set up the directional light
        Color3f lightColour = new Color3f(1.0f,1.0f,1.0f);
        Vector3f lightDir  = new Vector3f(-1.0f,-1.0f,-1.0f);
        DirectionalLight light = new DirectionalLight(lightColour,lightDir);
        light.setInfluencingBounds(bounds);
        //Add the lights to the BranchGroup
        b.addChild(ambientLight);
        b.addChild(light);
}
/**
 * This builds the content branch of our scene graph.
 * It creates a transform group so that the shape
 * is slightly tilted to reveal its 3D shape.
 * @param shape Node that represents the geometry for the content
 * @return BranchGroup that is the root of the content branch
 */
protected BranchGroup buildContentBranch() {
        BranchGroup contentBranch = new BranchGroup();
        Transform3D rotateCube = new Transform3D( );
        rotateCube.set(new AxisAngle4d(1.0,1.0,0.0,Math.PI/4.0));
        TransformGroup rotationGroup = new TransformGroup(rotateCube);
        contentBranch.addChild(rotationGroup);
        //Create a new appearance
        Appearance app = new Appearance();
        //Create the colours for the material
        Color3f ambientColour = new Color3f(1.0f, 0.0f, 0.0f);
        Color3f diffuseColour = new Color3f(1.0f, 0.0f, 0.0f);
        Color3f specularColour = new Color3f(1.0f, 1.0f, 1.0f);
```

```
              Color3f emissiveColour= new Color3f(0.0f, 0.0f, 0.0f);
              //Define the shininess
              float shininess = 20.0f;
              //Set the material of the appearance
              app.setMaterial(new Material(ambientColour,emissiveColour,
                              diffuseColour,specularColour,shininess));
              //Create and add a new sphere using the appearance
              rotationGroup.addChild(new Sphere(2.0f,
                              Sphere.GENERATE_NORMALS, 120, app));
              //Use the addLights function to add the lights to the branch
              addLights(contentBranch);
              //Return the root of the content branch
              return contentBranch;
       }
       /**
        * Handles the exit button action to quit the program.
        */
       public void actionPerformed(ActionEvent e) {
              dispose();
              System.exit(0);
       }
       /**
        * This creates a default universe and locale, creates a window
        * and uses the functions defined in this class to build the
        * view and content branches of the scene graph.
        */
       public SimpleDirLight() {
              VirtualUniverse myUniverse = new VirtualUniverse();
              Locale myLocale = new Locale(myUniverse);
              myLocale.addBranchGraph(buildViewBranch(myCanvas3D));
              myLocale.addBranchGraph(buildContentBranch());
              setTitle("SimpleDirLight");
              setSize(400,400);
              setLayout(new BorderLayout());
              add(BorderLayout.CENTER, myCanvas3D);
              add(BorderLayout.SOUTH,myButton);
              myButton.addActionListener(this);
              setVisible(true);
       }
       public static void main(String[] args) {
              SimpleDirLight sdl = new SimpleDirLight();
       }
}
```

SimpleSpotLights

This creates a white sphere with two different coloured spotlights to show the effect of combining different light colours.

```java
import javax.media.j3d.*;
import javax.vecmath.*;
import java.awt.*;
import java.awt.event.*;
import com.sun.j3d.utils.geometry.*;
/**
* This builds a red sphere using the Sphere utility class and
* adds lights so that you can see it shape. It creates a
* material for the sphere, creates an ambient light and a
* two spot lights of different colours.
* @author I.J.Palmer
* @version 1.0
*/
public class SimpleSpotLights extends Frame implements ActionListener {
    protected Canvas3D myCanvas3D = new Canvas3D(null);
    protected Button myButton = new Button("Exit");
    /**
    * This function builds the view branch of the scene
    * graph. It creates a branch group and then creates the
    * necessary view elements to give a useful view of our
    * content.
    * @param c Canvas3D that will display the view
    * @return BranchGroup that is the root of the view elements
    */
    protected BranchGroup buildViewBranch(Canvas3D c) {
        BranchGroup viewBranch = new BranchGroup();
        Transform3D viewXfm = new Transform3D();
        viewXfm.set(new Vector3f(0.0f,0.0f,10.0f));
        TransformGroup viewXfmGroup = new TransformGroup(viewXfm);
        ViewPlatform myViewPlatform = new ViewPlatform();
        PhysicalBody myBody = new PhysicalBody();
        PhysicalEnvironment myEnvironment = new PhysicalEnvironment();
        viewXfmGroup.addChild(myViewPlatform);
        viewBranch.addChild(viewXfmGroup);
        View myView = new View();
        myView.addCanvas3D(c);
```

```
        myView.attachViewPlatform(myViewPlatform);
        myView.setPhysicalBody(myBody);
        myView.setPhysicalEnvironment(myEnvironment);
        return viewBranch;
    }
/**
 * This creates some lights and adds them to the BranchGroup.
 * @param b BranchGroup that the lights are added to.
 */
    protected void addLights(BranchGroup b) {
        // Create a bounds for the lights
        BoundingSphere bounds =
            new BoundingSphere(new Point3d(0.0,0.0,0.0),100.0);
        //Set up the ambient light
        Color3f ambientColour = new Color3f(0.2f,0.2f,0.2f);
        AmbientLight ambientLight = new AmbientLight(ambientColour);
        ambientLight.setInfluencingBounds(bounds);
        Color3f blueColour = new Color3f(0.0f, 0.0f, 1.0f);
        Point3f bluePosition  = new Point3f(1.8f, 1.8f, 1.8f);
        Point3f blueAtten = new Point3f(1.0f, 0.0f, 0.0f);
        Vector3f blueDir = new Vector3f(-1.0f,-1.0f,-1.0f);
        SpotLight blueLight = new SpotLight(blueColour, bluePosition,
                                            blueAtten, blueDir
                                            (float)(Math.PI/2.0), 0.0f);
        blueLight.setInfluencingBounds(bounds);
        Color3f greenColour = new Color3f(0.0f, 1.0f, 0.0f);
        Point3f greenPosition = new Point3f(0.0f, 0.0f, 3.0f);
        Point3f greenAtten = new Point3f(1.0f, 0.0f, 0.0f);
        Vector3f greenDir = new Vector3f(0.0f, 0.0f, -1.0f);
        SpotLight greenLight = new SpotLight(greenColour, greenPosition,
                                             greenAtten, greenDir,
                                             (float)(Math.PI/2.0), 0.0f);
        greenLight.setInfluencingBounds(bounds);
        //Add the lights to the BranchGroup
        b.addChild(ambientLight);
        b.addChild(greenLight);
        b.addChild(blueLight);
    }
/**
 * This builds the content branch of our scene graph.
 * It creates a transform group so that the shape
 * is slightly tilted to reveal its 3D shape.
 * @param shape Node that represents the geometry for the content
 * @return BranchGroup that is the root of the content branch
```

```java
*/
protected BranchGroup buildContentBranch() {
    BranchGroup contentBranch = new BranchGroup();
    Transform3D rotateCube = new Transform3D( );
    rotateCube.set(new AxisAngle4d(1.0,1.0,0.0,Math.PI/4.0));
    TransformGroup rotationGroup = new TransformGroup(rotateCube);
    contentBranch.addChild(rotationGroup);
    //Create a new appearance
    Appearance app = new Appearance();
    //Create the colours for the material
    Color3f ambientColour = new Color3f(1.0f, 1.0f, 1.0f);
    Color3f diffuseColour = new Color3f(1.0f, 1.0f, 1.0f);
    Color3f specularColour = new Color3f(1.0f, 1.0f, 1.0f);
    Color3f emissiveColour= new Color3f(0.0f, 0.0f, 0.0f);
    //Define the shininess
    float shininess = 20.0f;
    //Set the material of the appearance
    app.setMaterial(new Material(ambientColour,emissiveColour,
                        diffuseColour,specularColour,shininess));
    //Create and add a new sphere using the appearance
    rotationGroup.addChild(new Sphere(2.0f,
                    Sphere.GENERATE_NORMALS, 120, app));
    //Use the addLights function to add the lights to the branch
    addLights(contentBranch);
    //Return the root of the content branch
    return contentBranch;
}
/**
 * Handles the exit button action to quit the program.
 */
public void actionPerformed(ActionEvent e) {
    dispose();
    System.exit(0);
}
/**
 * This creates a default universe and locale, creates a window
 * and uses the functions defined in this class to build the
 * view and content branches of the scene graph.
 */
public SimpleSpotLights() {
    VirtualUniverse myUniverse = new VirtualUniverse();
    Locale myLocale = new Locale(myUniverse);
    myLocale.addBranchGraph(buildViewBranch(myCanvas3D));
```

```
        myLocale.addBranchGraph(buildContentBranch());
        setTitle("SimpleDirLight");
        setSize(400,400);
        setLayout(new BorderLayout());
        add(BorderLayout.CENTER, myCanvas3D);
        add(BorderLayout.SOUTH,myButton);
        myButton.addActionListener(this);
        setVisible(true);
    }
    public static void main(String[] args) {
        SimpleSpotLights spl = new SimpleSpotLights();
    }
}
```

SimpleIndexedQuadNormals

This is similar to the program SimpleIndexedQuad but this time we define a red material and add some lights to the scene.

```
import javax.media.j3d.*;
import javax.vecmath.*;
import java.awt.*;
import java.awt.event.*;
/**
 * This builds a simple class using the an indexed quadrilateral
 * array.  This demonstrates the use of the IndexedQuadArray class.
 * It defines both the vertices and the normals of the cube such
 * that the shape is shaded with flat faces.
 * @author I.J.Palmer
 * @version 1.0
 */
public class SimpleIndexedQuadNormals extends Frame implements ActionListener
{
    protected Canvas3D myCanvas3D = new Canvas3D(null);
    protected Button myButton = new Button("Exit");
    /**
     * This function builds the view branch of the scene
     * graph.  It creates a branch group and then creates the
     * necessary view elements to give a useful view of our
     * content.
     * @param c Canvas3D that will display the view
```

```
   * @return BranchGroup that is the root of the view elements
   */
  protected BranchGroup buildViewBranch(Canvas3D c) {
        BranchGroup viewBranch = new BranchGroup();
        Transform3D viewXfm = new Transform3D();
        viewXfm.set(new Vector3f(0.0f,0.0f,5.0f));
        TransformGroup viewXfmGroup = new TransformGroup(viewXfm);
        ViewPlatform myViewPlatform = new ViewPlatform();
        PhysicalBody myBody = new PhysicalBody();
        PhysicalEnvironment myEnvironment = new PhysicalEnvironment();
        viewXfmGroup.addChild(myViewPlatform);
        viewBranch.addChild(viewXfmGroup);
        View myView = new View();
        myView.addCanvas3D(c);
        myView.attachViewPlatform(myViewPlatform);
        myView.setPhysicalBody(myBody);
        myView.setPhysicalEnvironment(myEnvironment);
        return viewBranch;
  }
  /**
   * Add some lights so that we can illuminate the scene.
   * This adds one ambient light to bring up the overall
   * lighting level and one directional shape to show
   * the shape of the objects in the scene.
   * @param b BranchGroup that the lights are to be added to.
   */
  protected void addLights(BranchGroup b) {
        BoundingSphere bounds =
                new BoundingSphere(new Point3d(0.0,0.0,0.0),100.0);
        Color3f lightColour = new Color3f(1.0f,1.0f,1.0f);
        Vector3f lightDir = new Vector3f(-1.0f, -1.0f,-1.0f);
        Color3f ambientColour = new Color3f(0.2f, 0.2f, 0.2f);
        AmbientLight ambientLight = new AmbientLight(ambientColour);
        ambientLight.setInfluencingBounds(bounds);
        DirectionalLight directionalLight =
                        new DirectionalLight(lightColour, lightDir);
        directionalLight.setInfluencingBounds(bounds);
        b.addChild(ambientLight);
        b.addChild(directionalLight);
  }
  /**
   * This builds the content branch of our scene graph.
   * It uses the buildShape function to create the actual shape,
```

```
* adding to to the transform group so that the shape
* is slightly tilted to reveal its 3D shape. It also uses
* the addLights function to add some lights to the scene.
* @param shape Node that represents the geometry for the content
* @return BranchGroup that is the root of the content branch
*/
protected BranchGroup buildContentBranch(Node shape) {
    BranchGroup contentBranch = new BranchGroup();
    Transform3D rotateCube = new Transform3D( );
    rotateCube.set(new AxisAngle4d(1.0,1.0,0.0,Math.PI/4.0));
    TransformGroup rotationGroup = new TransformGroup(rotateCube);
    contentBranch.addChild(rotationGroup);
    rotationGroup.addChild(shape);
    addLights(contentBranch);
    return contentBranch;
}
/**
* Build a cube from an IndexedQuadArray. This method creates
* the vertices as a set of eight points and the normals as a set of
* six vectors (one for each face). The data is then defined such
* that each vertex has a different normal associated with it when
* it is being used for a different face.
* @return Node that is the shape.
*/
protected Node buildShape() {
    //The shape. The constructor specifies 8 vertices, that both
    //vertices and normals are to be defined and that there are
    //24 normals to be specified (4 for each of the 6 faces).
    IndexedQuadArray indexedCube = new IndexedQuadArray(8,
                                    IndexedQuadArray.COORDINATES |
                                    IndexedQuadArray.NORMALS, 24);
    //The vertex coordinates defined as an array of points.
    Point3f[] cubeCoordinates = {    new Point3f( 1.0f, 1.0f, 1.0f),
                                     new Point3f(-1.0f, 1.0f, 1.0f),
                                     new Point3f(-1.0f,-1.0f, 1.0f),
                                     new Point3f( 1.0f,-1.0f, 1.0f),
                                     new Point3f( 1.0f, 1.0f,-1.0f),
                                     new Point3f(-1.0f, 1.0f,-1.0f),
                                     new Point3f(-1.0f,-1.0f,-1.0f),
                                     new Point3f( 1.0f,-1.0f,-1.0f)};
    //The vertex normals defined as an array of vectors
    Vector3f[] normals= { new Vector3f( 0.0f, 0.0f, 1.0f),
                          new Vector3f( 0.0f, 0.0f,-1.0f),
                          new Vector3f( 1.0f, 0.0f, 0.0f),
```

```
                              new Vector3f(-1.0f, 0.0f, 0.0f),
                              new Vector3f( 0.0f, 1.0f, 0.0f),
                              new Vector3f( 0.0f,-1.0f, 0.0f)};
     //Define the indices used to reference vertex array
     int coordIndices[] = {0,1,2,3,7,6,5,4,0,3,7,4,5,6,2,1,0,4,5,1,6,7,3,2};
     //Define the indices used to reference normal array
     int normalIndices[] = {0,0,0,0,1,1,1,1,2,2,2,2,3,3,3,3,4,4,4,4,5,5,5,5};
     //Set the data
     indexedCube.setCoordinates(0, cubeCoordinates);
     indexedCube.setNormals(0,normals);
     indexedCube.setCoordinateIndices(0, coordIndices);
     indexedCube.setNormalIndices(0, normalIndices);
     //Define an appearance for the shape
     Appearance app = new Appearance();
     Color3f ambientColour = new Color3f(1.0f,0.0f,0.0f);
     Color3f emissiveColour = new Color3f(0.0f,0.0f,0.0f);
     Color3f specularColour = new Color3f(1.0f,1.0f,1.0f);
     Color3f diffuseColour = new Color3f(1.0f,0.0f,0.0f);
     float shininess = 20.0f;
     app.setMaterial(new Material(ambientColour,emissiveColour,
                                  diffuseColour,specularColour,shininess));

     //Create and return the shape
     return new Shape3D(indexedCube, app);
}
/**
 * Handles the exit button action to quit the program.
 */
public void actionPerformed(ActionEvent e) {
     dispose();
     System.exit(0);
}
public SimpleIndexedQuadNormals() {
     VirtualUniverse myUniverse = new VirtualUniverse();
     Locale myLocale = new Locale(myUniverse);
     myLocale.addBranchGraph(buildViewBranch(myCanvas3D));
     myLocale.addBranchGraph(buildContentBranch(buildShape()));
     setTitle("SimpleIndexedQuadNormals");
     setSize(400,400);
     setLayout(new BorderLayout());
     add(BorderLayout.CENTER, myCanvas3D);
     add(BorderLayout.SOUTH,myButton);
     myButton.addActionListener(this);
     setVisible(true);
```

```
        }
    public static void main(String[] args) {
        SimpleIndexedQuadNormals siqn = new SimpleIndexedQuadNormals();
    }
}
```

SimpleIndexQuadSmooth

This is similar to the SimpleIndexedQuadNormals program but the normals are defined such that the corners of the cube share a comment normal.

```
import javax.media.j3d.*;
import javax.vecmath.*;
import java.awt.*;
import java.awt.event.*;
/**
* This builds a simple class using the an indexed quadrilateral
* array.  This demonstrates the use of the IndexedQuadArray class.
* It defines both the vertices and the normals of the shape such
* that each vertex has only one normal and it appears to have smooth
* edges.
* @author I.J.Palmer
* @version 1.0
*/
public class SimpleIndexedQuadSmooth extends Frame implements ActionListener {
    protected Canvas3D myCanvas3D = new Canvas3D(null);
    protected Button myButton = new Button("Exit");
    /**
    * This function builds the view branch of the scene
    * graph.  It creates a branch group and then creates the
    * necessary view elements to give a useful view of our
    * content.
    * @param c Canvas3D that will display the view
    * @return BranchGroup that is the root of the view elements
    */
    protected BranchGroup buildViewBranch(Canvas3D c) {
        BranchGroup viewBranch = new BranchGroup();
        Transform3D viewXfm = new Transform3D();
        viewXfm.set(new Vector3f(0.0f,0.0f,5.0f));
        TransformGroup viewXfmGroup = new TransformGroup(viewXfm);
        ViewPlatform myViewPlatform = new ViewPlatform();
```

```
        PhysicalBody myBody = new PhysicalBody();
        PhysicalEnvironment myEnvironment = new PhysicalEnvironment();
        viewXfmGroup.addChild(myViewPlatform);
        viewBranch.addChild(viewXfmGroup);
        View myView = new View();
        myView.addCanvas3D(c);
        myView.attachViewPlatform(myViewPlatform);
        myView.setPhysicalBody(myBody);
        myView.setPhysicalEnvironment(myEnvironment);
        return viewBranch;
}
/**
 * Add some lights so that we can illuminate the scene.
 * This adds one ambient light to bring up the overall
 * lighting level and one directional shape to show
 * the shape of the objects in the scene.
 * @param b BranchGroup that the lights are to be added to.
 */
protected void addLights(BranchGroup b) {
        BoundingSphere bounds =
                new BoundingSphere(new Point3d(0.0,0.0,0.0),100.0);
        Color3f lightColour = new Color3f(1.0f,1.0f,1.0f);
        Vector3f lightDir = new Vector3f(-1.0f, -1.0f,-1.0f);
        Color3f ambientColour = new Color3f(0.2f, 0.2f, 0.2f);
        AmbientLight ambientLight = new AmbientLight(ambientColour);
        ambientLight.setInfluencingBounds(bounds);
        DirectionalLight directionalLight =
                new DirectionalLight(lightColour, lightDir);
        directionalLight.setInfluencingBounds(bounds);
        b.addChild(ambientLight);
        b.addChild(directionalLight);
}
/**
 * This builds the content branch of our scene graph.
 * It uses the buildShape function to create the actual shape,
 * adding to to the transform group so that the shape
 * is slightly tilted to reveal its 3D shape. It also uses
 * the addLights function to add some lights to the scene.
 * @param shape Node that represents the geometry for the content
 * @return BranchGroup that is the root of the content branch
 */
protected BranchGroup buildContentBranch(Node shape) {
        BranchGroup contentBranch = new BranchGroup();
```

```java
    Transform3D rotateCube = new Transform3D( );
    rotateCube.set(new AxisAngle4d(1.0,1.0,0.0,Math.PI/4.0));
    TransformGroup rotationGroup = new TransformGroup(rotateCube);
    contentBranch.addChild(rotationGroup);
    rotationGroup.addChild(shape);
    addLights(contentBranch);
    return contentBranch;
}
/**
* Build a cube from an IndexedQuadArray.  This method creates
* the vertices as a set of eight points and the normals as a set of
* six vectors (one for each face).  The data is then defined such
* that each vertex has a different normal associated with it when
* it is being used for a different face.
* @return Node that is the shape.
*/
protected Node buildShape() {
    //The shape.  The constructor specifies 8 vertices, that both
    //vertices and normals are to be defined and that there are
    //24 normals to be specified (4 for each of the 6 faces).
    IndexedQuadArray indexedCube = new IndexedQuadArray(8,
            IndexedQuadArray.COORDINATES |
            IndexedQuadArray.NORMALS, 24);
    //The vertex coordinates defined as an array of points.
    Point3f[] cubeCoordinates = {    new Point3f( 1.0f, 1.0f, 1.0f),
                                     new Point3f(-1.0f, 1.0f, 1.0f),
                                     new Point3f(-1.0f,-1.0f, 1.0f),
                                     new Point3f( 1.0f,-1.0f, 1.0f),
                                     new Point3f( 1.0f, 1.0f,-1.0f),
                                     new Point3f(-1.0f, 1.0f,-1.0f),
                                     new Point3f(-1.0f,-1.0f,-1.0f),
                                     new Point3f( 1.0f,-1.0f,-1.0f)};
    //The vertex normals defined as an array of vectors
    Vector3f[] normals= {    new Vector3f( 1.0f, 1.0f, 1.0f),
                             new Vector3f(-1.0f, 1.0f, 1.0f),
                             new Vector3f(-1.0f,-1.0f, 1.0f),
                             new Vector3f( 1.0f,-1.0f, 1.0f),
                             new Vector3f( 1.0f, 1.0f,-1.0f),
                             new Vector3f(-1.0f, 1.0f,-1.0f),
                             new Vector3f(-1.0f,-1.0f,-1.0f),
                             new Vector3f( 1.0f,-1.0f,-1.0f)};
    //Define the indices used to reference vertex array
    int coordIndices[] = {0,1,2,3,7,6,5,4,0,3,7,4,5,6,2,1,0,4,5,1,6,7,3,2};
    //Define the indices used to reference normal array
```

```
    int normalIndices[] = {0,1,2,3,7,6,5,4,0,3,7,4,5,6,2,1,0,4,5,1,6,7,3,2};
    //Set the data
    indexedCube.setCoordinates(0, cubeCoordinates);
    indexedCube.setNormals(0,normals);
    indexedCube.setCoordinateIndices(0, coordIndices);
    indexedCube.setNormalIndices(0, normalIndices);
    //Define an appearance for the shape
    Appearance app = new Appearance();
    Color3f ambientColour = new Color3f(1.0f,0.0f,0.0f);
    Color3f emissiveColour = new Color3f(0.0f,0.0f,0.0f);
    Color3f specularColour = new Color3f(1.0f,1.0f,1.0f);
    Color3f diffuseColour = new Color3f(1.0f,0.0f,0.0f);
    float shininess = 20.0f;
    app.setMaterial(new Material(ambientColour,emissiveColour,
                          diffuseColour,specularColour,shininess));
    //Create and return the shape
    return new Shape3D(indexedCube, app);
}
/**
 * Handles the exit button action to quit the program.
 */
public void actionPerformed(ActionEvent e) {
    dispose();
    System.exit(0);
}
public SimpleIndexedQuadSmooth() {
    VirtualUniverse myUniverse = new VirtualUniverse();
    Locale myLocale = new Locale(myUniverse);
    myLocale.addBranchGraph(buildViewBranch(myCanvas3D));
    myLocale.addBranchGraph(buildContentBranch(buildShape()));
    setTitle("SimpleIndexedQuadSmooth");
    setSize(400,400);
    setLayout(new BorderLayout());
    add(BorderLayout.CENTER, myCanvas3D);
    add(BorderLayout.SOUTH,myButton);
    myButton.addActionListener(this);
    setVisible(true);
}
public static void main(String[] args) {
    SimpleIndexedQuadSmooth siqs = new SimpleIndexedQuadSmooth();
}
}
```

SimpleTexture

This loads an image from an external file and uses this as a texture map on a cube. The texture is mapped onto each surface once, i.e. the corners of the image are mapped to the corners of each face.

```java
import javax.media.j3d.*;
import javax.vecmath.*;
import java.awt.*;
import java.awt.event.*;
import com.sun.j3d.utils.image.*;
import com.sun.j3d.utils.geometry.*;
/**
 * This demonstrates the simple application of textures.
 * Each face of a cube has an image mapped onto it
 * exactly once. The image is loaded from an external file.
 * @author I.J.Palmer
 * @version 1.0
 */
public class SimpleTexture extends Frame implements ActionListener {
    protected Canvas3D myCanvas3D = new Canvas3D(null);
    protected Button myButton = new Button("Exit");
    /**
     * This function builds the view branch of the scene
     * graph. It creates a branch group and then creates the
     * necessary view elements to give a useful view of our
     * content.
     * @param c Canvas3D that will display the view
     * @return BranchGroup that is the root of the view elements
     */
    protected BranchGroup buildViewBranch(Canvas3D c) {
        BranchGroup viewBranch = new BranchGroup();
        Transform3D viewXfm = new Transform3D();
        viewXfm.set(new Vector3f(0.0f,0.0f,5.0f));
        TransformGroup viewXfmGroup = new TransformGroup(viewXfm);
        ViewPlatform myViewPlatform = new ViewPlatform();
        PhysicalBody myBody = new PhysicalBody();
        PhysicalEnvironment myEnvironment = new PhysicalEnvironment();
        viewXfmGroup.addChild(myViewPlatform);
        viewBranch.addChild(viewXfmGroup);
        View myView = new View();
        myView.addCanvas3D(c);
```

```
            myView.attachViewPlatform(myViewPlatform);
            myView.setPhysicalBody(myBody);
            myView.setPhysicalEnvironment(myEnvironment);
            return viewBranch;
    }
    /**
    * Add some lights so that we can illuminate the scene.
    * This adds one ambient light to bring up the overall
    * lighting level and one directional shape to show
    * the shape of the objects in the scene.
    * @param b BranchGroup that the lights are to be added to.
    */
    protected void addLights(BranchGroup b) {
        BoundingSphere bounds =
                    new BoundingSphere(new Point3d(0.0,0.0,0.0), 100.0);
        Color3f lightColour1 = new Color3f(1.0f,1.0f,1.0f);
        Vector3f lightDir1  = new Vector3f(-1.0f, -1.0f,-1.0f);
        Color3f lightColour2 = new Color3f(1.0f, 1.0f, 1.0f);
        Vector3f lightDir2  = new Vector3f(0.0f, 0.0f, -1.0f);
        Color3f ambientColour = new Color3f(0.2f, 0.2f, 0.2f);
        AmbientLight ambientLight1 = new AmbientLight(ambientColour);
        ambientLight1.setInfluencingBounds(bounds);
        DirectionalLight directionalLight1 =
                    new DirectionalLight(lightColour1, lightDir1);
        directionalLight1.setInfluencingBounds(bounds);
        b.addChild(ambientLight1);
        b.addChild(directionalLight1);
    }
    /**
    * This builds the content branch of our scene graph.
    * It uses the buildShape function to create the actual shape,
    * adding to to the transform group so that the shape
    * is slightly tilted to reveal its 3D shape. It also uses
    * the addLights function to add some lights to the scene.
    * @param shape Node that represents the geometry for the content
    * @return BranchGroup that is the root of the content branch
    */
    protected BranchGroup buildContentBranch(Node shape) {
        BranchGroup contentBranch = new BranchGroup();
        Transform3D rotateCube = new Transform3D( );
        rotateCube.set(new AxisAngle4d(1.0,1.0,0.0,Math.PI/4.0));
        TransformGroup rotationGroup = new TransformGroup(rotateCube);
        contentBranch.addChild(rotationGroup);
```

```
        rotationGroup.addChild(shape);
        addLights(contentBranch);
        return contentBranch;
}
/**
 * This defines the appearance with a texture.
 * The texture is loaded from an external file.
 * @return Appearance that uses the texture.
 */
protected Appearance DefineAppearance() {
        //Load the texture from the external image file
        TextureLoader textLoad = new TextureLoader("housebrick.jpg", this);
        //Access the image from the loaded texture
        ImageComponent2D textImage = textLoad.getImage();
        //Create a two dimensional texture
        Texture2D texture =
                new Texture2D(Texture2D.BASE_LEVEL, Texture.RGB,
                                textImage.getWidth(), textImage.getHeight());
        //Set the texture from the image loaded
        texture.setImage(0, textImage);
        //Create the appearance that will use the texture
        Appearance app = new Appearance();
        app.setTexture(texture);
        //Define how the texture will be mapped onto the surface
        //by creating the appropriate texture attributes
        TextureAttributes textAttr = new TextureAttributes();
        textAttr.setTextureMode(TextureAttributes.REPLACE);
        app.setTextureAttributes(textAttr);
        app.setMaterial(new Material());
        return app;
}
/**
 * Build a cube from an IndexedQuadArray. This method creates
 * the vertices as a set of eight points and the normals as a set of
 * six vectors (one for each face). The data is then defined such
 * that each vertex has a different normal associated with it when
 * it is being used for a different face. The shape is created with
 * texture coordinates so that when the appearance is set it will
 * use the appearance texture on the surface.
 * @return Node that is the shape.
 */
protected Node buildShape() {
        IndexedQuadArray indexedCube = new IndexedQuadArray(8,
                        IndexedQuadArray.COORDINATES|
```

```
                    IndexedQuadArray.NORMALS|
                    IndexedQuadArray.TEXTURE_COORDINATE_2, 24);
    Point3f[] cubeCoordinates = {    new Point3f( 1.0f, 1.0f, 1.0f),
                                     new Point3f(-1.0f, 1.0f, 1.0f),
                                     new Point3f(-1.0f,-1.0f, 1.0f),
                                     new Point3f( 1.0f,-1.0f, 1.0f),
                                     new Point3f( 1.0f, 1.0f,-1.0f),
                                     new Point3f(-1.0f, 1.0f,-1.0f),
                                     new Point3f(-1.0f,-1.0f,-1.0f),
                                     new Point3f( 1.0f,-1.0f,-1.0f)};
    Vector3f[] normals= { new Vector3f( 0.0f, 0.0f, 1.0f),
                          new Vector3f( 0.0f, 0.0f,-1.0f),
                          new Vector3f( 1.0f, 0.0f, 0.0f),
                          new Vector3f(-1.0f, 0.0f, 0.0f),
                          new Vector3f( 0.0f, 1.0f, 0.0f),
                          new Vector3f( 0.0f,-1.0f, 0.0f)};
    //Define the texture coordinates.  These are defined
    //as floating point pairs of values that are used to
    //map the corners of the texture image onto the vertices
    //of the face.  We then define the indices into this
    //array of values in a similar way to that used for
    //the vertices and normals.
    TexCoord2f[] textCoord = {    new TexCoord2f(1.0f,1.0f),
                                  new TexCoord2f(0.0f,1.0f),
                                  new TexCoord2f(0.0f,0.0f),
                                  new TexCoord2f(1.0f,0.0f)};
    int coordIndices[] = {0,1,2,3,7,6,5,4,0,3,7,4,5,6,2,1,0,4,5,1,6,7,3,2};
    int normalIndices[] = {0,0,0,0,1,1,1,1,2,2,2,2,3,3,3,3,4,4,4,4,5,5,5,5};
    int textIndices[] =  {0,1,2,3,3,0,1,2,1,2,3,0,1,2,3,0,3,0,1,2,1,2,3,0};
    indexedCube.setCoordinates(0, cubeCoordinates);
    indexedCube.setCoordinateIndices(0, coordIndices);
    indexedCube.setNormals(0,normals);
    indexedCube.setNormalIndices(0, normalIndices);
    indexedCube.setTextureCoordinates(0,0,textCoord);
    indexedCube.setTextureCoordinateIndices(0,0,textIndices);
    return new Shape3D(indexedCube, DefineAppearance());
}
/**
* Handles the exit button action to quit the program.
*/
public void actionPerformed(ActionEvent e) {
    dispose();
    System.exit(0);
```

```
        }

    public SimpleTexture() {
        VirtualUniverse myUniverse = new VirtualUniverse();
        Locale myLocale = new Locale(myUniverse);
      myLocale.addBranchGraph(buildViewBranch(myCanvas3D));
      myLocale.addBranchGraph(buildContentBranch(buildShape()));
        setTitle("SimpleTexture");
        setSize(400,400);
        setLayout(new BorderLayout());
        add(BorderLayout.CENTER, myCanvas3D);
        add(BorderLayout.SOUTH,myButton);
        myButton.addActionListener(this);
        setVisible(true);
    }
    public static void main(String[] args) {
        SimpleTexture st = new SimpleTexture();
    }
}
```

SimpleTextureGen

This generates the coordinates for the textures automatically. It uses an instance of the class **TexCoordGeneration** to do this.

```
import javax.media.j3d.*;
import javax.vecmath.*;
import java.awt.*;
import java.awt.event.*;
import com.sun.j3d.utils.image.*;
/**
 * This uses a TexCoordGeneration class to automatically define the
 * texture coordinates.
 * @author I.J.Palmer
 * @version 1.0
 */
public class SimpleTextureGen extends Frame implements ActionListener {
    protected Canvas3D myCanvas3D = new Canvas3D(null);
    protected Button myButton = new Button("Exit");
    /**
     * This function builds the view branch of the scene
```

```
 * graph.  It creates a branch group and then creates the
 * necessary view elements to give a useful view of our
 * content.
 * @param c Canvas3D that will display the view
 * @return BranchGroup that is the root of the view elements
 */
protected BranchGroup buildViewBranch(Canvas3D c) {
    BranchGroup viewBranch = new BranchGroup();
    Transform3D viewXfm = new Transform3D();
    viewXfm.set(new Vector3f(0.0f,0.0f,10.0f));
    TransformGroup viewXfmGroup = new TransformGroup(viewXfm);
    ViewPlatform myViewPlatform = new ViewPlatform();
    PhysicalBody myBody = new PhysicalBody();
    PhysicalEnvironment myEnvironment = new PhysicalEnvironment();
    viewXfmGroup.addChild(myViewPlatform);
    viewBranch.addChild(viewXfmGroup);
    View myView = new View();
    myView.addCanvas3D(c);
    myView.attachViewPlatform(myViewPlatform);
    myView.setPhysicalBody(myBody);
    myView.setPhysicalEnvironment(myEnvironment);
    return viewBranch;
}
/**
 * Add some lights so that we can illuminate the scene.
 * This adds one ambient light to bring up the overall
 * lighting level and one directional shape to show
 * the shape of the objects in the scene.
 * @param b BranchGroup that the lights are to be added to.
 */
protected void addLights(BranchGroup b) {
    BoundingSphere bounds =
                new BoundingSphere(new Point3d(0.0,0.0,0.0), 100.0);
    Color3f lightColour1 = new Color3f(1.0f,1.0f,1.0f);
    Vector3f lightDir1  = new Vector3f(-1.0f, -1.0f,-1.0f);
   Color3f lightColour2 = new Color3f(1.0f, 1.0f, 1.0f);
   Vector3f lightDir2  = new Vector3f(0.0f, 0.0f, -1.0f);
   Color3f ambientColour = new Color3f(0.2f, 0.2f, 0.2f);
    AmbientLight ambientLight1 = new AmbientLight(ambientColour);
    ambientLight1.setInfluencingBounds(bounds);
    DirectionalLight directionalLight1 =
                new DirectionalLight(lightColour1, lightDir1);
    directionalLight1.setInfluencingBounds(bounds);
```

```
            b.addChild(ambientLight1);
            b.addChild(directionalLight1);
    }
    /**
     * This builds the content branch of our scene graph.
     * The shape supplied as a parameter
     * is slightly tilted to reveal its 3D shape. It also uses
     * the addLights function to add some lights to the scene.
     * @param shape Node that represents the geometry for the content
     * @return BranchGroup that is the root of the content branch
     */
    protected BranchGroup buildContentBranch(Node shape) {
        BranchGroup contentBranch = new BranchGroup();
        Transform3D rotateCube = new Transform3D( );
        rotateCube.set(new AxisAngle4d(1.0,1.0,0.0,Math.PI/4.0));
        TransformGroup rotationGroup = new TransformGroup(rotateCube);
        contentBranch.addChild(rotationGroup);
        rotationGroup.addChild(shape);
        addLights(contentBranch);
        return contentBranch;
    }
    /**
     * This defines the appearance for the shape using a texture.
     * It uses a TextureLoader to load the texture image from an
     * external file and a TexCoordGeneration to define the
     * texture coordinates.
     * @return Appearance that uses a texture.
     */
    protected Appearance defineAppearance() {
            //This is used to automatically define the texture coordinates.
            //The coordinates are generated in object coordinates, but by
            //commented out the line with 'OBJECT_LINEAR' and uncommenting
            //the line 'EYE_LINEAR' the program will use eye coordinates.
            TexCoordGeneration textCoorder =
                        new TexCoordGeneration(
                            TexCoordGeneration.OBJECT_LINEAR,
                            //TexCoordGeneration.EYE_LINEAR,
                            TexCoordGeneration.TEXTURE_COORDINATE_2);
            //Load the texture from the external image file
            TextureLoader textLoad = new TextureLoader("housebrick.jpg", this);
            //Access the image from the loaded texture
            ImageComponent2D textImage = textLoad.getImage();
            //Create a two dimensional texture
            Texture2D texture =
```

```
                    new Texture2D(Texture2D.BASE_LEVEL, Texture.RGB,
                                    textImage.getWidth(), textImage.getHeight());
        //Set the texture from the image loaded
        texture.setImage(0, textImage);
        //Create the appearance that will use the texture
        Appearance app = new Appearance();
        app.setTexture(texture);
        //Pass the coordinate generator to the appearance
        app.setTexCoordGeneration(textCoorder);
        //Define how the texture will be mapped onto the surface
        //by creating the appropriate texture attributes
        TextureAttributes textAttr = new TextureAttributes();
        textAttr.setTextureMode(TextureAttributes.REPLACE);
        app.setTextureAttributes(textAttr);
        app.setMaterial(new Material());
        return app;
}
/**
 * Build a cube from an IndexedQuadArray.  This method creates
 * the vertices as a set of eight points and the normals as a set of
 * six vectors (one for each face).  The data is then defined such
 * that each vertex has a different normal associated with it when
 * it is being used for a different face.  The shape doesn't have
 * texture coordinates or nornmals defined since the texture
 * coordinate generator will define the necessary data.
 * @return Node that is the shape.
 */
protected Node buildShape() {
    IndexedQuadArray indexedCube = new IndexedQuadArray(8,
                                IndexedQuadArray.COORDINATES, 24);
    Point3f[] cubeCoordinates = {    new Point3f( 1.0f, 1.0f, 1.0f),
                                     new Point3f(-1.0f, 1.0f, 1.0f),
                                     new Point3f(-1.0f,-1.0f, 1.0f),
                                     new Point3f( 1.0f,-1.0f, 1.0f),
                                     new Point3f( 1.0f, 1.0f,-1.0f),
                                     new Point3f(-1.0f, 1.0f,-1.0f),
                                     new Point3f(-1.0f,-1.0f,-1.0f),
                                     new Point3f( 1.0f,-1.0f,-1.0f)};
    int coordIndices[] = {0,1,2,3,7,6,5,4,0,3,7,4,5,6,2,1,0,4,5,1,6,7,3,2};
    indexedCube.setCoordinates(0, cubeCoordinates);
    indexedCube.setCoordinateIndices(0, coordIndices);
    return new Shape3D(indexedCube, defineAppearance());
}
```

```java
/**
 * Handles the exit button action to quit the program.
 */
public void actionPerformed(ActionEvent e) {
    dispose();
    System.exit(0);
}
public SimpleTextureGen() {
    VirtualUniverse myUniverse = new VirtualUniverse();
    Locale myLocale = new Locale(myUniverse);
    myLocale.addBranchGraph(buildViewBranch(myCanvas3D));
    myLocale.addBranchGraph(buildContentBranch(buildShape()));
    setTitle("SimpleWorld");
    setSize(400,400);
    setLayout(new BorderLayout());
    add(BorderLayout.CENTER, myCanvas3D);
    add(BorderLayout.SOUTH,myButton);
    myButton.addActionListener(this);
    setVisible(true);
}
public static void main(String[] args) {
    SimpleTextureGen stg = new SimpleTextureGen();
}
}
```

Chapter 5

SimpleCombine

This builds up a hieararchical scene from primitives and transform groups.

```java
import javax.media.j3d.*;
import javax.vecmath.*;
import java.awt.*;
import java.awt.event.*;
import com.sun.j3d.utils.geometry.*;
/**
* This builds up a simple scene from primitives.
* It builds a circular 'house' with a conical 'roof',
* and then creates three 'trees' made up of cylinders
* and spheres.  All this is place on a ground made up
* of a cube.
* @author I.J.Palmer
* @version 1.0
*/
public class SimpleCombine extends Frame implements ActionListener {
    protected Canvas3D myCanvas3D = new Canvas3D(null);
    protected Button myButton = new Button("Exit");
    /**
     * This function builds the view branch of the scene
     * graph.  It creates a branch group and then creates the
     * necessary view elements to give a useful view of our
     * content.
     * @param c Canvas3D that will display the view
     * @return BranchGroup that is the root of the view elements
     */
    protected BranchGroup buildViewBranch(Canvas3D c) {
        BranchGroup viewBranch = new BranchGroup();
        Transform3D viewXfm = new Transform3D();
        viewXfm.set(new Vector3f(0.0f,0.0f,7.0f));
        TransformGroup viewXfmGroup = new TransformGroup(viewXfm);
        ViewPlatform myViewPlatform = new ViewPlatform();
```

```java
        PhysicalBody myBody = new PhysicalBody();
        PhysicalEnvironment myEnvironment = new PhysicalEnvironment();
        viewXfmGroup.addChild(myViewPlatform);
        viewBranch.addChild(viewXfmGroup);
        View myView = new View();
        myView.addCanvas3D(c);
        myView.attachViewPlatform(myViewPlatform);
    myView.setPhysicalBody(myBody);
        myView.setPhysicalEnvironment(myEnvironment);
        return viewBranch;
}
/**
 * Add some lights so that we can illuminate the scene.
 * This adds one ambient light to bring up the overall
 * lighting level and one directional shape to show
 * the shape of the objects in the scene.
 * @param b BranchGroup that the lights are to be added to.
 */
protected void addLights(BranchGroup b) {
        BoundingSphere bounds =
                    new BoundingSphere(new Point3d(0.0,0.0,0.0), 100.0);
        Color3f lightColour1 = new Color3f(1.0f, 1.0f, 1.0f);
        Vector3f lightDir1  = new Vector3f(-1.0f, -1.0f, -1.0f);
        Color3f lightColour2 = new Color3f(1.0f, 1.0f, 1.0f);
        Vector3f lightDir2  = new Vector3f(1.0f, -1.0f, -1.0f);
        DirectionalLight light1 = new DirectionalLight(lightColour1, lightDir1);
        light1.setInfluencingBounds(bounds);
        DirectionalLight light2 = new DirectionalLight(lightColour2, lightDir2);
        light2.setInfluencingBounds(bounds);
        b.addChild(light1);
        b.addChild(light2);
}
/**
 * This builds the content branch of our scene graph.
 * The root of the shapes supplied as a parameter
 * is slightly tilted to reveal its 3D shape. It also uses
 * the addLights function to add some lights to the scene.
 * @param shape Node that represents the geometry for the content
 * @return BranchGroup that is the root of the content branch
 */
protected BranchGroup buildContentBranch(Node shape) {
        BranchGroup contentBranch = new BranchGroup();
        Transform3D rotateCube = new Transform3D( );
    rotateCube.set(new AxisAngle4d(1.0,1.0,0.0,Math.PI/4.0));
```

```
        TransformGroup rotationGroup = new TransformGroup(rotateCube);
        contentBranch.addChild(rotationGroup);
        rotationGroup.addChild(shape);
    addLights(contentBranch);
        return contentBranch;
}
/**
* This defines the shapes used in the scene.
* The function uses the utility geometries sphere, box, cone
* and cylinder to build a simple scene.  This demonstrates
* the use of transformations to group and position items.
* @return Node that is the root of the shape hierarchy.
*/
protected Node buildShape() {
        //Create a root for the shapes in the scene
        BranchGroup theScene = new BranchGroup();
        //Create an appearance for the ground
        Appearance groundApp = new Appearance();
        Color3f groundColour = new Color3f(0.0f,0.5f,0.0f);
        Color3f emissiveColour = new Color3f(0.0f,0.0f,0.0f);
        Color3f specularColour = new Color3f(0.5f,0.5f,0.5f);
        float shininess = 10.0f;
        groundApp.setMaterial(new Material(groundColour,emissiveColour,
                                    groundColour,specularColour,shininess));
        //Create a box that will be the ground
        Box ground = new Box(100.0f,0.1f,100.0f,groundApp);
        //Create a transform and a transform group that
        //will position the ground
        Transform3D grndXfm = new Transform3D();
        grndXfm.set(new Vector3f(0.0f,-1.0f,0.0f));
        TransformGroup grndXfmGrp = new TransformGroup(grndXfm);
        //Add the ground shape to the group
        grndXfmGrp.addChild(ground);
        //Add the ground group to the scene group
        theScene.addChild(grndXfmGrp);
        //Create an appearance for the wall of the house
        Appearance wallApp = new Appearance();
        Color3f wallColour = new Color3f(0.5f,0.5f,0.5f);
        wallApp.setMaterial(new Material(wallColour,emissiveColour,
                                    wallColour,specularColour,shininess));
        //Create a cylinder that is the wall of the house
        Cylinder walls = new Cylinder(1.0f,1.0f,
                Primitive.GENERATE_NORMALS,wallApp);
```

```
//Create a group that will be the root of the house
TransformGroup house = new TransformGroup();
//Add the walls to the house group
house.addChild(walls);
//Create an appearance for the roof
Appearance roofApp = new Appearance();
Color3f roofColour = new Color3f(0.5f,0.0f,0.0f);
roofApp.setMaterial(new Material(roofColour,emissiveColour,
                    roofColour,specularColour,shininess));
//Create a cone that will be the roof
Cone myRoof =
    new Cone(1.0f,1.0f,Primitive.GENERATE_NORMALS,roofApp);
//Create the transform and transform group that will position the
//roof on the house
Transform3D roofXfm = new Transform3D();
roofXfm.set(new Vector3f(0.0f,1.0f,0.0f));
TransformGroup roofXfmGrp = new TransformGroup(roofXfm);
//Add the roof to the roof transform group
roofXfmGrp.addChild(myRoof);
//Add the roof group to the house
house.addChild(roofXfmGrp);
//Create an appearance for the tree trunks
Appearance trunkApp = new Appearance();
Color3f trunkColour = new Color3f(0.2f,0.2f,0.0f);
trunkApp.setMaterial(new Material(trunkColour,emissiveColour,
                       trunkColour,specularColour,shininess));
//Create an appearance for the tree leaves
Appearance leafApp = new Appearance();
Color3f leafColour = new Color3f(0.0f,0.2f,0.0f);
leafApp.setMaterial(new Material(leafColour,emissiveColour,
                    leafColour,specularColour,shininess));
//Create a transform and transform group for the tree
Transform3D treeXfm = new Transform3D();
treeXfm.set(new Vector3f(-2.0f,0.0f,0.5f));
TransformGroup treeXfmGrp = new TransformGroup(treeXfm);
//Create a cylinder for the tree trunk
Cylinder myTrunk = new Cylinder(0.1f,1.0f,trunkApp);
//Add the trunk to the tree group
treeXfmGrp.addChild(myTrunk);
//Create a transform and transform group for the tree leaves
Transform3D leafXfm = new Transform3D();
leafXfm.set(new Vector3f(0.0f,1.0f,0.0f));
TransformGroup leafXfmGrp = new TransformGroup(leafXfm);
//Create the leaves
```

```
        Sphere myLeaf = new Sphere(0.5f,leafApp);
        //Add the leaves to the leaf group
        leafXfmGrp.addChild(myLeaf);
        //Add the leaf group to the tree group
        treeXfmGrp.addChild(leafXfmGrp);
        //Create another tree
        Transform3D tree1Xfm = new Transform3D();
        tree1Xfm.set(new Vector3f(1.4f,0.0f,-0.5f));
        TransformGroup tree1XfmGrp = new TransformGroup(tree1Xfm);
        Cylinder myTrunk1 = new Cylinder(0.1f,1.0f,trunkApp);
        tree1XfmGrp.addChild(myTrunk1);
        Transform3D leaf1Xfm = new Transform3D();
        leaf1Xfm.set(new Vector3f(0.0f,1.0f,0.0f));
        TransformGroup leaf1XfmGrp = new TransformGroup(leaf1Xfm);
        Sphere myLeaf1 = new Sphere(0.5f,leafApp);
        leaf1XfmGrp.addChild(myLeaf1);
        tree1XfmGrp.addChild(leaf1XfmGrp);
        //Create the final tree
        Transform3D tree2Xfm = new Transform3D();
        tree2Xfm.set(new Vector3f(1.2f,0.0f,1.0f));
        TransformGroup tree2XfmGrp = new TransformGroup(tree2Xfm);
        Cylinder myTrunk2 = new Cylinder(0.1f,1.0f,trunkApp);
        tree2XfmGrp.addChild(myTrunk2);
        Transform3D leaf2Xfm = new Transform3D();
        leaf2Xfm.set(new Vector3f(0.0f,1.0f,0.0f));
        TransformGroup leaf2XfmGrp = new TransformGroup(leaf2Xfm);
        Sphere myLeaf2 = new Sphere(0.5f,leafApp);
        leaf2XfmGrp.addChild(myLeaf2);
    tree2XfmGrp.addChild(leaf2XfmGrp);
  //Put the scene together by adding all the groups
    //to the scene group
    theScene.addChild(house);
    theScene.addChild(treeXfmGrp);
    theScene.addChild(tree1XfmGrp);
    theScene.addChild(tree2XfmGrp);
    return theScene;
}
/**
 * Handles the AWT event to exit the program.
 */
public void actionPerformed(ActionEvent e) {
    dispose();
    System.exit(0);
```

```
        }
        public SimpleCombine() {
            VirtualUniverse myUniverse = new VirtualUniverse();
            Locale myLocale = new Locale(myUniverse);
            myLocale.addBranchGraph(buildViewBranch(myCanvas3D));
            myLocale.addBranchGraph(buildContentBranch(buildShape()));
            setTitle("SimpleWorld");
            setSize(400,400);
            setLayout(new BorderLayout());
            add(BorderLayout.CENTER, myCanvas3D);
            add(BorderLayout.SOUTH,myButton);
            myButton.addActionListener(this);
            setVisible(true);
        }
        public static void main(String[] args) {
            SimpleCombine sc = new SimpleCombine();
        }
}
```

SimpleTransform

```
import javax.media.j3d.*;
import javax.vecmath.*;
import java.awt.*;
import java.awt.event.*;
import com.sun.j3d.utils.geometry.*;
/**
* This program uses AWT buttons to allow the user
* to rotate an object.  This is achieved by altering
* the transform of a transform group.
* @author I.J.Palmer
* @version 1.0
*/
public class SimpleTransform extends Frame implements ActionListener {
        protected Canvas3D myCanvas3D = new Canvas3D(null);
        /** The exit button */
        protected Button exitButton = new Button("Exit");
        /** The rotate left button */
        protected Button leftButton = new Button("<-");
        /** The rotate right button */
        protected Button rightButton = new Button("->");
        /** The transform group used to rotate the shape */
```

```java
    protected TransformGroup rotationGroup;
/**
 * This function builds the view branch of the scene
 * graph.  It creates a branch group and then creates the
 * necessary view elements to give a useful view of our
 * content.
 * @param c Canvas3D that will display the view
 * @return BranchGroup that is the root of the view elements
 */
    protected BranchGroup buildViewBranch(Canvas3D c) {
        BranchGroup viewBranch = new BranchGroup();
        Transform3D viewXfm = new Transform3D();
        viewXfm.set(new Vector3f(0.0f,0.0f,10.0f));
        TransformGroup viewXfmGroup = new TransformGroup(viewXfm);
        ViewPlatform myViewPlatform = new ViewPlatform();
        PhysicalBody myBody = new PhysicalBody();
        PhysicalEnvironment myEnvironment = new PhysicalEnvironment();
        viewXfmGroup.addChild(myViewPlatform);
        viewBranch.addChild(viewXfmGroup);
        View myView = new View();
        myView.addCanvas3D(c);
        myView.attachViewPlatform(myViewPlatform);
        myView.setPhysicalBody(myBody);
        myView.setPhysicalEnvironment(myEnvironment);
        return viewBranch;
    }
/**
 * Add some lights so that we can illuminate the scene.
 * This adds one ambient light to bring up the overall
 * lighting level and one directional shape to show
 * the shape of the objects in the scene.
 * @param b BranchGroup that the lights are to be added to.
 */
    protected void addLights(BranchGroup b) {
        BoundingSphere bounds =
                new BoundingSphere(new Point3d(0.0,0.0,0.0), 100.0);
        Color3f ambLightColour = new Color3f(0.5f, 0.5f, 0.5f);
        AmbientLight ambLight = new AmbientLight(ambLightColour);
        ambLight.setInfluencingBounds(bounds);
        Color3f dirLightColour = new Color3f(1.0f, 1.0f, 1.0f);
        Vector3f dirLightDir = new Vector3f(-1.0f, -1.0f, -1.0f);
        DirectionalLight dirLight =
                        new DirectionalLight(dirLightColour, dirLightDir);
```

```
            dirLight.setInfluencingBounds(bounds);
            b.addChild(ambLight);
            b.addChild(dirLight);
    }
    /**
    * This builds the content branch of our scene graph.
    * The root of the shapes supplied as a parameter
    * is slightly tilted to reveal its 3D shape. It also uses
    * the addLights function to add some lights to the scene.
    * The group that the shape is added to has its capabilities
    * set so that we can read and write it.
    * @param shape Node that represents the geometry for the content
    * @return BranchGroup that is the root of the content branch
    */
    protected BranchGroup buildContentBranch(Node shape) {
            BranchGroup contentBranch = new BranchGroup();
            Transform3D rotateCube = new Transform3D( );
            rotateCube.set(new AxisAngle4d(1.0,1.0,0.0,Math.PI/4.0));
            rotationGroup = new TransformGroup(rotateCube);
            //Set the capabilities so that the transform can be accessed
            rotationGroup.setCapability(
                            TransformGroup.ALLOW_TRANSFORM_READ);
            rotationGroup.setCapability(
                            TransformGroup.ALLOW_TRANSFORM_WRITE);
            contentBranch.addChild(rotationGroup);
            rotationGroup.addChild(shape);
            addLights(contentBranch);
            return contentBranch;
    }
    /**
    * This defines the shapes used in the scene. It creates
    * a simple cube using a Box utility class.
    * @return Node that is the root of the shape hierarchy.
    */
    protected Node buildShape() {
            Appearance app = new Appearance();
            Color3f ambientColour = new Color3f(1.0f,0.0f,0.0f);
            Color3f emissiveColour = new Color3f(0.0f,0.0f,0.0f);
            Color3f specularColour = new Color3f(1.0f,1.0f,1.0f);
            Color3f diffuseColour = new Color3f(1.0f,0.0f,0.0f);
            float shininess = 20.0f;
            app.setMaterial(new Material(ambientColour,emissiveColour,
                            diffuseColour,specularColour,shininess));
            return new Box(2.0f, 2.0f, 2.0f, app);
```

```
}
/**
* This processes the AWT events and performs the appropriate
* operations.  The exit button causes the program to terminate,
* the left button causes a rotation to be applied to the
* shape's transformation to spin it to the left and the right
* has the similar effect but to the right button.
* @param e ActionEvent that has been performed
*/
public void actionPerformed(ActionEvent e) {
    if (e.getSource() == exitButton) {
        dispose();
        System.exit(0);
    } else if (e.getSource() == leftButton) {
        //Create a temporary transform
        Transform3D temp = new Transform3D();
        //Read the transform from the shape
        rotationGroup.getTransform(temp);
        //Create a rotation that will be applied
        Transform3D tempDelta = new Transform3D();
        tempDelta.rotY(-0.3);
        //Apply the rotation
        temp.mul(tempDelta);
        //Write the value back into the scene graph
        rotationGroup.setTransform(temp);
    } else if (e.getSource() == rightButton) {
        //Do the same for the right rotation
        Transform3D temp = new Transform3D();
        rotationGroup.getTransform(temp);
        Transform3D tempDelta = new Transform3D();
        tempDelta.rotY(0.3);
        temp.mul(tempDelta);
        rotationGroup.setTransform(temp);
    }
}
public SimpleTransform() {
    VirtualUniverse myUniverse = new VirtualUniverse();
    Locale myLocale = new Locale(myUniverse);
    myLocale.addBranchGraph(buildViewBranch(myCanvas3D));
    myLocale.addBranchGraph(buildContentBranch(buildShape()));
    setTitle("SimpleWorld");
    setSize(400,400);
    setLayout(new BorderLayout());
```

```
        Panel bottom = new Panel();
        bottom.add(leftButton);
        bottom.add(rightButton);
        bottom.add(exitButton);
        add(BorderLayout.CENTER, myCanvas3D);
        add(BorderLayout.SOUTH, bottom);
        exitButton.addActionListener(this);
        leftButton.addActionListener(this);
        rightButton.addActionListener(this);
        setVisible(true);
    }
    public static void main(String[] args) {
        SimpleTransform st = new SimpleTransform();
    }
}
```

SimpleSwitch

This demonstrates the use of a switch node to swap between two shapes.

```java
import javax.media.j3d.*;
import javax.vecmath.*;
import java.awt.*;
import java.awt.event.*;
import com.sun.j3d.utils.geometry.*;
/**
* This application uses a switch node to swap between two shapes.
* The switch is driven by two AWT buttons.
* @author I.J.Palmer
* @version 1.0
*/
public class SimpleSwitch extends Frame implements ActionListener {
    protected Canvas3D myCanvas3D = new Canvas3D(null);
    /** The exit button */
    protected Button exitButton = new Button("Exit");
    /** Set the shape to a box */
    protected Button boxButton = new Button("Box");
    /** Set the shape to a cone */
    protected Button coneButton = new Button("Cone");
    /** The switch that is used to swap between the shapes */
    protected Switch firstSwitch = new Switch(0);
```

```java
/**
 * This function builds the view branch of the scene
 * graph. It creates a branch group and then creates the
 * necessary view elements to give a useful view of our
 * content.
 * @param c Canvas3D that will display the view
 * @return BranchGroup that is the root of the view elements
 */
protected BranchGroup buildViewBranch(Canvas3D c) {
    BranchGroup viewBranch = new BranchGroup();
    Transform3D viewXfm = new Transform3D();
    viewXfm.set(new Vector3f(0.0f,0.0f,10.0f));
    TransformGroup viewXfmGroup = new TransformGroup(viewXfm);
    ViewPlatform myViewPlatform = new ViewPlatform();
    PhysicalBody myBody = new PhysicalBody();
    PhysicalEnvironment myEnvironment = new PhysicalEnvironment();
    viewXfmGroup.addChild(myViewPlatform);
    viewBranch.addChild(viewXfmGroup);
    View myView = new View();
    myView.addCanvas3D(c);
    myView.attachViewPlatform(myViewPlatform);
    myView.setPhysicalBody(myBody);
    myView.setPhysicalEnvironment(myEnvironment);
    return viewBranch;
}
/**
 * Add some lights so that we can illuminate the scene.
 * This adds one ambient light to bring up the overall
 * lighting level and one directional shape to show
 * the shape of the objects in the scene.
 * @param b BranchGroup that the lights are to be added to.
 */
protected void addLights(BranchGroup b) {
    BoundingSphere bounds =
            new BoundingSphere(new Point3d(0.0,0.0,0.0), 100.0);
    Color3f lightColour1 = new Color3f(1.0f, 1.0f, 1.0f);
    Vector3f lightDir1 = new Vector3f(0.0f, -1.0f, 0.0f);
    Color3f lightColour2 = new Color3f(1.0f, 1.0f, 1.0f);
    Vector3f lightDir2 = new Vector3f(0.0f, 1.0f, 0.0f);
    DirectionalLight light1 = new DirectionalLight(lightColour1, lightDir1);
    light1.setInfluencingBounds(bounds);
    DirectionalLight light2 = new DirectionalLight(lightColour2, lightDir2);
    light2.setInfluencingBounds(bounds);
```

```
        b.addChild(light1);
        b.addChild(light2);
}
/**
 * This builds the content branch of our scene graph.
 * The root of the shapes supplied as a parameter
 * is slightly tilted to reveal its 3D shape. It also uses
 * the addLights function to add some lights to the scene.
 * @param shape Node that represents the geometry for the content
 * @return BranchGroup that is the root of the content branch
 */
protected BranchGroup buildContentBranch(Node shape) {
        BranchGroup contentBranch = new BranchGroup();
        Transform3D rotateCube = new Transform3D( );
        rotateCube.set(new AxisAngle4d(1.0,1.0,0.0,Math.PI/4.0));
        TransformGroup rotationGroup = new TransformGroup(rotateCube);
        contentBranch.addChild(rotationGroup);
        rotationGroup.addChild(shape);
        addLights(contentBranch);
        return contentBranch;
}
/**
 * This creates the shapes used in the program.
 * A switch node is created that has its write capability set so that
 * we can swap the rendered shape.  Then a box and a cone are
 * created and added to the switch.
 * @return Node that is the switch node
 */
protected Node buildShape() {
        Appearance app = new Appearance();
        Color3f ambientColour = new Color3f(1.0f,0.0f,0.0f);
        Color3f emissiveColour = new Color3f(0.0f,0.0f,0.0f);
        Color3f specularColour = new Color3f(1.0f,1.0f,1.0f);
        Color3f diffuseColour = new Color3f(1.0f,0.0f,0.0f);
        float shininess = 20.0f;
        app.setMaterial(new Material(ambientColour,emissiveColour,
                        diffuseColour,specularColour,shininess));
        //Set the capability so that we can change the switch value
        firstSwitch.setCapability(Switch.ALLOW_SWITCH_WRITE);
        //Add the two shapes to the switch
        firstSwitch.addChild(
                new Box(2.0f,2.0f,2.0f,Box.GENERATE_NORMALS,app));
        firstSwitch.addChild(
                new Cone(2.0f,4.0f,Cone.GENERATE_NORMALS,app));
```

```java
            return firstSwitch;
    }
    /**
     * Process the AWT events and perform the appropriate actions.
     * If the exit button has been pressed, quit the application,
     * if the box button has been pressed, select the box child
     * of the switch and if its the cone button select the cone
     * child.
     * @param e ActionEvent that is to be processed.
     */
    public void actionPerformed(ActionEvent e) {
        if (e.getSource() == exitButton) {
            dispose();
            System.exit(0);
        } else if (e.getSource() == boxButton) {
            firstSwitch.setWhichChild(0);
        } else if (e.getSource() == coneButton) {
            firstSwitch.setWhichChild(1);
        }
    }
    public SimpleSwitch() {
        VirtualUniverse myUniverse = new VirtualUniverse();
        Locale myLocale = new Locale(myUniverse);
        myLocale.addBranchGraph(buildViewBranch(myCanvas3D));
        myLocale.addBranchGraph(buildContentBranch(buildShape()));
        setTitle("SimpleWorld");
        setSize(400,400);
        setLayout(new BorderLayout());
        Panel bottom = new Panel();
        bottom.add(boxButton);
        bottom.add(coneButton);
        bottom.add(exitButton);
        add(BorderLayout.CENTER,myCanvas3D);
        add(BorderLayout.SOUTH,bottom);
        exitButton.addActionListener(this);
        boxButton.addActionListener(this);
        coneButton.addActionListener(this);
        setVisible(true);
    }
    public static void main(String[] args) {
        SimpleSwitch ss = new SimpleSwitch();
    }
}
```

Chapter 6

SimpleRotator

```
import javax.media.j3d.*;
import javax.vecmath.*;
import java.awt.*;
import java.awt.event.*;
import com.sun.j3d.utils.geometry.*;
/**
 * This creates a rotation interpolator and applies it to a shape.
 * @author I.J.Palmer
 * @version 1.0
 /
public class SimpleRotator extends Frame implements ActionListener {
        protected Canvas3D myCanvas3D = new Canvas3D(null);
        protected Button exitButton = new Button("Exit");
        /**
         * This function builds the view branch of the scene
         * graph.  It creates a branch group and then creates the
         * necessary view elements to give a useful view of our
         * content.
         * @param c Canvas3D that will display the view
         * @return BranchGroup that is the root of the view elements
         */
        protected BranchGroup buildViewBranch(Canvas3D c) {
                BranchGroup viewBranch = new BranchGroup();
                Transform3D viewXfm = new Transform3D();
                viewXfm.set(new Vector3f(0.0f,0.0f,10.0f));
                TransformGroup viewXfmGroup =
                                    new TransformGroup(viewXfm);
                ViewPlatform myViewPlatform = new ViewPlatform();
                PhysicalBody myBody = new PhysicalBody();
                PhysicalEnvironment myEnvironment =
                                    new PhysicalEnvironment();
                viewXfmGroup.addChild(myViewPlatform);
                viewBranch.addChild(viewXfmGroup);
                View myView = new View();
```

```
        myView.addCanvas3D(c);
        myView.attachViewPlatform(myViewPlatform);
        myView.setPhysicalBody(myBody);
        myView.setPhysicalEnvironment(myEnvironment);
        return viewBranch;
}
/**
 * Add some lights so that we can illuminate the scene.
 * This adds one ambient light to bring up the overall
 * lighting level and one directional shape to show
 * the shape of the objects in the scene.
 * @param b BranchGroup that the lights are to be added to.
 */
protected void addLights(BranchGroup b) {
        BoundingSphere bounds = new BoundingSphere(new
                                Point3d(0.0,0.0,0.0), 100.0);
        Color3f ambLightColour = new Color3f(0.5f, 0.5f, 0.5f);
        AmbientLight ambLight = new AmbientLight(ambLightColour);
        ambLight.setInfluencingBounds(bounds);
        Color3f dirLightColour = new Color3f(1.0f, 1.0f, 1.0f);
        Vector3f dirLightDir  = new Vector3f(-1.0f, -1.0f, -1.0f);
        DirectionalLight dirLight = new
                                DirectionalLight(dirLightColour, dirLightDir);
        dirLight.setInfluencingBounds(bounds);
        b.addChild(ambLight);
        b.addChild(dirLight);

}
/**
 * This builds the content branch of our scene graph.
 * The root of the shapes supplied as a parameter
 * is slightly tilted to reveal its 3D shape. It also uses
 * the addLights function to add some lights to the scene.
 * We also create the alpha generator and the rotation
 * interpolator to perform the animation.
 * @param shape Node that represents the geometry for the content
 * @return BranchGroup that is the root of the content branch
 /
protected BranchGroup buildContentBranch(Node shape) {
        BranchGroup contentBranch = new BranchGroup();
        //Create the transform and group used for the rotation
        Transform3D rotateCube = new Transform3D( );
        TransformGroup rotationGroup = new
                                TransformGroup(rotateCube);
```

```java
        //Set the capability so we can write the transform
        rotationGroup.setCapability(
                TransformGroup.ALLOW_TRANSFORM_WRITE);
        //Create the alpha generator
        Alpha rotationAlpha = new Alpha(
                -1,Alpha.INCREASING_ENABLE,0,0,4000,0,0,0,0,0);
        //Build the interpolator
        Transform3D yAxis = new Transform3D();
        RotationInterpolator rotator = new
                RotationInterpolator(rotationAlpha, rotationGroup,
                        yAxis, 0.0f, (float) Math.PI*2.0f);
        BoundingSphere bounds = new BoundingSphere(new
                        Point3d(0.0,0.0,0.0), 100.0);
        rotator.setSchedulingBounds(bounds);
        //Put all this together
        contentBranch.addChild(rotationGroup);
        rotationGroup.addChild(shape);
        rotationGroup.addChild(rotator);
        addLights(contentBranch);
        return contentBranch;
}
/**
 * This creates the shapes used in the program.
 * @return Node that is the switch node
 /
protected Node buildShape() {
        Appearance app = new Appearance();
        Color3f ambientColour = new Color3f(1.0f,0.0f,0.0f);
        Color3f emissiveColour = new Color3f(0.0f,0.0f,0.0f);
        Color3f specularColour = new Color3f(1.0f,1.0f,1.0f);
        Color3f diffuseColour = new Color3f(1.0f,0.0f,0.0f);
        float shininess = 20.0f;
        app.setMaterial(new Material(ambientColour,emissiveColour,
                        diffuseColour,specularColour,shininess));
        return new Box(2.0f, 2.0f, 2.0f, app);
}
/**
 * Process the button action to exit the program.
 */
public void actionPerformed(ActionEvent e) {
        if (e.getSource() == exitButton) {
                dispose();
                System.exit(0);
        }
```

```
        }
        public SimpleRotator() {
                VirtualUniverse myUniverse = new VirtualUniverse();
                Locale myLocale = new Locale(myUniverse);
                myLocale.addBranchGraph(buildViewBranch(myCanvas3D));
                myLocale.addBranchGraph(buildContentBranch(buildShape()));
                setTitle("SimpleRotator");
                setSize(400,400);
                setLayout(new BorderLayout());
                Panel bottom = new Panel();
                bottom.add(exitButton);
                add(BorderLayout.CENTER, myCanvas3D);
                add(BorderLayout.SOUTH, bottom);
                exitButton.addActionListener(this);
                setVisible(true);
        }
        public static void main(String[] args) {
                SimpleRotator sr = new SimpleRotator();
        }
}
```

SimpleInterpolator

Animate the size, position and rotation of a shape using an interpolator.

```
import javax.media.j3d.*;
import javax.vecmath.*;
import java.awt.*;
import java.awt.event.*;
import com.sun.j3d.utils.geometry.*;
/**
 * This program uses an interpolator to animate the size, position and
 * rotation of a shape.
 * @author I.J.Palmer
 * @version 1.0
 */
public class SimpleInterpolator extends Frame implements ActionListener {
        protected Canvas3D myCanvas3D = new Canvas3D(null);
        protected Button exitButton = new Button("Exit");
        /** The group that is used to animate the shape */
        protected TransformGroup interpolatorGroup;
```

```java
/**
 * This function builds the view branch of the scene
 * graph.  It creates a branch group and then creates the
 * necessary view elements to give a useful view of our
 * content.
 * @param c Canvas3D that will display the view
 * @return BranchGroup that is the root of the view elements
 */
protected BranchGroup buildViewBranch(Canvas3D c) {
    BranchGroup viewBranch = new BranchGroup();
    Transform3D viewXfm = new Transform3D();
    viewXfm.set(new Vector3f(0.0f,0.0f,10.0f));
    TransformGroup viewXfmGroup = new TransformGroup(viewXfm);
    ViewPlatform myViewPlatform = new ViewPlatform();
    PhysicalBody myBody = new PhysicalBody();
    PhysicalEnvironment myEnvironment = new PhysicalEnvironment();
    viewXfmGroup.addChild(myViewPlatform);
    viewBranch.addChild(viewXfmGroup);
    View myView = new View();
    myView.addCanvas3D(c);
    myView.attachViewPlatform(myViewPlatform);
    myView.setPhysicalBody(myBody);
    myView.setPhysicalEnvironment(myEnvironment);
    return viewBranch;
}
/**
 * Add some lights so that we can illuminate the scene.
 * This adds one ambient light to bring up the overall
 * lighting level and one directional shape to show
 * the shape of the objects in the scene.
 * @param b BranchGroup that the lights are to be added to.
 */
protected void addLights(BranchGroup b) {
    BoundingSphere bounds =
                new BoundingSphere(new Point3d(0.0,0.0,0.0), 100.0);
    Color3f ambLightColour = new Color3f(0.5f, 0.5f, 0.5f);
    AmbientLight ambLight = new AmbientLight(ambLightColour);
    ambLight.setInfluencingBounds(bounds);
    Color3f dirLightColour = new Color3f(1.0f, 1.0f, 1.0f);
    Vector3f dirLightDir = new Vector3f(-1.0f, -1.0f, -1.0f);
    DirectionalLight dirLight =
                new DirectionalLight(dirLightColour, dirLightDir);
    dirLight.setInfluencingBounds(bounds);
    b.addChild(ambLight);
```

```
            b.addChild(dirLight);
    }
    /**
     * This method creates the required interpolator.
     * @param TG TransformGroup that the interpolator is applied to.
     * @return RotPosScaleInterpolator that changes the transform group
     */
    protected RotPosScalePathInterpolator
                        createInterpolator(TransformGroup TG) {
        //Create the alpha generator
        Alpha RPSAlpha =
                new Alpha(-1,Alpha.INCREASING_ENABLE,0,2000,4000,0,0,0,0,0);
        //Create the array for the interpolation positions
        float[] knots = {0.0f,0.1f,0.8f,1.0f};
        //Create the scale key values
        float[] scales = {1.0f,0.5f,2.0f,1.0f};
        //Create the rotation key values
        Quat4f[] rotations = {  new Quat4f(0.0f,0.0f,0.0f,0.0f),
                                new Quat4f(0.0f,1.0f,0.0f,0.0f),
                                new Quat4f(0.0f,2.0f,0.0f,0.0f),
                                new Quat4f(1.0f,0.0f,1.0f,0.0f)};
        //Create the position key values
        Point3f[] positions = {  new Point3f(0.0f,0.0f,0.0f),
                                new Point3f(-1.0f,0.0f,0.0f),
                                new Point3f(0.0f,1.0f,0.0f),
                                new Point3f(0.0f,0.0f,0.0f)};
        //Create the axis for the inerpolator
        Transform3D yAxis = new Transform3D();
        //Build the interpolator from the data that we've created
        RotPosScalePathInterpolator RPSInterpolator =
                new RotPosScalePathInterpolator(RPSAlpha,TG,
                            yAxis,knots,rotations,positions,scales);

        BoundingSphere bounds =
                new BoundingSphere(new Point3d(0.0,0.0,0.0), 100.0);
        RPSInterpolator.setSchedulingBounds(bounds);
        return RPSInterpolator;
    }
    /**
     * This builds the content branch of our scene graph.
     * The root of the shapes supplied as a parameter
     * is slightly tilted to reveal its 3D shape. It also uses
     * the addLights function to add some lights to the scene
     * and sets up a transform group that can be written to.
```

```
    * @param shape Node that represents the geometry for the content
    * @return BranchGroup that is the root of the content branch
    */
    protected BranchGroup buildContentBranch(Node shape) {
        BranchGroup contentBranch = new BranchGroup();
        interpolatorGroup = new TransformGroup();
        interpolatorGroup.setCapability(
                            TransformGroup.ALLOW_TRANSFORM_WRITE);
        contentBranch.addChild(interpolatorGroup);
        interpolatorGroup.addChild(shape);
        addLights(contentBranch);
        contentBranch.addChild(createInterpolator(interpolatorGroup));
        return contentBranch;
    }
    /**
    * This creates the shape used in the program.
    * @return Node that is the switch node
    */
    protected Node buildShape() {
        Appearance app = new Appearance();
        Color3f ambientColour = new Color3f(1.0f,0.0f,0.0f);
        Color3f emissiveColour = new Color3f(0.0f,0.0f,0.0f);
        Color3f specularColour = new Color3f(1.0f,1.0f,1.0f);
        Color3f diffuseColour = new Color3f(1.0f,0.0f,0.0f);
        float shininess = 20.0f;
        app.setMaterial(new Material(ambientColour,emissiveColour,
                            diffuseColour,specularColour,shininess));
        return new Box(1.0f, 1.0f, 1.0f, app);
    }
    /**
    * Process the button action to end the program.
    */
    public void actionPerformed(ActionEvent e) {
        if (e.getSource() == exitButton) {
            dispose();
            System.exit(0);
        }
    }
    public SimpleInterpolator() {
        VirtualUniverse myUniverse = new VirtualUniverse();
        Locale myLocale = new Locale(myUniverse);
        myLocale.addBranchGraph(buildViewBranch(myCanvas3D));
        myLocale.addBranchGraph(buildContentBranch(buildShape()));
        setTitle("SimpleInterpolator");
```

```
        setSize(400,400);
        setLayout(new BorderLayout());
        Panel bottom = new Panel();
        bottom.add(exitButton);
        add(BorderLayout.CENTER, myCanvas3D);
        add(BorderLayout.SOUTH, bottom);
        exitButton.addActionListener(this);
        setVisible(true);
    }
    public static void main(String[] args) {
        SimpleInterpolator si = new SimpleInterpolator();
    }
}
```

SimpleMorph

```
import javax.media.j3d.*;
import javax.vecmath.*;
import java.awt.*;
import java.awt.event.*;
/**
* This uses a morph node to animate the geometry of an object.  The
* animation is started and stopped by use of two AWT buttons.
* @author I.J.Palmer
* @version 1.0
/
public class SimpleMorph extends Frame implements ActionListener {
    protected Canvas3D myCanvas3D = new Canvas3D(null);
    /** The button that changes the shape into a cube */
    protected Button cubeButton = new Button("Cube");
    /** The button that changes the shape into a pyramid */
    protected Button pyraButton = new Button("Pyramid");
    /** The button to exit the program */
    protected Button exitButton = new Button("Exit");
    /** The morph that performs the animation */
    protected Morph myMorph;
    /** The weights for the morph */
    protected double[] weights = {0.5,0.5};
    /**
    * This function builds the view branch of the scene
    * graph.  It creates a branch group and then creates the
```

```
    * necessary view elements to give a useful view of our
    * content.
    * @param c Canvas3D that will display the view
    * @return BranchGroup that is the root of the view elements
    */
    protected BranchGroup buildViewBranch(Canvas3D c) {
        BranchGroup viewBranch = new BranchGroup();
        Transform3D viewXfm = new Transform3D();
        viewXfm.set(new Vector3f(0.0f,0.0f,5.0f));
        TransformGroup viewXfmGroup =
                                    new TransformGroup(viewXfm);
        ViewPlatform myViewPlatform = new ViewPlatform();
        PhysicalBody myBody = new PhysicalBody();
        PhysicalEnvironment myEnvironment =
                                    new PhysicalEnvironment();
        viewXfmGroup.addChild(myViewPlatform);
        viewBranch.addChild(viewXfmGroup);
        View myView = new View();
        myView.addCanvas3D(c);
        myView.attachViewPlatform(myViewPlatform);
        myView.setPhysicalBody(myBody);
        myView.setPhysicalEnvironment(myEnvironment);
        return viewBranch;
    }
    /**
    * Add some lights so that we can illuminate the scene.
    * This adds one ambient light to bring up the overall
    * lighting level and one directional shape to show
    * the shape of the objects in the scene.
    * @param b BranchGroup that the lights are to be added to.
    */
    protected void addLights(BranchGroup b) {
        BoundingSphere bounds = new
                        BoundingSphere(new Point3d(0.0,0.0,0.0), 100.0);
        Color3f ambLightColour = new Color3f(0.5f, 0.5f, 0.5f);
        AmbientLight ambLight = new AmbientLight(ambLightColour);
        ambLight.setInfluencingBounds(bounds);
        Color3f dirLightColour = new Color3f(1.0f, 1.0f, 1.0f);
        Vector3f dirLightDir  = new Vector3f(-1.0f, -1.0f, -1.0f);
        DirectionalLight dirLight =
                        new DirectionalLight(dirLightColour, dirLightDir);
        dirLight.setInfluencingBounds(bounds);
        b.addChild(ambLight);
        b.addChild(dirLight);
```

```
}
/**
 * Create the morph node that will perform the animation
 * @param theShapes GeometryArray[] that holds the shapes to be
 * morphed between
 * @param app Appearance used for the shapes
 * @return Morph that performs the animation
 */
protected Morph createMorph(GeometryArray[] theShapes,
                                      Appearance app) {
    //Create the morph node from the shapes given
    myMorph = new Morph(theShapes,app);
    //Set the initial weights
    myMorph.setWeights(weights);
    //Set the access rights to the weight values
    myMorph.setCapability(Morph.ALLOW_WEIGHTS_READ);
    myMorph.setCapability(Morph.ALLOW_WEIGHTS_WRITE);
    return myMorph;
}
    /**
 * This builds the content branch of our scene graph.
 * The root of the shapes supplied as a parameter
 * is slightly tilted to reveal its 3D shape.
 * It uses the CreateMorph function to build the content,
 * which consists of morph node made up of a cube and
 * pyramid.  It also uses
 * the addLights function to add some lights to the scene.
 * @param shape Node that represents the geometry for the content
 * @return BranchGroup that is the root of the content branch
 */
protected BranchGroup buildContentBranch() {
    Appearance app = new Appearance();
    Color3f ambientColour = new Color3f(1.0f,0.0f,0.0f);
    Color3f emissiveColour = new Color3f(0.0f,0.0f,0.0f);
    Color3f specularColour = new Color3f(1.0f,1.0f,1.0f);
    Color3f diffuseColour = new Color3f(1.0f,0.0f,0.0f);
    float shininess = 20.0f;
    app.setMaterial(new Material(ambientColour,emissiveColour,
                        diffuseColour,specularColour,shininess));
    //Create a cube from an indexed quadrilateral array
    IndexedQuadArray indexedCube = new IndexedQuadArray(8,
                        IndexedQuadArray.COORDINATES |
                        IndexedQuadArray.NORMALS, 24);
```

```
Point3f[] cubeCoordinates = { new Point3f( 1.0f, 1.0f, 1.0f),
                               new Point3f(-1.0f, 1.0f, 1.0f),
                               new Point3f(-1.0f,-1.0f, 1.0f),
                               new Point3f( 1.0f,-1.0f, 1.0f),
                               new Point3f( 1.0f, 1.0f,-1.0f),
                               new Point3f(-1.0f, 1.0f,-1.0f),
                               new Point3f(-1.0f,-1.0f,-1.0f),
                               new Point3f( 1.0f,-1.0f,-1.0f)};
Vector3f[] cubeNormals = {     new Vector3f( 0.0f, 0.0f, 1.0f),
                               new Vector3f( 0.0f, 0.0f,-1.0f),
                               new Vector3f( 1.0f, 0.0f, 0.0f),
                               new Vector3f(-1.0f, 0.0f, 0.0f),
                               new Vector3f( 0.0f, 1.0f, 0.0f),
                               new Vector3f( 0.0f,-1.0f, 0.0f)};
int cubeCoordIndices[] =
                {0,1,2,3,7,6,5,4,0,3,7,4,5,6,2,1,0,4,5,1,6,7,3,2};
int cubeNormalIndices[] =
                {0,0,0,0,1,1,1,1,2,2,2,2,3,3,3,3,4,4,4,4,5,5,5,5};
indexedCube.setCoordinates(0, cubeCoordinates);
indexedCube.setNormals(0, cubeNormals);
indexedCube.setCoordinateIndices(0, cubeCoordIndices);
indexedCube.setNormalIndices(0, cubeNormalIndices);
//Create the pyramid from an indexed quadrilateral array.
//This is created with more vertices than would normally
//be required so that each vertex in the pyramid will
//map to a vertex in the cube so that the morph will
//operate correctly.
IndexedQuadArray indexedPyramid = new IndexedQuadArray(8,
                            IndexedQuadArray.COORDINATES |
                            IndexedQuadArray.NORMALS, 24);
Point3f[] pyramidCoordinates = { new Point3f( 0.0f, 1.0f, 0.0f),
                               new Point3f(0.0f, 1.0f, 0.0f),
                               new Point3f(-1.0f,-1.0f, 1.0f),
                               new Point3f( 1.0f,-1.0f, 1.0f),
                               new Point3f( 0.0f, 1.0f,0.0f),
                               new Point3f(0.0f, 1.0f,0.0f),
                               new Point3f(-1.0f,-1.0f,-1.0f),
                               new Point3f( 1.0f,-1.0f,-1.0f)};
Vector3f[] pyramidNormals= {new Vector3f( 0.0f, 0.0f, 1.0f),
                               new Vector3f( 0.0f, 0.0f,-1.0f),
                               new Vector3f( 1.0f, 0.0f, 0.0f),
                               new Vector3f(-1.0f, 0.0f, 0.0f),
                               new Vector3f( 0.0f, 1.0f, 0.0f),
                               new Vector3f( 0.0f,-1.0f, 0.0f)};
```

```
        int pyramidCoordIndices[] =
                        {0,1,2,3,7,6,5,4,0,3,7,4,5,6,2,1,0,4,5,1,6,7,3,2};
        int pyramidNormalIndices[] =
                        {0,0,0,0,1,1,1,1,2,2,2,2,3,3,3,3,4,4,4,4,5,5,5,5};
        indexedPyramid.setCoordinates(0, pyramidCoordinates);
        indexedPyramid.setNormals(0,pyramidNormals);
        indexedPyramid.setCoordinateIndices(0, pyramidCoordIndices);
        indexedPyramid.setNormalIndices(0, pyramidNormalIndices);
        //Write the shapes into the array
        GeometryArray[] theShapes = new GeometryArray[2];
        theShapes[0] = indexedCube;
        theShapes[1] = indexedPyramid;
        //Put them into the group to return
        BranchGroup contentBranch = new BranchGroup();
        Transform3D rotateCube = new Transform3D( );
        rotateCube.set(new AxisAngle4d(1.0,1.0,0.0,Math.PI/4.0));
        TransformGroup rotationGroup =
                                new TransformGroup(rotateCube);
        contentBranch.addChild(rotationGroup);
        addLights(contentBranch);
        rotationGroup.addChild(createMorph(theShapes,app));
        return contentBranch;
}
/**
 * Process the button actions and perform the appropriate
 * action.
 */
public void actionPerformed(ActionEvent e) {
        if (e.getSource() == exitButton) {
                dispose();
                System.exit(0);
        } else if (e.getSource() == cubeButton) {
                //If the cube button is pressed, change the
                //weights so that the shape is nearer to a cube.
                if (weights[0] <= 0.9) {
                        weights[0] += 0.1;
                        weights[1] -= 0.1;
                        myMorph.setWeights(weights);
                }
        } else if (e.getSource() == pyraButton) {
                //If the pyramid button is pressed, change the
                //weights so that the shape is nearer to a pyramid.
                if (weights[1] <= 0.9) {
```

```
                    weights[0] -= 0.1;
                    weights[1] += 0.1;
                    myMorph.setWeights(weights);
                }
            }
    }
    public SimpleMorph () {
        VirtualUniverse myUniverse = new VirtualUniverse();
        Locale myLocale = new Locale(myUniverse);
        myLocale.addBranchGraph(buildViewBranch(myCanvas3D));
        myLocale.addBranchGraph(buildContentBranch());
        setTitle("SimpleMorph");
        setSize(400,400);
        setLayout(new BorderLayout());
        Panel bottom = new Panel();
        bottom.add(pyraButton);
        bottom.add(cubeButton);
        bottom.add(exitButton);
        add(BorderLayout.CENTER, myCanvas3D);
        add(BorderLayout.SOUTH, bottom);
        pyraButton.addActionListener(this);
        cubeButton.addActionListener(this);
        exitButton.addActionListener(this);
        setVisible(true);
    }
    public static void main(String[] args) {
        SimpleMorph sm = new SimpleMorph();
    }
}
```

Chapter 7

SimpleMorphBehaviour

This class is used in the application *SimpleMorph2*.

```java
import javax.media.j3d.*;
import javax.vecmath.*;
import java.util.*;
import java.awt.event.*;
/**
* This class uses an alpha generator to change the weights
* of a Morph node.  It morphs a shape between two key shapes
* repeatedly once a key has been pressed. Subsequent key presses
* toggle the running state of the animation.
* @author I.J.Palmer
* @version 1.0
* @see SimpleMorph2
*/
public class SimpleMorphBehaviour extends Behavior {
    /** Used to drive the animation */
    protected Alpha theAlpha;
    /** The weights of this are changed by the alpha values */
    protected Morph theMorph;
    /** Used to define the Morph weights */
    protected double theWeights[] = new double[2];
    /** Defines whether the animation is running or not */
    protected boolean running = false;
    /** The triggers for the animation to start */
    protected WakeupCriterion[] wakeConditions;
    /** The combined triggers */
    protected WakeupOr oredConditions;
    /** Set up the criteria to trigger after zero time or when a key is pressed */
    public void initialize() {
        wakeConditions = new WakeupCriterion[2];
        wakeConditions[0] =
            new WakeupOnAWTEvent(KeyEvent.KEY_PRESSED);
        wakeConditions[1] = new WakeupOnElapsedFrames(0);
```

```
                oredConditions = new WakeupOr(wakeConditions);
                wakeupOn(wakeConditions[0]);
        }
        /** If the behaviour is not running and and a key has been pressed,
         * start the animation and vice-versa.  Otherwise calculate a new
         * set of weights.
         */
        public void processStimulus(Enumeration criteria) {
                WakeupCriterion theCriteria;
                theCriteria = (WakeupCriterion) criteria.nextElement();
                //If a key has been pressed, toggle the running state
                if (theCriteria instanceof WakeupOnAWTEvent) {
                        running = !running;
                }
                if (running) {
                        //Get the alpha value
                        double alphaValue = theAlpha.value();
                        //Set the two weights according to this value
                        theWeights[0] = 1.0 - alphaValue;
                        theWeights[1] = alphaValue;
                        //Use the weights in the Morph
                        theMorph.setWeights(theWeights);
                }
                //Set the trigger conditions again
                wakeupOn(oredConditions);
        }
        /**
         * Set up the data for the behaviour.
         * @param a Alpha that is used to drive the animation
         * @param m Morph that is affected by this behaviour
         */
        public SimpleMorphBehaviour(Alpha a, Morph m) {
                theAlpha = a;
                theMorph = m;
        }
}
```

SimpleMorph2

```
import javax.media.j3d.*;
import javax.vecmath.*;
import java.awt.*;
```

```java
import java.awt.event.*;
/**
 * This uses the class SimpleMorphBehaviour to animate a shape between two
 * key shapes: a cube and a pyramid.  The Morph object is the same as
 * that used in the program SimpleMorph, but this time we use an alpha
 * generator to drive the animation.
 * @author I.J.Palmer
 * @version 1.0
 * @see SimpleMorphBehaviour
 * @see SimpleMorph
 */
public class SimpleMorph2 extends Frame implements ActionListener {
    protected Canvas3D myCanvas3D = new Canvas3D(null);
    protected Button exitButton = new Button("Exit");
    /** This performs the animation */
    protected Morph myMorph;
    /** This drives the Morph object */
    protected SimpleMorphBehaviour myBehave;
    /** The active bounds for the behaviour */
    protected BoundingSphere bounds =
            new BoundingSphere(new Point3d(0.0,0.0,0.0), 100.0);
    /**
     * Build the view branch of the scene graph
     * @return BranchGroup that is the root of the view branch
     */
    protected BranchGroup buildViewBranch(Canvas3D c) {
        BranchGroup viewBranch = new BranchGroup();
        Transform3D viewXfm = new Transform3D();
        viewXfm.set(new Vector3f(0.0f,0.0f,5.0f));
        TransformGroup viewXfmGroup = new TransformGroup(viewXfm);
        ViewPlatform myViewPlatform = new ViewPlatform();
        PhysicalBody myBody = new PhysicalBody();
        PhysicalEnvironment myEnvironment = new PhysicalEnvironment();
        viewXfmGroup.addChild(myViewPlatform);
        viewBranch.addChild(viewXfmGroup);
        View myView = new View();
        myView.addCanvas3D(c);
        myView.attachViewPlatform(myViewPlatform);
        myView.setPhysicalBody(myBody);
        myView.setPhysicalEnvironment(myEnvironment);
        return viewBranch;
    }
    /**
```

```
     * Add some lights to the scene graph
     * @param b BranchGroup that the lights are added to
     */
    protected void addLights(BranchGroup b) {
        Color3f ambLightColour = new Color3f(0.5f, 0.5f, 0.5f);
        AmbientLight ambLight = new AmbientLight(ambLightColour);
        ambLight.setInfluencingBounds(bounds);
        Color3f dirLightColour = new Color3f(1.0f, 1.0f, 1.0f);
        Vector3f dirLightDir  = new Vector3f(-1.0f, -1.0f, -1.0f);
        DirectionalLight dirLight =
                    new DirectionalLight(dirLightColour, dirLightDir);
        dirLight.setInfluencingBounds(bounds);
        b.addChild(ambLight);
        b.addChild(dirLight);
    }
    /**
     * Create the Morph from the given shapes
     * @param theShapes GeometryArray that stores the shapes for the Morph
     * @param app Appearnce used for the shapes
     * @return Morph that uses the given shapes
     */
    protected Morph createMorph(GeometryArray[] theShapes, Appearance app) {
        double[] weights = {1.0,0.0};
        Alpha morphAlpha = new Alpha(-1,
                Alpha.INCREASING_ENABLE | Alpha.DECREASING_ENABLE,
                0,0,4000,2000,0,4000,2000,0);
        myMorph = new Morph(theShapes,app);
        myMorph.setWeights(weights);
        myMorph.setCapability(Morph.ALLOW_WEIGHTS_WRITE);
        myBehave = new SimpleMorphBehaviour(morphAlpha,myMorph);
        myBehave.setSchedulingBounds(bounds);
        return myMorph;
    }
    /**
     * Build the content branch for the scene graph
     * @return BranchGroup that is the root of the content
     */
    protected BranchGroup buildContentBranch() {
        Appearance app = new Appearance();
        Color3f ambientColour = new Color3f(1.0f,0.0f,0.0f);
        Color3f emissiveColour = new Color3f(0.0f,0.0f,0.0f);
        Color3f specularColour = new Color3f(1.0f,1.0f,1.0f);
        Color3f diffuseColour = new Color3f(1.0f,0.0f,0.0f);
        float shininess = 20.0f;
```

```
app.setMaterial(new Material(ambientColour,emissiveColour,
                             diffuseColour,specularColour,shininess));
//Make the cube key shape
IndexedQuadArray indexedCube = new IndexedQuadArray(8,
      IndexedQuadArray.COORDINATES|IndexedQuadArray.NORMALS, 24);
Point3f[] cubeCoordinates = {    new Point3f( 1.0f, 1.0f, 1.0f),
                                 new Point3f(-1.0f, 1.0f, 1.0f),
                                 new Point3f(-1.0f,-1.0f, 1.0f),
                                 new Point3f( 1.0f,-1.0f, 1.0f),
                                 new Point3f( 1.0f, 1.0f,-1.0f),
                                 new Point3f(-1.0f, 1.0f,-1.0f),
                                 new Point3f(-1.0f,-1.0f,-1.0f),
                                 new Point3f( 1.0f,-1.0f,-1.0f)};
Vector3f[] cubeNormals= {new Vector3f( 0.0f, 0.0f, 1.0f),
                         new Vector3f( 0.0f, 0.0f,-1.0f),
                         new Vector3f( 1.0f, 0.0f, 0.0f),
                         new Vector3f(-1.0f, 0.0f, 0.0f),
                         new Vector3f( 0.0f, 1.0f, 0.0f),
                         new Vector3f( 0.0f,-1.0f, 0.0f)};
int cubeCoordIndices[] = {0,1,2,3,7,6,5,4,0,3,7,4,5,6,2,1,0,4,5,1,6,7,3,2};
int cubeNormalIndices[] = {0,0,0,0,1,1,1,1,2,2,2,2,3,3,3,3,4,4,4,4,5,5,5,5};
indexedCube.setCoordinates(0, cubeCoordinates);
indexedCube.setNormals(0,cubeNormals);
indexedCube.setCoordinateIndices(0, cubeCoordIndices);
indexedCube.setNormalIndices(0, cubeNormalIndices);
//Make the pyramid key shape.  Although this needs
//only five vertices to create the desired shape, we
//need to use six vertices so that it has the same
//number as the cube.
IndexedQuadArray indexedPyramid = new IndexedQuadArray(8,
      IndexedQuadArray.COORDINATES|IndexedQuadArray.NORMALS, 24);
Point3f[] pyramidCoordinates = {    new Point3f( 0.0f, 1.0f, 0.0f),
                                 new Point3f(0.0f, 1.0f, 0.0f),
                                 new Point3f(-1.0f,-1.0f, 1.0f),
                                 new Point3f( 1.0f,-1.0f, 1.0f),
                                 new Point3f( 0.0f, 1.0f,0.0f),
                                 new Point3f(0.0f, 1.0f,0.0f),
                                 new Point3f(-1.0f,-1.0f,-1.0f),
                                 new Point3f( 1.0f,-1.0f,-1.0f)};
Vector3f[] pyramidNormals= {    new Vector3f( 0.0f, 0.0f, 1.0f),
                                 new Vector3f( 0.0f, 0.0f,-1.0f),
                                 new Vector3f( 1.0f, 0.0f, 0.0f),
                                 new Vector3f(-1.0f, 0.0f, 0.0f),
```

```
                               new Vector3f( 0.0f, 1.0f, 0.0f),
                          new Vector3f( 0.0f,-1.0f, 0.0f)};
    int pyramidCoordIndices[] =
              {0,1,2,3,7,6,5,4,0,3,7,4,5,6,2,1,0,4,5,1,6,7,3,2};
    int pyramidNormalIndices[] =
                       {0,0,0,0,1,1,1,1,2,2,2,2,3,3,3,3,4,4,4,4,5,5,5,5};
    indexedPyramid.setCoordinates(0, pyramidCoordinates);
    indexedPyramid.setNormals(0,pyramidNormals);
    indexedPyramid.setCoordinateIndices(0, pyramidCoordIndices);
    indexedPyramid.setNormalIndices(0, pyramidNormalIndices);
    //Set the contents of the array to the two shapes
    GeometryArray[] theShapes = new GeometryArray[2];
    theShapes[0] = indexedCube;
    theShapes[1] = indexedPyramid;
    BranchGroup contentBranch = new BranchGroup();
    //Create a transform to rotate the shape slightly
    Transform3D rotateCube = new Transform3D( );
    rotateCube.set(new AxisAngle4d(1.0,1.0,0.0,Math.PI/4.0));
    TransformGroup rotationGroup = new TransformGroup(rotateCube);
    contentBranch.addChild(rotationGroup);
    addLights(contentBranch);
    //Call the function to build the morph
    rotationGroup.addChild(createMorph(theShapes,app));
    //Add the behaviour to the scene graph to activate it
    rotationGroup.addChild(myBehave);
    return contentBranch;
}
public void actionPerformed(ActionEvent e) {
    dispose();
    System.exit(0);
}
public SimpleMorph2() {
    VirtualUniverse myUniverse = new VirtualUniverse();
    Locale myLocale = new Locale(myUniverse);
    myLocale.addBranchGraph(buildViewBranch(myCanvas3D));
    myLocale.addBranchGraph(buildContentBranch());
    setTitle("SimpleMorph2");
    setSize(400,400);
    setLayout(new BorderLayout());
    Panel bottom = new Panel();
    bottom.add(exitButton);
    add(BorderLayout.CENTER, myCanvas3D);
    add(BorderLayout.SOUTH, bottom);
    exitButton.addActionListener(this);
```

```
            setVisible(true);
    }
    public static void main(String[] args) {
        SimpleMorph2 sm2 = new SimpleMorph2();
    }
}
```

SimpleMouse

```java
import javax.media.j3d.*;
import javax.vecmath.*;
import java.awt.*;
import java.awt.event.*;
import com.sun.j3d.utils.behaviors.mouse.*;
import com.sun.j3d.utils.geometry.*;
/**
 * This application demonstrates the use of the mouse
 * utility classes.  It allows rotation, translation and
 * resizing of the screen image of
 * a cube by clicking and dragging the mouse on the shape.
 * @author I.J.Palmer
 * @version 1.0
 */
public class SimpleMouse extends Frame implements ActionListener {
    protected Canvas3D myCanvas3D = new Canvas3D(null);
    protected Button exitButton = new Button("Exit");
    protected BoundingSphere bounds =
                    new BoundingSphere(new Point3d(0.0,0.0,0.0), 100.0);

    /**
     * Build the view branch of the scene graph
     * @return BranchGroup that is the root of the view branch
     */
    protected BranchGroup buildViewBranch(Canvas3D c) {
        BranchGroup viewBranch = new BranchGroup();
        Transform3D viewXfm = new Transform3D();
        viewXfm.set(new Vector3f(0.0f,0.0f,10.0f));
        TransformGroup viewXfmGroup = new TransformGroup(viewXfm);
        ViewPlatform myViewPlatform = new ViewPlatform();
        PhysicalBody myBody = new PhysicalBody();
        PhysicalEnvironment myEnvironment = new PhysicalEnvironment();
        viewXfmGroup.addChild(myViewPlatform);
```

```
        viewBranch.addChild(viewXfmGroup);
        View myView = new View();
        myView.addCanvas3D(c);
        myView.attachViewPlatform(myViewPlatform);
        myView.setPhysicalBody(myBody);
        myView.setPhysicalEnvironment(myEnvironment);
        return viewBranch;
}
/**
 * Add some lights to the scene graph
 * @param b BranchGroup that the lights are added to
 */
protected void addLights(BranchGroup b) {
        Color3f ambLightColour = new Color3f(0.5f, 0.5f, 0.5f);
        AmbientLight ambLight = new AmbientLight(ambLightColour);
        ambLight.setInfluencingBounds(bounds);
        Color3f dirLightColour = new Color3f(1.0f, 1.0f, 1.0f);
        Vector3f dirLightDir  = new Vector3f(-1.0f, -1.0f, -1.0f);
        DirectionalLight dirLight =
                    new DirectionalLight(dirLightColour, dirLightDir);
        dirLight.setInfluencingBounds(bounds);
        b.addChild(ambLight);
        b.addChild(dirLight);
}
/**
 * Build the content branch for the scene graph
 * @return BranchGroup that is the root of the content
 */
protected BranchGroup buildContentBranch() {
        Appearance app = new Appearance();
        Color3f ambientColour = new Color3f(1.0f,0.0f,0.0f);
        Color3f emissiveColour = new Color3f(0.0f,0.0f,0.0f);
        Color3f specularColour = new Color3f(1.0f,1.0f,1.0f);
        Color3f diffuseColour = new Color3f(1.0f,0.0f,0.0f);
        float shininess = 20.0f;
        app.setMaterial(new Material(ambientColour,emissiveColour,
                                    diffuseColour,specularColour,shininess));
        Box cube = new Box(2.0f,2.0f,2.0f, app);
        BranchGroup contentBranch = new BranchGroup();
        addLights(contentBranch);
        //Create the transform groups that will be
        //affected by the mouse utiltities
        TransformGroup spinGroup = new TransformGroup();
        TransformGroup zoomGroup = new TransformGroup();
```

```
        TransformGroup moveGroup = new TransformGroup();
        //Set the capabilities of the groups so that we can
        //manipulate them
        spinGroup.setCapability(
                        TransformGroup.ALLOW_TRANSFORM_WRITE);
        spinGroup.setCapability(
                        TransformGroup.ALLOW_TRANSFORM_READ);
        zoomGroup.setCapability(
                        TransformGroup.ALLOW_TRANSFORM_WRITE);
        zoomGroup.setCapability(
                        TransformGroup.ALLOW_TRANSFORM_READ);
        moveGroup.setCapability(
                        TransformGroup.ALLOW_TRANSFORM_WRITE);
        moveGroup.setCapability(
                        TransformGroup.ALLOW_TRANSFORM_READ);
        //Create and use the rotation utility
        MouseRotate mouseSpin = new MouseRotate();
        mouseSpin.setTransformGroup(spinGroup);
        contentBranch.addChild(mouseSpin);
        mouseSpin.setSchedulingBounds(bounds);
        //Create and use the zoom utility
        MouseZoom mouseSize = new MouseZoom();
        mouseSize.setTransformGroup(zoomGroup);
        contentBranch.addChild(mouseSize);
        mouseSize.setSchedulingBounds(bounds);
        //Create and use the translation utility
        MouseTranslate mouseMove = new MouseTranslate();
        mouseMove.setTransformGroup(moveGroup);
        contentBranch.addChild(mouseMove);
        mouseMove.setSchedulingBounds(bounds);
        //Put it all together
        spinGroup.addChild(cube);
        moveGroup.addChild(spinGroup);
        zoomGroup.addChild(moveGroup);
        contentBranch.addChild(zoomGroup);
        return contentBranch;
    }
    /** Use the action event of the exit button
     * to end the application.
     */
    public void actionPerformed(ActionEvent e) {
        dispose();
        System.exit(0);
```

```
        }
        public SimpleMouse() {
                VirtualUniverse myUniverse = new VirtualUniverse();
                Locale myLocale = new Locale(myUniverse);
                myLocale.addBranchGraph(buildViewBranch(myCanvas3D));
                myLocale.addBranchGraph(buildContentBranch());
                setTitle("SimpleMouse");
                setSize(400,400);
                setLayout(new BorderLayout());
                Panel bottom = new Panel();
                bottom.add(exitButton);
                add(BorderLayout.CENTER, myCanvas3D);
                add(BorderLayout.SOUTH, bottom);
                exitButton.addActionListener(this);
                setVisible(true);
        }
        public static void main(String[] args) {
                SimpleMouse sm = new SimpleMouse();
        }
}
```

SimpleKeyNav

```
import javax.media.j3d.*;
import javax.vecmath.*;
import java.awt.*;
import java.awt.event.*;
import com.sun.j3d.utils.behaviors.keyboard.*;
import com.sun.j3d.utils.geometry.*;
/**
 * This application uses the mouse keyboard utility
 * class to allow navigation around the scene.
 * The scene consists of a yellow and red cube.
 * @author I.J.Palmer
 * @version 1.0
 */
public class SimpleKeyNav extends Frame implements ActionListener {
        protected Canvas3D myCanvas3D = new Canvas3D(null);
        protected Button exitButton = new Button("Exit");
        protected BoundingSphere bounds =
                        new BoundingSphere(new Point3d(0.0,0.0,0.0), 100.0);
        /**
```

```
    * Build the view branch of the scene graph. In this case
    * a key navigation utility object is created and associated
    * with the view transform so that the view can be changed
    * via the keyboard.
    * @return BranchGroup that is the root of the view branch
    */
    protected BranchGroup buildViewBranch(Canvas3D c) {
        BranchGroup viewBranch = new BranchGroup();
        Transform3D viewXfm = new Transform3D();
        viewXfm.set(new Vector3f(0.0f,0.0f,10.0f));
        TransformGroup viewXfmGroup = new TransformGroup(viewXfm);
        //Set the capabilities so that we can access the view transform
        viewXfmGroup.setCapability(
                            TransformGroup.ALLOW_TRANSFORM_READ);
        viewXfmGroup.setCapability(
                            TransformGroup.ALLOW_TRANSFORM_WRITE);
        //Create a bounding leaf so that the key navigation is always
        //active
        BoundingSphere movingBounds =
                    new BoundingSphere(new Point3d(0.0,0.0,0.0), 100.0);
        BoundingLeaf boundLeaf = new BoundingLeaf(movingBounds);
        ViewPlatform myViewPlatform = new ViewPlatform();
        viewXfmGroup.addChild(boundLeaf);
        PhysicalBody myBody = new PhysicalBody();
        PhysicalEnvironment myEnvironment = new PhysicalEnvironment();
        viewXfmGroup.addChild(myViewPlatform);
        viewBranch.addChild(viewXfmGroup);
        View myView = new View();
        myView.addCanvas3D(c);
        myView.attachViewPlatform(myViewPlatform);
        myView.setPhysicalBody(myBody);
        myView.setPhysicalEnvironment(myEnvironment);
        //Create the object for the key navigation
        KeyNavigatorBehavior keyNav =
                    new KeyNavigatorBehavior(viewXfmGroup);
        keyNav.setSchedulingBounds(movingBounds);
        viewBranch.addChild(keyNav);
        return viewBranch;
    }
    /**
    * Add some lights to the scene graph
    * @param b BranchGroup that the lights are added to
    */
```

```
protected void addLights(BranchGroup b) {
       // Create a bounds for the background and lights
       // Set up the global lights
       Color3f ambLightColour = new Color3f(0.5f, 0.5f, 0.5f);
       AmbientLight ambLight = new AmbientLight(ambLightColour);
       ambLight.setInfluencingBounds(bounds);
       Color3f dirLightColour = new Color3f(1.0f, 1.0f, 1.0f);
       Vector3f dirLightDir = new Vector3f(-1.0f, -1.0f, -1.0f);
       DirectionalLight dirLight =
                       new DirectionalLight(dirLightColour, dirLightDir);
       dirLight.setInfluencingBounds(bounds);
       b.addChild(ambLight);
       b.addChild(dirLight);
}
/**
 * Build the content branch for the scene graph
 * @return BranchGroup that is the root of the content
 */
protected BranchGroup buildContentBranch() {
       //Create the appearance an appearance for the two cubes
       Appearance app1 = new Appearance();
       Appearance app2 = new Appearance();
       Color3f ambientColour1 = new Color3f(1.0f,0.0f,0.0f);
       Color3f ambientColour2 = new Color3f(1.0f,1.0f,0.0f);
       Color3f emissiveColour = new Color3f(0.0f,0.0f,0.0f);
       Color3f specularColour = new Color3f(1.0f,1.0f,1.0f);
       Color3f diffuseColour1 = new Color3f(1.0f,0.0f,0.0f);
       Color3f diffuseColour2 = new Color3f(1.0f,1.0f,0.0f);
       float shininess = 20.0f;
       app1.setMaterial(new Material(ambientColour1,emissiveColour,
                               diffuseColour1,specularColour,shininess));
       app2.setMaterial(new Material(ambientColour2, emissiveColour,
                               diffuseColour2,specularColour,shininess));
       //Make two cubes
       Box leftCube = new Box(1.0f,1.0f,1.0f,app1);
       Box rightCube = new Box(1.0f,1.0f,1.0f,app2);
       BranchGroup contentBranch = new BranchGroup();
       addLights(contentBranch);
       //Put it all together
       Transform3D leftGroupXfm = new Transform3D();
       leftGroupXfm.set(new Vector3d(-1.5,0.0,0.0));
       TransformGroup leftGroup = new TransformGroup(leftGroupXfm);
       Transform3D rightGroupXfm = new Transform3D();
       rightGroupXfm.set(new Vector3d(1.5,0.0,0.0));
```

```
            TransformGroup rightGroup = new TransformGroup(rightGroupXfm)
            leftGroup.addChild(leftCube);
            rightGroup.addChild(rightCube);
            contentBranch.addChild(leftGroup);
            contentBranch.addChild(rightGroup);
            return contentBranch;
    }
    /**
     * Use the action event of the exit button
     * to end the application.
     */
    public void actionPerformed(ActionEvent e) {
            dispose();
            System.exit(0);
    }
    public SimpleKeyNav() {
            VirtualUniverse myUniverse = new VirtualUniverse();
            Locale myLocale = new Locale(myUniverse);
            myLocale.addBranchGraph(buildViewBranch(myCanvas3D));
            myLocale.addBranchGraph(buildContentBranch());
            setTitle("SimpleKeyNav");
            setSize(400,400);
            setLayout(new BorderLayout());
            Panel bottom = new Panel();
            bottom.add(exitButton);
            add(BorderLayout.CENTER, myCanvas3D);
            add(BorderLayout.SOUTH, bottom);
            exitButton.addActionListener(this);
            setVisible(true);
    }
    public static void main(String[] args) {
            SimpleKeyNav skn = new SimpleKeyNav();
    }
}
```

SimplePickBehaviour

This class is uses in the application *SimplePick*.

```
import javax.media.j3d.*;
import com.sun.j3d.utils.picking.*;
import com.sun.j3d.utils. picking.behaviors. *;
```

```
import com.sun.j3d.utils.geometry.*;
/**
* This class implements a simple pick behaviour.
* It prints out a message identifying which object has been picked
* by using the userData of the object.  The use of this class is
* demonstrated in SimplePick.
* @author I.J.Palmer
* @version 1.0
* @see SimplePick
*/
public class SimplePickBehaviour extends PickMouseBehavior {
    /**
    * @param pickRoot BranchGroup that is the root of the picking operation.
    * @param pickCanvas Canvas3D used in the pick operation.
    * @param pickBounds Bounds that define the behaviour's active region.
    */
    public SimplePickBehaviour(Canvas3D pickCanvas, BranchGroup pickRoot,
                                                   Bounds pickBounds) {
        super(pickCanvas, pickRoot, pickBounds);
        setSchedulingBounds(pickBounds);
    }
    /**
    * Where the processing is carried out.
    * This checks if an object has been picked and if it
    * has prints out the user data for that shape.
    * @xpos int that stores the x-position of the mouse
    * @ypos int that stores the y-position of the mouse
    */
    public void updateScene(int xpos, int ypos) {
        Primitive pickedShape = null;
        pickCanvas.setShapeLocation(xpos,ypos);
        pickResult = pickCanvas.pickClosest();
        if (pickResult != null)
                pickedShape = (Primitive) pickResult.getNode(PickResult.PRIMITIVE);
        if (pickedShape != null)
                System.out.println("Picked the " + pickedShape.getUserData());
        else
                System.out.println("Picked nothing");
    }
}
```

SimplePickBehaviour (version 2)

This version of the picking behaviour only responds to left mouse button events.

```java
import java.util.*;
import java.awt.AWTEvent;
import java.awt.event.MouseEvent;
import javax.media.j3d.*;
import com.sun.j3d.utils.picking.*;
import com.sun.j3d.utils. picking.behaviors. *;
import com.sun.j3d.utils.geometry.*;
/**
 * This class implements a simple pick behaviour.
 * It prints out a message identifying which object has been picked
 * by using the userData of the object.  The use of this class is
 * demonstrated in SimplePick.
 * @author I.J.Palmer
 * @version 1.0
 * @see SimplePick
 */
public class SimplePickBehaviour extends PickMouseBehavior {
    /**
     * The wake up criteria.
     * This is set to trigger on mouse events using the MOUSE_EVENT_MASK.
     */
    WakeupOnAWTEvent buttonPressed =
        new WakeupOnAWTEvent(MouseEvent.MOUSE_EVENT_MASK);
    /**
     * @param pickRoot BranchGroup that is the root of the picking operation.
     * @param pickCanvas Canvas3D used in the pick operation.
     * @param pickBounds Bounds that define the behaviour's active region.
     */
    public SimplePickBehaviour(Canvas3D pickCanvas, BranchGroup pickRoot,
                               Bounds pickBounds) {
        super(pickCanvas, pickRoot, pickBounds);
        setSchedulingBounds(pickBounds);
    }
    /** Sets the wake up criterion to the mouse button criteria */
    public void initialize() {
        wakeupOn(buttonPressed);
    }
```

```java
/**
 * Where the processing is carried out.
 * This obtains the AWT mouse event, checks if it is the left mouse button
 * and then uses the x and y coodinates of the mouse position to
 * pick an object.  A message is printed according to which
 * object has been picked.
 * Finally the wake up condition is set to the mouse
 * criterion again.
 */
public void processStimulus(Enumeration criteria) {
    WakeupOnAWTEvent theCriterion =
                (WakeupOnAWTEvent) criteria.nextElement();
    AWTEvent theEvents[] = theCriterion.getAWTEvent();
    if (theEvents[0].getID() == MouseEvent.MOUSE_RELEASED) {
        MouseEvent theMouseEvent = (MouseEvent) theEvents[0];
        if ((theMouseEvent.getModifiers()
                    & MouseEvent.BUTTON1_MASK) != 0) {
            int xpos = theMouseEvent.getX();
            int ypos = theMouseEvent.getY();
            Primitive pickedShape = null;
            PickResult pickResult = null;
            pickCanvas.setShapeLocation(xpos,ypos);
            pickResult = pickCanvas.pickClosest();
            if (pickResult != null)
                pickedShape =
                    (Primitive) pickResult.getNode(PickResult.PRIMITIVE);
            if (pickedShape != null)
                System.out.println("Picked the " + pickedShape.getUserData());
            else
                System.out.println("Picked nothing");
        }
    }
    wakeupOn(buttonPressed);
}
/**
 * This performs no processing but is required
 * as the parent class is abstract.
 */
public void updateScene(int xpos, int ypos) {}
}
```

SimplePick

This uses a *SimplePickBehaviour* (either of the ones given above) to implement a simple picking operation.

```java
import javax.media.j3d.*;
import javax.vecmath.*;
import java.awt.*;
import java.awt.event.*;
import com.sun.j3d.utils. picking.behaviors. *;
/**
 * This demonstrates the use of the SimplePickBehaviour class.
 * When run, picking one of the cubes with the right mouse button
 * results in a messages being printed that identify which was picked.
 * @author I.J.Palmer
 * @version 1.0
 * @see SimplePickBehaviour
 */
public class SimplePick extends Frame implements ActionListener {
    protected Canvas3D myCanvas3D = new Canvas3D(null);
    protected Button exitButton = new Button("Exit");
    /** The bounds in which the behaviour is active */
    protected BoundingSphere bounds =
        new BoundingSphere(new Point3d(0.0,0.0,0.0), 100.0);
    /**
     * Build the view branch of the scene graph
     * @return BranchGroup that is the root of the view branch
     * @param c Canvas3D used to display the scene
     */
    protected BranchGroup buildViewBranch(Canvas3D c) {
        BranchGroup viewBranch = new BranchGroup();
        Transform3D viewXfm = new Transform3D();
        viewXfm.set(new Vector3f(0.0f,0.0f,10.0f));
        TransformGroup viewXfmGroup = new TransformGroup(viewXfm);
        ViewPlatform myViewPlatform = new ViewPlatform();
        PhysicalBody myBody = new PhysicalBody();
        PhysicalEnvironment myEnvironment = new PhysicalEnvironment();
        viewXfmGroup.addChild(myViewPlatform);
        viewBranch.addChild(viewXfmGroup);
        View myView = new View();
        myView.addCanvas3D(c);
        myView.attachViewPlatform(myViewPlatform);
```

```
            myView.setPhysicalBody(myBody);
            myView.setPhysicalEnvironment(myEnvironment);
            return viewBranch;
    }
    /**
     * Add some lights to the scene graph
     * @param b BranchGroup to add
     */
    protected void addLights(BranchGroup b) {
            Color3f ambLightColour = new Color3f(0.5f, 0.5f, 0.5f);
            AmbientLight ambLight = new AmbientLight(ambLightColour);
            ambLight.setInfluencingBounds(bounds);
            Color3f dirLightColour = new Color3f(1.0f, 1.0f, 1.0f);
            Vector3f dirLightDir  = new Vector3f(-1.0f, -1.0f, -1.0f);
            DirectionalLight dirLight =
                                new DirectionalLight(dirLightColour, dirLightDir);
            dirLight.setInfluencingBounds(bounds);
            b.addChild(ambLight);
            b.addChild(dirLight);
    }
    /**
     * Build the content branch
     * @return BranchGroup that is the root of the content branch
     */
    protected BranchGroup buildContentBranch() {
            //Create appearances for the two cubes
            Appearance app1 = new Appearance();
            Appearance app2 = new Appearance();
            Color3f ambientColour1 = new Color3f(1.0f,0.0f,0.0f);
            Color3f ambientColour2 = new Color3f(1.0f,1.0f,0.0f);
            Color3f emissiveColour = new Color3f(0.0f,0.0f,0.0f);
            Color3f specularColour = new Color3f(1.0f,1.0f,1.0f);
            Color3f diffuseColour1 = new Color3f(1.0f,0.0f,0.0f);
            Color3f diffuseColour2 = new Color3f(1.0f,1.0f,0.0f);
            float shininess = 20.0f;
            app1.setMaterial(new Material(ambientColour1,emissiveColour,
                                diffuseColour1,specularColour,shininess));
            app2.setMaterial(new Material(ambientColour2, emissiveColour,
                                diffuseColour2,specularColour,shininess));
            //Make the cubes
            Box leftCube = new Box(1.0f,1.0f,1.0f, app1);
            leftCube.setUserData(new String("left cube"));
            Box rightCube = new Box(1.0f,1.0f,1.0f, app2);
            rightCube.setUserData(new String("right cube"));
```

```
        BranchGroup contentBranch = new BranchGroup();
        addLights(contentBranch);
        Transform3D leftGroupXfm = new Transform3D();
        leftGroupXfm.set(new Vector3d(-1.5,0.0,0.0));
        TransformGroup leftGroup = new TransformGroup(leftGroupXfm);
        Transform3D rightGroupXfm = new Transform3D();
        rightGroupXfm.set(new Vector3d(1.5,0.0,0.0));
        TransformGroup rightGroup = new TransformGroup(rightGroupXfm);
        //Create the behaviour and add it to the scene
        SimplePickBehaviour simplePick =
            new SimplePickRightBehaviour(contentBranch,
                                        myCanvas3D, bounds);
        contentBranch.addChild(simplePick);
        //Put the hierarchy together
        leftGroup.addChild(leftCube);
        rightGroup.addChild(rightCube);
        contentBranch.addChild(leftGroup);
        contentBranch.addChild(rightGroup);
        return contentBranch;
    }
    /** Process button event to exit to quit application */
    public void actionPerformed(ActionEvent e) {
        dispose();
        System.exit(0);
    }
    public SimplePick() {
        VirtualUniverse myUniverse = new VirtualUniverse();
        Locale myLocale = new Locale(myUniverse);
        myLocale.addBranchGraph(buildViewBranch(myCanvas3D));
        myLocale.addBranchGraph(buildContentBranch());
        setTitle("SimplePick");
        setSize(400,400);
        setLayout(new BorderLayout());
        Panel bottom = new Panel();
        bottom.add(exitButton);
        add(BorderLayout.CENTER, myCanvas3D);
        add(BorderLayout.SOUTH, bottom);
        exitButton.addActionListener(this);
        setVisible(true);
    }
    public static void main(String[] args) {
        SimplePick sp = new SimplePick();
```

```
        }
}
```

CollisionDetector class

This class is used in the application *SimpleCollision*.

```java
import java.util.*;
import javax.media.j3d.*;

/**
 * A simple collision detector class.  This responds to a collision
 * event by printing a message with information about the type of
 * collision event and the object that has been collided with.
 * @author I.J.Palmer
 * @version 1.0
 */
public class CollisionDetector extends Behavior {
    /** The separate criteria used to wake up this beahvior. */
    protected WakeupCriterion[] theCriteria;
    /** The OR of the separate criteria. */
    protected WakeupOr oredCriteria;
    /** The shape that is watched for collision. */
    protected Shape3D collidingShape;

    /**
     * @param theShape Shape3D that is to be watched for collisions.
     * @param theBounds Bounds that define the active region for this behaviour
     */
    public CollisionDetector(Shape3D theShape, Bounds theBounds) {
        collidingShape = theShape;
        setSchedulingBounds(theBounds);
    }

    /**
     * This creates an entry, exit and movement collision criteria.
     * These are then OR'ed together, and the wake up condition set
     * to the result.
     */
    public void initialize() {
        theCriteria = new WakeupCriterion[3];
        theCriteria[0] = new WakeupOnCollisionEntry(collidingShape);
        theCriteria[1] = new WakeupOnCollisionExit(collidingShape);
```

```
        theCriteria[2] = new WakeupOnCollisionMovement(collidingShape);
        oredCriteria = new WakeupOr(theCriteria);
        wakeupOn(oredCriteria);
    }

    /**
     * Where the work is done in this class.  A message is printed out
     * using the userData of the object collided with.  The wake up
     * condition is then set to the OR'ed criterion again.
     */
    public void processStimulus(Enumeration criteria) {
        WakeupCriterion theCriterion = (WakeupCriterion) criteria.nextElement();
        if (theCriterion instanceof WakeupOnCollisionEntry) {
            Node theLeaf = ((WakeupOnCollisionEntry)
                              theCriterion).getTriggeringPath().getObject();
            System.out.println("Collided with " + theLeaf.getUserData());
        }
        else if (theCriterion instanceof WakeupOnCollisionExit) {
            Node theLeaf = ((WakeupOnCollisionExit)
                              theCriterion).getTriggeringPath().getObject();
            System.out.println("Stopped colliding with  " + theLeaf.getUserData());
        } else {
            Node theLeaf = ((WakeupOnCollisionMovement)
                              theCriterion).getTriggeringPath().getObject();
            System.out.println("Moved whilst colliding with " + theLeaf.getUserData());
        }
        wakeupOn(oredCriteria);
    }
}
```

SimpleCollision application

```
import javax.media.j3d.*;
import javax.vecmath.*;
import java.awt.*;
import java.awt.event.*;
import com.sun.j3d.utils. picking.behaviors. *;

/**
 * This class demonstrates the use of the CollisionDetector
 * class to perform processing when objects collide. When this
```

```
* program is run the white cube can be selected and moved by
* dragging on it with the right mouse button.
* You should notice that there is a problem
* if the movable cube comes into contact with both of the
* static cubes at one time. A way round this is given in the
* SimpleCollision2 application.
* @see CollisionDetector
* @see SimpleCollision2
* @author I.J.Palmer
* @version 1.0
*/
public class SimpleCollision extends Frame implements ActionListener {
        protected Canvas3D myCanvas3D = new Canvas3D(null);
        protected Button exitButton = new Button("Exit");
    protected BoundingSphere bounds =
            new BoundingSphere(new Point3d(0.0,0.0,0.0), 100.0);
        /** Transform for the left cube. */
        protected TransformGroup leftGroup;
        /** Transform for the right cube */
        protected TransformGroup rightGroup;
        /** Transform for the movable cube. This has read,
           write and pick reporting capabilities enabled. */
        protected TransformGroup moveGroup;
        /** The left static cube. */
        protected Shape3D leftCube;
        /** The right static cube. */
        protected Shape3D rightCube;
        /** The movable cube that will collide with the other two cubes */
        protected Shape3D moveCube;


        /**
        * This builds the view branch of the scene graph.
        */
        protected BranchGroup buildViewBranch(Canvas3D c) {
            BranchGroup viewBranch = new BranchGroup();
            Transform3D viewXfm = new Transform3D();
            viewXfm.set(new Vector3f(0.0f,0.0f,10.0f));
            TransformGroup viewXfmGroup = new TransformGroup(viewXfm);
            ViewPlatform myViewPlatform = new ViewPlatform();
            PhysicalBody myBody = new PhysicalBody();
            PhysicalEnvironment myEnvironment = new PhysicalEnvironment();
            viewXfmGroup.addChild(myViewPlatform);
            viewBranch.addChild(viewXfmGroup);
            View myView = new View();
```

```
            myView.addCanvas3D(c);
            myView.attachViewPlatform(myViewPlatform);
            myView.setPhysicalBody(myBody);
            myView.setPhysicalEnvironment(myEnvironment);
            return viewBranch;
        }


/**
 * This adds some lights to the content branch of the scene graph.
 * @param b The BranchGroup to add the lights to.
 */
protected void addLights(BranchGroup b) {
        Color3f ambLightColour = new Color3f(0.5f, 0.5f, 0.5f);
        AmbientLight ambLight = new AmbientLight(ambLightColour);
        ambLight.setInfluencingBounds(bounds);
        Color3f dirLightColour = new Color3f(1.0f, 1.0f, 1.0f);
        Vector3f dirLightDir  = new Vector3f(-1.0f, -1.0f, -1.0f);
        DirectionalLight dirLight =
                        new DirectionalLight(dirLightColour, dirLightDir);
        dirLight.setInfluencingBounds(bounds);
        b.addChild(ambLight);
        b.addChild(dirLight);
    }


/**
 * Creates the content branch of the scene graph.
 * @return BranchGroup with content attached.
 */
protected BranchGroup buildContentBranch() {
        //First create a different appearance for each cube
        Appearance app1 = new Appearance();
        Appearance app2 = new Appearance();
        Appearance app3 = new Appearance();
        Color3f ambientColour1 = new Color3f(1.0f,0.0f,0.0f);
        Color3f ambientColour2 = new Color3f(1.0f,1.0f,0.0f);
        Color3f ambientColour3 = new Color3f(1.0f,1.0f,1.0f);
        Color3f emissiveColour = new Color3f(0.0f,0.0f,0.0f);
        Color3f specularColour = new Color3f(1.0f,1.0f,1.0f);
        Color3f diffuseColour1 = new Color3f(1.0f,0.0f,0.0f);
        Color3f diffuseColour2 = new Color3f(1.0f,1.0f,0.0f);
        Color3f diffuseColour3 = new Color3f(1.0f,1.0f,1.0f);
        float shininess = 20.0f;
        app1.setMaterial(new Material(ambientColour1,emissiveColour,
```

```
                                    diffuseColour1,specularColour,shininess));
    app2.setMaterial(new Material(ambientColour2, emissiveColour,
                                    diffuseColour2,specularColour,shininess));
    app3.setMaterial(new Material(ambientColour3,emissiveColour,
                                    diffuseColour3,specularColour,shininess));


    //Create the vertex data for the cube.  Since each shape is
    //a cube we can use the same vertex data for each cube
    IndexedQuadArray indexedCube = new IndexedQuadArray(8,
                                    IndexedQuadArray.COORDINATES |
                                    IndexedQuadArray.NORMALS, 24);
    Point3f[] cubeCoordinates = {  new Point3f( 1.0f, 1.0f, 1.0f),
                                    new Point3f(-1.0f, 1.0f, 1.0f),
                                    new Point3f(-1.0f,-1.0f, 1.0f),
                                    new Point3f( 1.0f,-1.0f, 1.0f),
                                    new Point3f( 1.0f, 1.0f,-1.0f),
                                    new Point3f(-1.0f, 1.0f,-1.0f),
                                    new Point3f(-1.0f,-1.0f,-1.0f),
                                    new Point3f( 1.0f,-1.0f,-1.0f)};
    Vector3f[] cubeNormals= {new Vector3f( 0.0f, 0.0f, 1.0f),
                                    new Vector3f( 0.0f, 0.0f,-1.0f),
                                    new Vector3f( 1.0f, 0.0f, 0.0f),
                                    new Vector3f(-1.0f, 0.0f, 0.0f),
                                    new Vector3f( 0.0f, 1.0f, 0.0f),
                                    new Vector3f( 0.0f,-1.0f, 0.0f)};
    int cubeCoordIndices[] = {0,1,2,3,7,6,5,4,0,3,7,4,5,6,2,1,0,4,5,1,6,7,3,2};
    int cubeNormalIndices[] = {0,0,0,0,1,1,1,1,2,2,2,2,3,3,3,3,4,4,4,4,5,5,5,5};
    indexedCube.setCoordinates(0, cubeCoordinates);
    indexedCube.setNormals(0,cubeNormals);
    indexedCube.setCoordinateIndices(0, cubeCoordIndices);
    indexedCube.setNormalIndices(0, cubeNormalIndices);


    //Create the three cubes
    leftCube = new Shape3D(indexedCube, app1);
    rightCube = new Shape3D(indexedCube, app2);
    moveCube = new Shape3D(indexedCube, app3);


    //Define the user data so that we can print out the
    //name of the colliding cube.
    leftCube.setUserData(new String("left cube"));
    rightCube.setUserData(new String("right cube"));


    //Create the content branch and add the lights
    BranchGroup contentBranch = new BranchGroup();
```

```
        addLights(contentBranch);

        //Create and set up the movable cube's TransformGroup.
        //This scales and translates the cube and then sets the
        // read, write and pick reporting capabilities.
        Transform3D moveXfm = new Transform3D();
        moveXfm.set(0.7,new Vector3d(0.0,2.0,1.0));
        moveGroup = new TransformGroup(moveXfm);
        moveGroup.setCapability(
                        TransformGroup.ALLOW_TRANSFORM_WRITE);
moveGroup.setCapability(
                        TransformGroup.ALLOW_TRANSFORM_READ);
        moveGroup.setCapability(
                        TransformGroup.ENABLE_PICK_REPORTING);

        //Create the left cube's TransformGroup
        Transform3D leftGroupXfm = new Transform3D();
        leftGroupXfm.set(new Vector3d(-1.5,0.0,0.0));
        leftGroup = new TransformGroup(leftGroupXfm);

        //Create the right cube's TransformGroup
        Transform3D rightGroupXfm = new Transform3D();
        rightGroupXfm.set(new Vector3d(1.5,0.0,0.0));
        rightGroup = new TransformGroup(rightGroupXfm);

        //Add the behaviour to allow us to move the cube
        PickTranslateBehavior pickTranslate =
                new PickTranslateBehavior(contentBranch, myCanvas3D, bounds);
        contentBranch.addChild(pickTranslate);

        //Add our CollisionDetector class to detect collisions with
        //the movable cube.
        CollisionDetector myColDet = new CollisionDetector(moveCube, bounds);
        contentBranch.addChild(myColDet);

        //Create the content branch hierarchy.
        contentBranch.addChild(moveGroup);
        contentBranch.addChild(leftGroup);
        contentBranch.addChild(rightGroup);
        moveGroup.addChild(moveCube);
        leftGroup.addChild(leftCube);
        rightGroup.addChild(rightCube);
```

```
            return contentBranch;
    }


    /**
     * Process the exit button action to exit the application.
     */
    public void actionPerformed(ActionEvent e) {
        dispose();
        System.exit(0);
    }

    public SimpleCollision() {
        VirtualUniverse myUniverse = new VirtualUniverse();
        Locale myLocale = new Locale(myUniverse);
        myLocale.addBranchGraph(buildViewBranch(myCanvas3D));
        myLocale.addBranchGraph(buildContentBranch());
        setTitle("SimpleCollision");
        setSize(400,400);
        setLayout(new BorderLayout());
        Panel bottom = new Panel();
        bottom.add(exitButton);
        add(BorderLayout.CENTER, myCanvas3D);
        add(BorderLayout.SOUTH, bottom);
        exitButton.addActionListener(this);
        setVisible(true);
    }

    public static void main(String[] args) {
        SimpleCollision sc = new SimpleCollision();
    }
}
```

CollisionDetector2 class

This class is used in the *SimpleCollision2* application.

```
import java.util.*;
import javax.media.j3d.*;

/**
 * A simple collision detector class.  This responds to a collision
 * event by printing a message with information about the type of
 * collision event and the object involved.  This is a variation
```

```
* of the CollisionDetector class that prints information about
* the object that is associated with this behaviour rather than
* the object that has been collided with. An example of its use
* is given in the SimpleCollision2 class.
* @author I.J.Palmer
* @version 1.0
* @see CollisionDetector
* @see SimpleCollision2
*/
public class CollisionDetector2 extends Behavior {
    /** The shape that is being watched for collisions. */
    protected Shape3D collidingShape;
    /** The separate criteria that trigger this behaviour */
    protected WakeupCriterion[] theCriteria;
    /** The result of the 'OR' of the separate criteria */
    protected WakeupOr oredCriteria;

    /**
     * @param theShape Shape3D that is to be watched for collisions.
     * @param theBounds Bounds that define the active region for this behaviour
     */
    public CollisionDetector2(Shape3D theShape, Bounds theBounds) {
        collidingShape = theShape;
        setSchedulingBounds(theBounds);
    }

    /**
     * This sets up the criteria for triggering the behaviour.
     * It creates an entry, exit and movement trigger, OR's these
     * together and then sets the OR'ed criterion as the wake up
     * condition.
     */
    public void initialize() {
        theCriteria = new WakeupCriterion[3];
        WakeupOnCollisionEntry startsCollision =
                                new WakeupOnCollisionEntry(collidingShape);
        WakeupOnCollisionExit endsCollision =
                                new WakeupOnCollisionExit(collidingShape);
        WakeupOnCollisionMovement moveCollision =
                                new WakeupOnCollisionMovement(collidingShape);
        theCriteria[0] = startsCollision;
        theCriteria[1] = endsCollision;
        theCriteria[2] = moveCollision;
```

```
        oredCriteria = new WakeupOr(theCriteria);
        wakeupOn(oredCriteria);
    }


    /**
     * This is where the work is done.
     * This identifies the type of collision (entry, exit or movement) and
     * prints a message stating that an object has collided with this object.
     * The userData field of the shape associated with this collision detector
     * is used to identify the object.  Finally, the wake up condition is set
     * to be the OR'ed criterion again.
     */
    public void processStimulus(Enumeration criteria) {
        while (criteria.hasMoreElements()) {
            WakeupCriterion theCriterion = (WakeupCriterion) criteria.nextElement();
            if (theCriterion instanceof WakeupOnCollisionEntry) {
                System.out.println("Collided with " + collidingShape.getUserData());
            }
            else if (theCriterion instanceof WakeupOnCollisionExit) {
                System.out.println("Stopped colliding with  " +
                                                        collidingShape.getUserData());
            } else {
                System.out.println("Moved whilst colliding with " +
                                                        collidingShape.getUserData());
            }
        }
        wakeupOn(oredCriteria);
    }
}
```

SimpleCollision2 application

```
import javax.media.j3d.*;
import javax.vecmath.*;
import java.awt.*;
import java.awt.event.*;
import com.sun.j3d.utils. picking.behaviors. *;


/**
 * This class demonstrates the use of two collision detectors
 * to overcome the problem of an object colliding with more
 * than one object at a time.  The white cube is movable by
```

```
* dragging it with the right mouse button.
* @see CollisionDetector2
* @author I.J.Palmer
* @version 1.0
*/
public class SimpleCollision2 extends Frame implements ActionListener {
    protected Canvas3D myCanvas3D = new Canvas3D(null);
    protected Button exitButton = new Button("Exit");
  protected BoundingSphere bounds =
                        new BoundingSphere(new Point3d(0.0,0.0,0.0), 100.0);
    /** Transform for the left cube. */
    protected TransformGroup leftGroup;
    /** Transform for the right cube */
    protected TransformGroup rightGroup;
    /** Transform for the movable cube. This has read,
      write and pick reporting capabilities enabled. */
    protected TransformGroup moveGroup;
    /** The left static cube. */
    protected Shape3D leftCube;
    /** The right static cube. */
    protected Shape3D rightCube;
    /** The movable cube that will collide with the other two cubes */
    protected Shape3D moveCube;

    /**
     * This builds the view branch of the scene graph.
    * @return BranchGroup with viewing objects attached.
     */
    protected BranchGroup buildViewBranch(Canvas3D c) {
        BranchGroup viewBranch = new BranchGroup();
        Transform3D viewXfm = new Transform3D();
        viewXfm.set(new Vector3f(0.0f,0.0f,10.0f));
        TransformGroup viewXfmGroup = new TransformGroup(viewXfm);
        ViewPlatform myViewPlatform = new ViewPlatform();
        PhysicalBody myBody = new PhysicalBody();
        PhysicalEnvironment myEnvironment = new PhysicalEnvironment();
        viewXfmGroup.addChild(myViewPlatform);
        viewBranch.addChild(viewXfmGroup);
        View myView = new View();
        myView.addCanvas3D(c);
        myView.attachViewPlatform(myViewPlatform);
        myView.setPhysicalBody(myBody);
        myView.setPhysicalEnvironment(myEnvironment);
```

```
            return viewBranch;
    }


    /**
     * This adds some lights to the content branch of the scene graph.
     * @param b The BranchGroup to add the lights to.
     */
    protected void addLights(BranchGroup b) {
        Color3f ambLightColour = new Color3f(0.5f, 0.5f, 0.5f);
        AmbientLight ambLight = new AmbientLight(ambLightColour);
        ambLight.setInfluencingBounds(bounds);
        Color3f dirLightColour = new Color3f(1.0f, 1.0f, 1.0f);
        Vector3f dirLightDir = new Vector3f(-1.0f, -1.0f, -1.0f);
        DirectionalLight dirLight =
                                    new DirectionalLight(dirLightColour, dirLightDir);
        dirLight.setInfluencingBounds(bounds);
        b.addChild(ambLight);
        b.addChild(dirLight);
    }


    /**
     * Creates the content branch of the scene graph.
     * @return BranchGroup with content attached.
     */
    protected BranchGroup buildContentBranch() {
        //First create a different appearance for each cube
        Appearance app1 = new Appearance();
        Appearance app2 = new Appearance();
        Appearance app3 = new Appearance();
        Color3f ambientColour1 = new Color3f(1.0f,0.0f,0.0f);
        Color3f ambientColour2 = new Color3f(1.0f,1.0f,0.0f);
        Color3f ambientColour3 = new Color3f(1.0f,1.0f,1.0f);
        Color3f emissiveColour = new Color3f(0.0f,0.0f,0.0f);
        Color3f specularColour = new Color3f(1.0f,1.0f,1.0f);
        Color3f diffuseColour1 = new Color3f(1.0f,0.0f,0.0f);
        Color3f diffuseColour2 = new Color3f(1.0f,1.0f,0.0f);
        Color3f diffuseColour3 = new Color3f(1.0f,1.0f,1.0f);
        float shininess = 20.0f;
        app1.setMaterial(new Material(ambientColour1,emissiveColour,
                                    diffuseColour1,specularColour,shininess));
        app2.setMaterial(new Material(ambientColour2, emissiveColour,
                                    diffuseColour2,specularColour,shininess));
        app3.setMaterial(new Material(ambientColour3,emissiveColour,
                                    diffuseColour3,specularColour,shininess));
```

```
//Build the vertex array for the cubes.  We can use the same
//data for each cube so we just define one set of data
IndexedQuadArray indexedCube = new IndexedQuadArray(8,
                        IndexedQuadArray.COORDINATES |
                        IndexedQuadArray.NORMALS, 24);
Point3f[] cubeCoordinates = {  new Point3f( 1.0f, 1.0f, 1.0f),
                        new Point3f(-1.0f, 1.0f, 1.0f),
                        new Point3f(-1.0f,-1.0f, 1.0f),
                        new Point3f( 1.0f,-1.0f, 1.0f),
                        new Point3f( 1.0f, 1.0f,-1.0f),
                        new Point3f(-1.0f, 1.0f,-1.0f),
                        new Point3f(-1.0f,-1.0f,-1.0f),
                        new Point3f( 1.0f,-1.0f,-1.0f)};
Vector3f[] cubeNormals= {new Vector3f( 0.0f, 0.0f, 1.0f),
                        new Vector3f( 0.0f, 0.0f,-1.0f),
                        new Vector3f( 1.0f, 0.0f, 0.0f),
                        new Vector3f(-1.0f, 0.0f, 0.0f),
                        new Vector3f( 0.0f, 1.0f, 0.0f),
                        new Vector3f( 0.0f,-1.0f, 0.0f)};
int cubeCoordIndices[] = {0,1,2,3,7,6,5,4,0,3,7,4,5,6,2,1,0,4,5,1,6,7,3,2};
int cubeNormalIndices[] = {0,0,0,0,1,1,1,1,2,2,2,2,3,3,3,3,4,4,4,4,5,5,5,5};
indexedCube.setCoordinates(0, cubeCoordinates);
indexedCube.setNormals(0,cubeNormals);
indexedCube.setCoordinateIndices(0, cubeCoordIndices);
indexedCube.setNormalIndices(0, cubeNormalIndices);

//Create the three cubes
leftCube = new Shape3D(indexedCube,app1);
rightCube = new Shape3D(indexedCube,app2);
moveCube = new Shape3D(indexedCube,app3);

//Define some user data so that we can print meaningful messages
leftCube.setUserData(new String("left cube"));
rightCube.setUserData(new String("right cube"));

//Create the content branch and add the lights
BranchGroup contentBranch = new BranchGroup();
addLights(contentBranch);

//Set up the transform to position the left cube
Transform3D leftGroupXfm = new Transform3D();
leftGroupXfm.set(new Vector3d(-1.5,0.0,0.0));
```

```java
leftGroup = new TransformGroup(leftGroupXfm);

//Set up the transform to position the right cube
Transform3D rightGroupXfm = new Transform3D();
rightGroupXfm.set(new Vector3d(1.5,0.0,0.0));
rightGroup = new TransformGroup(rightGroupXfm);

//Create the movable cube's transform with a scale and
//a translation. Set up the
//capabilities so it can be moved by the behaviour
Transform3D moveXfm = new Transform3D();
moveXfm.set(0.7,new Vector3d(0.0,2.0,1.0));
moveGroup = new TransformGroup(moveXfm);
moveGroup.setCapability(
                    TransformGroup.ALLOW_TRANSFORM_WRITE);
moveGroup.setCapability(
                    TransformGroup.ALLOW_TRANSFORM_READ);
moveGroup.setCapability(
                    TransformGroup.ENABLE_PICK_REPORTING);
//Create the behaviour to move the movable cube
PickTranslateBehavior pickTranslate =
        new PickTranslateBehavior(contentBranch, myCanvas3D, bounds);
contentBranch.addChild(pickTranslate);

//Create and add the two colision detectors
CollisionDetector2 myColDetLeft =
                        new CollisionDetector2(leftCube, bounds);
contentBranch.addChild(myColDetLeft);
CollisionDetector2 myColDetRight =
                        new CollisionDetector2(rightCube, bounds);
contentBranch.addChild(myColDetRight);

//Set up the scene graph
contentBranch.addChild(moveGroup);
contentBranch.addChild(leftGroup);
contentBranch.addChild(rightGroup);
moveGroup.addChild(moveCube);
leftGroup.addChild(leftCube);
rightGroup.addChild(rightCube);

return contentBranch;
}

/** Process exit button's action to quit */
```

```java
    public void actionPerformed(ActionEvent e) {
        dispose();
        System.exit(0);
    }

    public SimpleCollision2() {
        VirtualUniverse myUniverse = new VirtualUniverse();
        Locale myLocale = new Locale(myUniverse);
        myLocale.addBranchGraph(buildViewBranch(myCanvas3D));
        myLocale.addBranchGraph(buildContentBranch());
        setTitle("SimpleCollision");
        setSize(400,400);
        setLayout(new BorderLayout());
        Panel bottom = new Panel();
        bottom.add(exitButton);
        add(BorderLayout.CENTER, myCanvas3D);
        add(BorderLayout.SOUTH, bottom);
        exitButton.addActionListener(this);
        setVisible(true);
    }

    public static void main(String[] args) {
        SimpleCollision2 sc = new SimpleCollision2();
    }
}
```

Chapter 8

SimpleBillboard

```
import javax.media.j3d.*;
import javax.vecmath.*;
import java.awt.*;
import java.awt.event.*;
import com.sun.j3d.utils.geometry.*;
import com.sun.j3d.utils.behaviors.keyboard.*;
/**
* This application demonstrates the use of a billboard node.
* Two cubes are created, one yellow and the other with a
* a different colour on each face.  The billboard is
* created so that the red face of the right cube is always
* facing the viewer.  A key board utility class is used to
* allow modification of the view angle.
* @author I.J.Palmer
* @version 1.0
*/
public class SimpleBillboard extends Frame implements ActionListener {
    protected Canvas3D myCanvas3D = new Canvas3D(null);
    protected Button exitButton = new Button("Exit");
    protected BoundingSphere bounds =
                    new BoundingSphere(new Point3d(0.0,0.0,0.0), 100.0);
    /**
        * Build the view branch of the scene graph.  In this case
        * a key navigation utility object is created and associated
        * with the view transform so that the view can be changed
        * via the keyboard.
        * @return BranchGroup that is the root of the view branch
        */
    protected BranchGroup buildViewBranch(Canvas3D c) {
        BranchGroup viewBranch = new BranchGroup();
        Transform3D viewXfm = new Transform3D();
        viewXfm.set(new Vector3f(0.0f,0.0f,10.0f));
        TransformGroup viewXfmGroup = new TransformGroup(viewXfm);
        viewXfmGroup.setCapability(
```

```
                            TransformGroup.ALLOW_TRANSFORM_READ);
        viewXfmGroup.setCapability(
                            TransformGroup.ALLOW_TRANSFORM_WRITE);
        BoundingSphere movingBounds =
                            new BoundingSphere(new Point3d(0.0,0.0,0.0), 100.0);
        BoundingLeaf boundLeaf = new BoundingLeaf(movingBounds);
        ViewPlatform myViewPlatform = new ViewPlatform();
        viewXfmGroup.addChild(boundLeaf);
        PhysicalBody myBody = new PhysicalBody();
        PhysicalEnvironment myEnvironment = new PhysicalEnvironment();
        viewXfmGroup.addChild(myViewPlatform);
        viewBranch.addChild(viewXfmGroup);
        View myView = new View();
        myView.addCanvas3D(c);
        myView.attachViewPlatform(myViewPlatform);
        myView.setPhysicalBody(myBody);
        myView.setPhysicalEnvironment(myEnvironment);
        KeyNavigatorBehavior keyNav =
                    new KeyNavigatorBehavior(viewXfmGroup);
        keyNav.setSchedulingBounds(movingBounds);
        viewBranch.addChild(keyNav);
        return viewBranch;
    }
    /**
     * Add some lights to the scene graph
     * @param b BranchGroup that the lights are added to
     */
    protected void addLights(BranchGroup b) {
        Color3f ambLightColour = new Color3f(0.5f, 0.5f, 0.5f);
        AmbientLight ambLight = new AmbientLight(ambLightColour);
        ambLight.setInfluencingBounds(bounds);
        Color3f dirLightColour = new Color3f(1.0f, 1.0f, 1.0f);
        Vector3f dirLightDir  = new Vector3f(-1.0f, -1.0f, -1.0f);
        DirectionalLight dirLight =
                    new DirectionalLight(dirLightColour, dirLightDir);
        dirLight.setInfluencingBounds(bounds);
        b.addChild(ambLight);
        b.addChild(dirLight);
    }
    /**
     * Build the content branch for the scene graph.
     * This creates two cubes and uses a billboard node
     * to keep one face of one of the cubes facing the viewer.
```

```java
 * @return BranchGroup that is the root of the content
 */
protected BranchGroup buildContentBranch() {
    //Create the appearance
    Appearance app = new Appearance();
    Color3f ambientColour = new Color3f(1.0f,1.0f,0.0f);
    Color3f emissiveColour = new Color3f(0.0f,0.0f,0.0f);
    Color3f specularColour = new Color3f(1.0f,1.0f,1.0f);
    Color3f diffuseColour = new Color3f(1.0f,1.0f,0.0f);
    float shininess = 20.0f;
    app.setMaterial(new Material(ambientColour,emissiveColour,
                        diffuseColour,specularColour,shininess));
    //Make the cubes
    Box leftCube = new Box(1.0f,1.0f,1.0f, app);
    ColorCube rightCube = new ColorCube();
    //Create the transformgroup used for the billboard
    TransformGroup billBoardGroup = new TransformGroup();
    //Set the access rights to the group
    billBoardGroup.setCapability(
                    TransformGroup.ALLOW_TRANSFORM_WRITE);
    //Add the cube to the group
    billBoardGroup.addChild(rightCube);
    //Create and activate the billboard
    Billboard myBillboard =
        new Billboard(billBoardGroup, Billboard.ROTATE_ABOUT_AXIS,
                            new Vector3f(0.0f,1.0f,0.0f));
    myBillboard.setSchedulingBounds(bounds);
    BranchGroup contentBranch = new BranchGroup();
    contentBranch.addChild(myBillboard);
    addLights(contentBranch);
    //Position the cubes
    TransformGroup bothGroup = new TransformGroup();
    Transform3D leftGroupXfm = new Transform3D();
    leftGroupXfm.set(new Vector3d(-1.5,0.0,0.0));
    TransformGroup leftGroup = new TransformGroup(leftGroupXfm);
    Transform3D rightGroupXfm = new Transform3D();
    rightGroupXfm.set(new Vector3d(1.5,0.0,0.0));
    TransformGroup rightGroup = new TransformGroup(rightGroupXfm);
    //Put it all together
    bothGroup.addChild(leftGroup);
    leftGroup.addChild(leftCube);
    bothGroup.addChild(rightGroup);
    rightGroup.addChild(billBoardGroup);
    contentBranch.addChild(bothGroup);
```

```
            return contentBranch;
    }
    /**
     * Use the action event of the exit button
     * to end the application.
     */
    public void actionPerformed(ActionEvent e) {
        dispose();
        System.exit(0);
    }
    public SimpleBillboard() {
        VirtualUniverse myUniverse = new VirtualUniverse();
        Locale myLocale = new Locale(myUniverse);
        myLocale.addBranchGraph(buildViewBranch(myCanvas3D));
        myLocale.addBranchGraph(buildContentBranch());
        setTitle("SimpleBillboard");
        setSize(400,400);
        setLayout(new BorderLayout());
        Panel bottom = new Panel();
        bottom.add(exitButton);
        add(BorderLayout.CENTER, myCanvas3D);
        add(BorderLayout.SOUTH, bottom);
        exitButton.addActionListener(this);
        setVisible(true);
    }
    public static void main(String[] args) {
        SimpleBillboard sb = new SimpleBillboard();
    }
}
```

SimpleLOD

```
import javax.media.j3d.*;
import javax.vecmath.*;
import java.awt.*;
import java.awt.event.*;
import com.sun.j3d.utils.geometry.*;
import com.sun.j3d.utils.behaviors.keyboard.*;
/**
 * This uses three resolutions of a cylinder to demonstrate
 * the operation of a level of detail node.
```

```
* @author I.J.Palmer
* @version 1.0
*/
public class SimpleLOD extends Frame implements ActionListener {
        protected Canvas3D myCanvas3D = new Canvas3D(null);
        protected Button exitButton = new Button("Exit");
        protected BoundingSphere bounds =
                        new BoundingSphere(new Point3d(0.0,0.0,0.0), 100.0);
        /**
        * Build the view branch of the scene graph.  In this case
        * a key navigation utility object is created and associated
        * with the view transform so that the view can be changed
        * via the keyboard.
        * @return BranchGroup that is the root of the view branch
        */
        protected BranchGroup buildViewBranch(Canvas3D c) {
                BranchGroup viewBranch = new BranchGroup();
                Transform3D viewXfm = new Transform3D();
                viewXfm.set(new Vector3f(0.0f,0.0f,10.0f));
                TransformGroup viewXfmGroup = new TransformGroup(viewXfm);
                viewXfmGroup.setCapability(
                                        TransformGroup.ALLOW_TRANSFORM_READ);
                viewXfmGroup.setCapability(
                                        TransformGroup.ALLOW_TRANSFORM_WRITE);
                BoundingSphere movingBounds =
                                new BoundingSphere(new Point3d(0.0,0.0,0.0), 100.0);
                BoundingLeaf boundLeaf = new BoundingLeaf(movingBounds);
                ViewPlatform myViewPlatform = new ViewPlatform();
                viewXfmGroup.addChild(boundLeaf);
                PhysicalBody myBody = new PhysicalBody();
                PhysicalEnvironment myEnvironment = new PhysicalEnvironment();
                viewXfmGroup.addChild(myViewPlatform);
                viewBranch.addChild(viewXfmGroup);
                View myView = new View();
                myView.addCanvas3D(c);
                myView.attachViewPlatform(myViewPlatform);
                myView.setPhysicalBody(myBody);
                myView.setPhysicalEnvironment(myEnvironment);
                KeyNavigatorBehavior keyNav =
                                        new KeyNavigatorBehavior(viewXfmGroup);
                keyNav.setSchedulingBounds(movingBounds);
                viewBranch.addChild(keyNav);
                return viewBranch;
        }
```

```java
/**
 * Add some lights to the scene graph
 * @param b BranchGroup that the lights are added to
 */
protected void addLights(BranchGroup b) {
    Color3f ambLightColour = new Color3f(0.5f, 0.5f, 0.5f);
    AmbientLight ambLight = new AmbientLight(ambLightColour);
    ambLight.setInfluencingBounds(bounds);
    Color3f dirLightColour = new Color3f(1.0f, 1.0f, 1.0f);
    Vector3f dirLightDir = new Vector3f(-1.0f, -1.0f, -1.0f);
    DirectionalLight dirLight =
                        new DirectionalLight(dirLightColour, dirLightDir);
    dirLight.setInfluencingBounds(bounds);
    b.addChild(ambLight);
    b.addChild(dirLight);
}
/**
 * Build the content branch for the scene graph
 * This creates three cylinders, each with a different
 * resolution.  These are then used with a LOD node
 * to implement a crude level of detail.
 * @return BranchGroup that is the root of the content
 */
protected BranchGroup buildContentBranch() {
    //Create the appearance
    Appearance app = new Appearance();
    Color3f ambientColour = new Color3f(1.0f,1.0f,0.0f);
    Color3f emissiveColour = new Color3f(0.0f,0.0f,0.0f);
    Color3f specularColour = new Color3f(1.0f,1.0f,1.0f);
    Color3f diffuseColour = new Color3f(1.0f,1.0f,0.0f);
    float shininess = 20.0f;
    app.setMaterial(new Material(ambientColour, emissiveColour,
            diffuseColour,specularColour,shininess));
    //Make the switch node that is to used with the LOD
    //and make it writable
    Switch LODswitch = new Switch();
    LODswitch.setCapability(Switch.ALLOW_SWITCH_WRITE);
    //Add the three cylinders
    LODswitch.addChild(new
                Cylinder(1.0f,1.0f,Cylinder.GENERATE_NORMALS,

10,10,app));
    LODswitch.addChild(new
```

```
                        Cylinder(1.0f,1.0f,Cylinder.GENERATE_NORMALS,
                                                          5,5,app));
        LODswitch.addChild(new
                        Cylinder(1.0f,1.0f,Cylinder.GENERATE_NORMALS,
                                                          3,3,app));
        //Define the distances for the LOD
        float[] LODdistances = {5.0f,10.0f,15.0f};
        DistanceLOD myLOD =
                new DistanceLOD(LODdistances,new Point3f(0.0f,0.0f,0.0f));
        myLOD.setSchedulingBounds(bounds);
        //Add the switch to the LOD
        myLOD.addSwitch(LODswitch);
        BranchGroup contentBranch = new BranchGroup();
        contentBranch.addChild(myLOD);
        addLights(contentBranch);
        contentBranch.addChild(LODswitch);
        return contentBranch;
}
/**
 * Use the action event of the exit button
 * to end the application.
 *
public void actionPerformed(ActionEvent e) {
        dispose();
        System.exit(0);
}
public SimpleLOD() {
        VirtualUniverse myUniverse = new VirtualUniverse();
        Locale myLocale = new Locale(myUniverse);
        myLocale.addBranchGraph(buildViewBranch(myCanvas3D));
        myLocale.addBranchGraph(buildContentBranch());
        setTitle("SimpleLOD");
        setSize(400,400);
        setLayout(new BorderLayout());
        Panel bottom = new Panel();
        bottom.add(exitButton);
        add(BorderLayout.CENTER, myCanvas3D);
        add(BorderLayout.SOUTH, bottom);
        exitButton.addActionListener(this);
        setVisible(true);
}
public static void main(String[] args) {
        SimpleLOD sl = new SimpleLOD();
```

```
        }
}
```

SimpleSounds

```java
import javax.media.j3d.*;
import javax.vecmath.*;
import java.awt.*;
import java.awt.event.*;
import com.sun.j3d.utils.behaviors.keyboard.*;
import com.sun.j3d.audioengines.javasound.*;
import com.sun.j3d.utils.geometry.*;
/**
 * This application demonstrates the use of 3D sound.
 * It loads three sounds: loop3.wav is an ambient background sound and
 * loop1.wav and loop2.wav are point sounds.  The two point
 * sounds can be switched on and off use AWT buttons. The user can
 * navigate around the scene using the keyboard.
 * @author I.J.Palmer
 * @version 1.0
 */
public class SimpleSounds extends Frame implements ActionListener {
        protected Canvas3D myCanvas3D = new Canvas3D(null);
        /** The exit button to quit the application */
        protected Button exitButton = new Button("Exit");
        /** The button to switch on and off the first sound */
        protected Button sound1Button = new Button("Sound 1");
        /** The button to switch on and off the second sound */
        protected Button sound2Button = new Button("Sound 2");
        protected BoundingSphere bounds =
                        new BoundingSphere(new Point3d(0.0,0.0,0.0), 10000.0);
        //Create the two point sounds
        PointSound sound1 = new PointSound();
        PointSound sound2 = new PointSound();
        /**
         * Build the view branch of the scene graph.  In this case
         * a key navigation utility object is created and associated
         * with the view transform so that the view can be changed
         * via the keyboard. It also creates and initialises the
         * sound mixer object.
         * @return BranchGroup that is the root of the view branch
```

```java
*/
protected BranchGroup buildViewBranch(Canvas3D c) {
    BranchGroup viewBranch = new BranchGroup();
    Transform3D viewXfm = new Transform3D();
    viewXfm.set(new Vector3f(0.0f,0.0f,30.0f));
    TransformGroup viewXfmGroup = new TransformGroup(viewXfm);
    viewXfmGroup.setCapability(
                    TransformGroup.ALLOW_TRANSFORM_READ);
    viewXfmGroup.setCapability(
                    TransformGroup.ALLOW_TRANSFORM_WRITE);
    ViewPlatform myViewPlatform = new ViewPlatform();
    BoundingSphere movingBounds =
                    new BoundingSphere(new Point3d(0.0,0.0,0.0),100.0);
    BoundingLeaf boundLeaf = new BoundingLeaf(movingBounds);
    PhysicalBody myBody = new PhysicalBody();
    PhysicalEnvironment myEnvironment = new PhysicalEnvironment();
    viewXfmGroup.addChild(myViewPlatform);
    viewBranch.addChild(viewXfmGroup);
    View myView = new View();
    myView.addCanvas3D(c);
    myView.attachViewPlatform(myViewPlatform);
    myView.setPhysicalBody(myBody);
    myView.setPhysicalEnvironment(myEnvironment);
    KeyNavigatorBehavior keyNav =
                    new KeyNavigatorBehavior(viewXfmGroup);
    keyNav.setSchedulingBounds(movingBounds);
    viewBranch.addChild(keyNav);
    //Create a sounds mixer to use our sounds with
    //and initialise it
    JavaSoundMixer myMixer = new JavaSoundMixer(myEnvironment);
    myMixer.initialize();
    return viewBranch;
}
/**
 * Add some lights to the scene graph
 * @param b BranchGroup that the lights are added to
 */
protected void addLights(BranchGroup b) {
    Color3f ambLightColour = new Color3f(0.5f, 0.5f, 0.5f);
    AmbientLight ambLight = new AmbientLight(ambLightColour);
    ambLight.setInfluencingBounds(bounds);
    Color3f dirLightColour = new Color3f(1.0f, 1.0f, 1.0f);
    Vector3f dirLightDir  = new Vector3f(-1.0f, -1.0f, -1.0f);
    DirectionalLight dirLight =
```

```
                        new DirectionalLight(dirLightColour, dirLightDir);
        dirLight.setInfluencingBounds(bounds);
        b.addChild(ambLight);
        b.addChild(dirLight);
}
/**
 * This adds a continuous background sound to the branch group.
 * @param b BranchGroup to add the sound to.
 * @param soundFile String that is the name of the sound file.
 */
protected void addBackgroundSound (BranchGroup b,String soundFile) {
        //Create a media container to load the file
        MediaContainer droneContainer = new MediaContainer(soundFile);
        //Create the background sound from the media container
        BackgroundSound drone = new BackgroundSound(droneContainer,1.0f);
        //Activate the sound
        drone.setSchedulingBounds(bounds);
        drone.setEnable(true);
        //Set the sound to loop forever
        drone.setLoop(BackgroundSound.INFINITE_LOOPS);
        Add it to the group
        b.addChild(drone);
}
/**
 * Add a sound to the transform group.
 * This takes a point sound object and loads into it a
 * sounds from a given file.  The edge of the sound's extent
 * is also defined in a parameter.
 * @param tg TransformGroup that the sound is to be added to
 * @param sound PointSound to be used
 * @param soundFile String that is the name of the sound
 * file to be loaded
 * @param edge float that represents the sound's maximum extent
 */
protected void addObjectSound(TransformGroup tg, PointSound sound,
                                        String soundFile, float edge) {
        //First we get the current transform so that we can
        //position the sound in the same place
        Transform3D objXfm = new Transform3D();
        Vector3f objPosition = new Vector3f();
        tg.getTransform(objXfm);
        objXfm.get(objPosition);
        //Create the media container to load the sound
```

```
      MediaContainer soundContainer = new MediaContainer(soundFile);
      //Use the loaded data in the sound
      sound.setSoundData(soundContainer);
      sound.setInitialGain(1.0f);
      //Set the position to that of the given transform
      sound.setPosition(new Point3f(objPosition));
      //Allow use to switch the sound on and off
      sound.setCapability(PointSound.ALLOW_ENABLE_READ);
      sound.setCapability(PointSound.ALLOW_ENABLE_WRITE);
      sound.setSchedulingBounds(bounds);
      //Set it off to start with
      sound.setEnable(false);
      //Set it to loop forever
      sound.setLoop(BackgroundSound.INFINITE_LOOPS);
      //Use the edge value to set to extent of the sound
      Point2f[] attenuation = {new Point2f(0.0f,1.0f),
                                new Point2f(edge,0.1f)};
      sound.setDistanceGain(attenuation);
      //Add the sound to the transform group
      tg.addChild(sound);
}
/**
 * Create the content branch. This uses the sound functions
 * to load and create the sounds used.
 * @return BranchGroup that is the root of the content
 */
protected BranchGroup buildContentBranch() {
      //Create the appearance
      Appearance app = new Appearance();
      Color3f ambientColour = new Color3f(1.0f,0.0f,0.0f);
      Color3f emissiveColour = new Color3f(0.0f,0.0f,0.0f);
      Color3f specularColour = new Color3f(1.0f,1.0f,1.0f);
      Color3f diffuseColour = new Color3f(1.0f,0.0f,0.0f);
      float shininess = 20.0f;
      app.setMaterial(new Material(ambientColour,emissiveColour,
                            diffuseColour,specularColour,shininess));
      //Make the cube
      Box myCube = new Box(1.0f,1.0f,1.0f,app);
      TransformGroup cubeGroup = new TransformGroup();
      BranchGroup contentBranch = new BranchGroup();
      addLights(contentBranch);
      addObjectSound(cubeGroup,sound1,new String("file:./loop1.wav"),10.0f);
      addObjectSound(cubeGroup,sound2,new String("file:./loop2.wav"),20.0f);
      addBackgroundSound(contentBranch,new String("file:./loop3.wav"));
```

```
        cubeGroup.addChild(myCube);
        contentBranch.addChild(cubeGroup);
        return contentBranch;
    }
    /**
     * Process the action and act accordingly.
     *  End the prohgram if the exit button was pressed or turn the
     * appropriate sound on/off.
     * @param e ActionEvent that has occurred
     */
    public void actionPerformed(ActionEvent e) {
        if (e.getSource() == exitButton) {
            dispose();
            System.exit(0);
        } else if (e.getSource() == sound1Button) {
            sound1.setEnable(!sound1.getEnable());
        } else if (e.getSource() == sound2Button) {
            sound2.setEnable(!sound2.getEnable());
        }
    }
    public SimpleSounds() {
        VirtualUniverse myUniverse = new VirtualUniverse();
        Locale myLocale = new Locale(myUniverse);
        myLocale.addBranchGraph(buildContentBranch());
        myLocale.addBranchGraph(buildViewBranch(myCanvas3D));
        setTitle("SimpleSounds");
        setSize(400,400);
        setLayout(new BorderLayout());
        Panel bottom = new Panel();
        bottom.add(sound1Button);
        bottom.add(sound2Button);
        bottom.add(exitButton);
        add(BorderLayout.CENTER, myCanvas3D);
        add(BorderLayout.SOUTH, bottom);
        exitButton.addActionListener(this);
        sound1Button.addActionListener(this);
        sound2Button.addActionListener(this);
        setVisible(true);
    }
    public static void main(String[] args) {
        SimpleSounds ss = new SimpleSounds();
    }
}
```

Chapter 9

DuckBehaviour

```
import java.util.*;
import javax.media.j3d.*;
import java.awt.event.*;
import java.awt.*;
/**
* This is used in the SimpleGame application.
* It defines the behaviour for the duck, which is the
* target in the shooting game.  If something collides
* with the duck, it swaps a switch value to 'kill' the duck
* The duck is revived when it's alpha value passes through zero.
* @author I.J.Palmer
* @version 1.0
* @see SimpleGame
*/
public class DuckBehaviour extends Behavior {
        /** The shape that is being watched for collisions. */
        protected Node collidingShape;
        /** The separate criteria that trigger this behaviour */
        protected WakeupCriterion[] theCriteria;
        /** The result of the 'OR' of the separate criteria */
        protected WakeupOr oredCriteria;
        /** The switch that is used to swap the duck shapes */
        protected Switch theSwitch;
        /** The alpha generator that drives the animation */
        protected Alpha theTargetAlpha;
        /** Defines whether the duck is dead or alive */
        protected boolean dead = false;
        /**
        * This sets up the data for the behaviour.
        * @param theShape Node that is to be watched for collisions.
        * @param sw Switch that is used to swap shapes.
        * @param a1 Alpha that drives the duck's animation.
        * @param theBounds Bounds that define the active region for this behaviour.
        */
        public DuckBehaviour(Node theShape, Switch sw,Alpha a1,Bounds theBounds) {
```

```
            collidingShape = theShape;
            theSwitch = sw;
            theTargetAlpha = a1;
            setSchedulingBounds(theBounds);
    }
    /**
    * This sets up the criteria for triggering the behaviour.
    * It creates an collision crtiterion and a time elapsed criterion, OR's these
    * together and then sets the OR'ed criterion as the wake up
    * condition.
    */
    public void initialize() {
            theCriteria = new WakeupCriterion[2];
            theCriteria[0] = new WakeupOnCollisionEntry(collidingShape);
            theCriteria[1] = new WakeupOnElapsedTime(1);
            oredCriteria = new WakeupOr(theCriteria);
            wakeupOn(oredCriteria);
    }
    /**
    * This is where the work is done.
    * If there is a collision, then if the duck is
    * alive we switch to the dead duck.  If the duck
    * was already dead then we take no action.
    * The other case we need to check for is when the
    * alpha value is zero, when we need to set the duck back
    * to the live one for its next traversal of the screen.
    * Finally, the wake up condition is set
    * to be the OR'ed criterion again.
    */
    public void processStimulus(Enumeration criteria) {
            while (criteria.hasMoreElements()) {
                WakeupCriterion theCriterion =
                        (WakeupCriterion) criteria.nextElement();
                if (theCriterion instanceof WakeupOnCollisionEntry) {
                    //There's a collision so if the duck is alive swap
                    //it to the dead one
                    if (dead == false) {
                            theSwitch.setWhichChild(1);
                            dead = true;
                    }
                }
                else if (theCriterion instanceof WakeupOnElapsedTime) {
                    //If there isn't a collision, then check the alpha
```

```
                    //value and if it's zero, revive the duck
                    if (theTargetAlpha.value() < 0.1) {
                            theSwitch.setWhichChild(0);
                            dead = false;
                    }
                }
            }
        wakeupOn(oredCriteria);
    }
}
```

GunBehaviour

```java
import java.util.*;
import javax.media.j3d.*;
import javax.vecmath.*;
import java.awt.event.*;
import java.awt.AWTEvent;
/**
* This is used in the SimpleGame application.
* It defines a behaviour that allows a 'gun' to be rotated when left and right
* cursor keys are pressed and then a ball is 'fired' when the space bar is
* pressed.  The 'firing' is achieved by setting the start time of an
* interpolator to the current time.
* @author I.J.Palmer
* @version 1.0
* @see SimpleGame
*/
public class GunBehaviour extends Behavior {
        /** The separate criteria that trigger this behaviour */
        protected WakeupCriterion theCriterion;
        /** The alpha that is used to 'fire' the ball */
        protected Alpha theGunAlpha;
        /** Used to animate the ball */
        protected PositionInterpolator theInterpolator;
        /** Used to calculate the current direction of the gun */
        protected int aim = 0;
        /** This is used to rotate the gun */
        protected TransformGroup aimXfmGrp;
        /** Used to aim the ball */
        protected Matrix3d aimShotMat = new Matrix3d();
        /** Used to aim the gun */
```

```java
protected Matrix3d aimGunMat = new Matrix3d();
/** Used to define the ball's direction */
protected Transform3D aimShotXfm = new Transform3D();
/** Used to define the gun's direction */
protected Transform3D aimGunXfm = new Transform3D();
/**
 * Set up the data for the behaviour.
 * @param a1 Alpha that drives the ball's animation.
 * @param pi PositionInterpolator used for the ball.
 * @param gunRotGrp TransformGroup that is used to rotate the gun.
 * @param theBounds Bounds that define the active region for this behaviour.
 */
public GunBehaviour(Alpha a1, PositionInterpolator pi,
                                TransformGroup gunRotGrp, Bounds theBounds) {
    theGunAlpha = a1;
    theInterpolator = pi;
    setSchedulingBounds(theBounds);
    aimXfmGrp = gunRotGrp;
}
/**
 * This sets up the criteria for triggering the behaviour.
 * We simple want to wait for a key to be pressed.
 */
public void initialize() {
    theCriterion = new WakeupOnAWTEvent(KeyEvent.KEY_PRESSED);
    wakeupOn(theCriterion);
}
/**
 * This is where the work is done.
 * This identifies which key has been pressed and acts
 * accordingly: left key cursor rotate left, right cursor key
 * rotate right, spacebar fire.
 * @criteria Enumeration that represents the trigger conditions.
 */
public void processStimulus(Enumeration criteria) {
    while (criteria.hasMoreElements()) {
        WakeupCriterion theCriterion =
                        (WakeupCriterion) criteria.nextElement();
        if (theCriterion instanceof WakeupOnAWTEvent) {
            AWTEvent[] triggers =
                ((WakeupOnAWTEvent)theCriterion).getAWTEvent();
            //Check if it's a keyboard event
            if (triggers[0] instanceof KeyEvent) {
```

```
                        int keyPressed = ((KeyEvent)triggers[0]).getKeyCode();
                        if (keyPressed == KeyEvent.VK_LEFT) {
                                //It's a left key so move the turret
                                //and the aim of the gun left unless
                                //we're at our maximum angle
                                if (aim < 8)
                                        aim += 1;
                                aimShotMat.rotY(((aim/32.0) + 0.5)*Math.PI);
                                aimGunMat.rotZ(((aim/-32.0))*Math.PI);
                                aimShotXfm.setRotation(aimShotMat);
                                aimGunXfm.setRotation(aimGunMat);
                                aimXfmGrp.setTransform(aimGunXfm);
                                theInterpolator.setAxisOfTranslation(aimShotXfm);
                        } else if (keyPressed == KeyEvent.VK_RIGHT) {
                                //It's the right key so do the same but rotate right
                                if (aim > -8)
                                        aim -= 1;
                                aimShotMat.rotY(((aim/32.0) + 0.5)*Math.PI);
                                aimGunMat.rotZ(((aim/-32.0))*Math.PI);
                                aimGunXfm.setRotation(aimGunMat);
                                aimShotXfm.setRotation(aimShotMat);
                                aimXfmGrp.setTransform(aimGunXfm);
                                theInterpolator.setAxisOfTranslation(aimShotXfm);
                        } else if (keyPressed == KeyEvent.VK_SPACE) {
                                //It's the spacebar so reset the start time
                                //of the ball's animation
                                theGunAlpha.setStartTime(System.currentTimeMillis());
                        }
                }
            }
        }
    }
    wakeupOn(theCriterion);
  }
}
```

SimpleGame

```
import javax.media.j3d.*;
import javax.vecmath.*;
import java.awt.*;
import java.awt.event.*;
import com.sun.j3d.utils.geometry.*;
```

```java
import com.sun.j3d.loaders.*;
import com.sun.j3d.loaders.objectfile.*;
/**
 * This application demonstrates a number of things in the
 * implementation of a simple shooting game. The object of the
 * the game is to shoot a duck that repeatedly moves across the
 * screen from left to right.  There are two duck models, one
 * for the 'live' duck and one for the 'dead' one.  These are
 * loaded from 'duck.obj' and 'deadduck.obj' files.  The 'gun'
 * is built from primitives.  The duck and the ball that is
 * used to shoot the duck use interpolators for their animation.
 * The gun uses key board input to aim and fire it, and
 * collision detection is used to 'kill' the duck.
 * @author I.J.Palmer
 * @version 1.0
 */
public class SimpleGame extends Frame implements ActionListener {
    protected Canvas3D myCanvas3D = new Canvas3D(null);
    protected Button exitButton = new Button("Exit");
    protected BoundingSphere bounds =
                new BoundingSphere(new Point3d(0.0,0.0,0.0), 100.0);
    /** Switch that is used to swap the duck models */
    Switch duckSwitch;
    /** Alpha used to drive the duck animation */
    Alpha duckAlpha;
    /** Used to drive the ball animation */
    Alpha ballAlpha;
    /** Used to move the ball */
    PositionInterpolator moveBall;
    /** Used to rotate the gun */
    TransformGroup gunXfmGrp= new TransformGroup();
    /**
     * This builds the view branch of the scene graph.
     * @return BranchGroup with viewing objects attached.
     */
    protected BranchGroup buildViewBranch(Canvas3D c) {
        BranchGroup viewBranch = new BranchGroup();
        Transform3D viewXfm = new Transform3D();
        Matrix3d viewTilt = new Matrix3d();
        viewTilt.rotX(Math.PI/-6);
        viewXfm.set(viewTilt,new Vector3d(0.0,10.0,10.0),1.0);
        TransformGroup viewXfmGroup = new TransformGroup(viewXfm);
        ViewPlatform myViewPlatform = new ViewPlatform();
```

```java
        PhysicalBody myBody = new PhysicalBody();
        PhysicalEnvironment myEnvironment = new PhysicalEnvironment();
        viewXfmGroup.addChild(myViewPlatform);
        viewBranch.addChild(viewXfmGroup);
        View myView = new View();
        myView.addCanvas3D(c);
        myView.attachViewPlatform(myViewPlatform);
        myView.setPhysicalBody(myBody);
        myView.setPhysicalEnvironment(myEnvironment);
        return viewBranch;
    }
/**
 * This adds some lights to the content branch of the scene graph.
 * @param b The BranchGroup to add the lights to.
 */
protected void addLights(BranchGroup b) {
        Color3f ambLightColour = new Color3f(0.5f, 0.5f, 0.5f);
        AmbientLight ambLight = new AmbientLight(ambLightColour);
        ambLight.setInfluencingBounds(bounds);
        Color3f dirLightColour = new Color3f(1.0f, 1.0f, 1.0f);
        Vector3f dirLightDir  = new Vector3f(-1.0f, -1.0f, -1.0f);
        DirectionalLight dirLight =
                    new DirectionalLight(dirLightColour, dirLightDir);
        dirLight.setInfluencingBounds(bounds);
        b.addChild(ambLight);
        b.addChild(dirLight);
    }
/**
 * This builds the gun geometry.
 * It uses box and cylinder primitives and sets up a
 * transform group so that we can rotate the gun.
 * @return BranchGroup with gun geometry attached
 */
protected BranchGroup buildGun() {
        BranchGroup theGun = new BranchGroup();
        Appearance gunApp = new Appearance();
        Color3f ambientColour = new Color3f(0.5f,0.5f,0.5f);
        Color3f emissiveColour = new Color3f(0.0f,0.0f,0.0f);
        Color3f specularColour = new Color3f(1.0f,1.0f,1.0f);
        Color3f diffuseColour = new Color3f(0.5f,0.5f,0.5f);
        float shininess = 20.0f;
        gunApp.setMaterial(new Material(ambientColour,emissiveColour,
                                   diffuseColour,specularColour,shininess));
        TransformGroup init = new TransformGroup();
```

```java
        TransformGroup barrel = new TransformGroup();
        Transform3D gunXfm = new Transform3D();
        Transform3D barrelXfm = new Transform3D();
        barrelXfm.set(new Vector3d(0.0,-2.0,0.0));
        barrel.setTransform(barrelXfm);
        Matrix3d gunXfmMat = new Matrix3d();
        gunXfmMat.rotX(Math.PI/2);
        gunXfm.set(gunXfmMat,new Vector3d(0.0,0.0,0.0),1.0);
        init.setTransform(gunXfm);
        gunXfmGrp.setCapability(
                TransformGroup.ALLOW_TRANSFORM_WRITE);
        gunXfmGrp.addChild(new Box(1.0f,1.0f,0.5f,gunApp));
        barrel.addChild(new Cylinder(0.3f,4.0f,gunApp));
        gunXfmGrp.addChild(barrel);
        theGun.addChild(init);
        init.addChild(gunXfmGrp);
        return theGun;
}
/**
 * Creates the duck.  This loads the two duck geometries
 * from the files 'duck.obj' and 'deadduck.obj' and loads
 * these into a switch.  The access rights to the switch
 * are then set so we can write to this switch to swap
 * between the two duck models.  It also creates a
 * transform group and an interpolator to move the duck.
 * @return BranchGroup with content attached.
 */
protected BranchGroup buildDuck() {
        BranchGroup theDuck = new BranchGroup();
        duckSwitch = new Switch(0);
        duckSwitch.setCapability(Switch.ALLOW_SWITCH_WRITE);
        ObjectFile f1 = new ObjectFile();
        ObjectFile f2 = new ObjectFile();
        Scene s1 = null;
        Scene s2 = null;
        try {
                s1 = f1.load("duck.obj");
                s2 = f2.load("deadduck.obj");
        } catch (Exception e) {
                System.exit(1);
        }
        TransformGroup duckRotXfmGrp = new TransformGroup();
        Transform3D duckRotXfm = new Transform3D();
```

```
        Matrix3d duckRotMat = new Matrix3d();
        duckRotMat.rotY(Math.PI/2);
        duckRotXfm.set(duckRotMat,new Vector3d(0.0,0.0,-30.0),1.0);
        duckRotXfmGrp.setTransform(duckRotXfm);
        duckRotXfmGrp.addChild(duckSwitch);
        duckSwitch.addChild(s1.getSceneGroup());
        duckSwitch.addChild(s2.getSceneGroup());
        TransformGroup duckMovXfmGrp = new TransformGroup();
        duckMovXfmGrp.setCapability(
                        TransformGroup.ALLOW_TRANSFORM_READ);
        duckMovXfmGrp.setCapability(
                        TransformGroup.ALLOW_TRANSFORM_WRITE);
        duckMovXfmGrp.addChild(duckRotXfmGrp);
        duckAlpha = new Alpha(-1,0,0,3000,0,0);
        Transform3D axis = new Transform3D();
        PositionInterpolator moveDuck = new
            PositionInterpolator(duckAlpha,duckMovXfmGrp,axis,-30.0f,30.0f);
        moveDuck.setSchedulingBounds(bounds);
        theDuck.addChild(moveDuck);
        theDuck.addChild(duckMovXfmGrp);
        return theDuck;
}
/**
 * This builds the ball that acts as the bullet for our gun.
 * The ball is created from a sphere primitive, and a transform
 * group and interpolator are added so that we can 'fire' the
 * bullet.
 * @return BranchGroup that is the root of the ball branch.
 */
protected BranchGroup buildBall() {
        BranchGroup theBall = new BranchGroup();
        Appearance ballApp = new Appearance();
        Color3f ambientColour = new Color3f(1.0f,0.0f,0.0f);
        Color3f emissiveColour = new Color3f(0.0f,0.0f,0.0f);
        Color3f specularColour = new Color3f(1.0f,1.0f,1.0f);
        Color3f diffuseColour = new Color3f(1.0f,0.0f,0.0f);
        float shininess = 20.0f;
        ballApp.setMaterial(new Material(ambientColour,emissiveColour,
                                diffuseColour,specularColour,shininess));
        Sphere ball = new Sphere(0.2f,ballApp);
        TransformGroup ballMovXfmGrp = new TransformGroup();
        ballMovXfmGrp.setCapability(
                        TransformGroup.ALLOW_TRANSFORM_READ);
        ballMovXfmGrp.setCapability(
```

```
                              TransformGroup.ALLOW_TRANSFORM_WRITE);
        ballMovXfmGrp.addChild(ball);
        theBall.addChild(ballMovXfmGrp);
        ballAlpha = new Alpha(1,0,0,500,0,0);
        Transform3D axis = new Transform3D();
        axis.rotY(Math.PI/2);
        moveBall = new
                PositionInterpolator(ballAlpha,ballMovXfmGrp,axis,0.0f,50.0f);
        moveBall.setSchedulingBounds(bounds);
        theBall.addChild(moveBall);
        return theBall;
}
/**
 * This puts all the content togther.  It used the three 'build' functions
 * to create the duck, the gun and the ball.  It also creates the two
 * behaviours from the DuckBehaviour and GunBehaviour classes.  It then
 * puts all this together.
 * @return BranchGroup that is the root of the content.
 */
protected BranchGroup buildContentBranch() {
        BranchGroup contentBranch = new BranchGroup();
        Node theDuck = buildDuck();
        contentBranch.addChild(theDuck);
        Node theBall = buildBall();
        contentBranch.addChild(theBall);
        DuckBehaviour hitTheDuck = new
                DuckBehaviour(theDuck,duckSwitch,duckAlpha,bounds);
        GunBehaviour shootTheGun = new
                GunBehaviour(ballAlpha,moveBall,gunXfmGrp,bounds);
        contentBranch.addChild(hitTheDuck);
        contentBranch.addChild(shootTheGun);
        contentBranch.addChild(buildGun());
        addLights(contentBranch);
        return contentBranch;
}
/** Exit the application */
public void actionPerformed(ActionEvent e) {
        dispose();
        System.exit(0);
}
public SimpleGame() {
        VirtualUniverse myUniverse = new VirtualUniverse();
        Locale myLocale = new Locale(myUniverse);
```

```
        myLocale.addBranchGraph(buildViewBranch(myCanvas3D));
        myLocale.addBranchGraph(buildContentBranch());
        setTitle("Duck Shoot!");
        setSize(400,400);
        setLayout(new BorderLayout());
        add(BorderLayout.CENTER, myCanvas3D);
        exitButton.addActionListener(this);
        add(BorderLayout.SOUTH, exitButton);
        setVisible(true);
    }
    public static void main(String[] args) {
        SimpleGame sg = new SimpleGame();
    }
}
```

Appendix B

Example Data Files

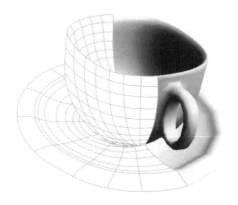

Introduction

This appendix contains examples of data files that are used in the various examples throughout the book.

Lightwave scene file

```
LWSC
1

FirstFrame 0
LastFrame 4
FrameStep 1
PreviewFirstFrame 1
PreviewLastFrame 60
PreviewFrameStep 1
FramesPerSecond 30.000000

LoadObject heraldbody.lwo
ShowObject 8 7
ObjectMotion (unnamed)
 9
 1
 000000111
 00000
EndBehavior 1
ShadowOptions 7

LoadObject heraldfrontwheels.lwo
ShowObject 8 7
ObjectMotion (unnamed)
 9
 1
 000000111
 00000
EndBehavior 1
ParentObject 1
ShadowOptions 7
```

```
LoadObject heraldrearwheels.lwo
ShowObject 8 7
ObjectMotion (unnamed)
 9
 1
 0 0 0 0 0 0 1 1 1
 0 0 0 0 0
EndBehavior 1
ParentObject 1
ShadowOptions 7

AmbientColor 255 255 255
AmbIntensity 0.250000

AddLight
LightName Light
ShowLight 1 7
LightMotion (unnamed)
 9
 1
 -2 2 -2 45 35 0 1 1 1
 0 0 0 0 0
EndBehavior 1
LockedChannels 48
LightColor 255 255 255
LgtIntensity 1.000000
LightType 0
ShadowType 1

AddLight
LightName Light
ShowLight 1 7
LightMotion (unnamed)
 9
 1
 -2 2 -2 45 35 0 1 1 1
 0 0 0 0 0
EndBehavior 1
LightColor 255 255 255
LgtIntensity 1.000000
LightType 0
ShadowType 1
```

```
ShowCamera 1 7
CameraMotion (unnamed)
1
 -9.644999 1.169036 -0.001490281 90 0 0 1 1 1
 0 0 0 0 0
EndBehavior 1
LockedChannels 54
ZoomFactor 3.200000
Resolution 1
PixelAspectRatio 2
SegmentMemory 2200000
Antialiasing 0
AdaptiveSampling 1
AdaptiveThreshold 16
FilmSize 2
FieldRendering 0
MotionBlur 0
DepthOfField 0

SolidBackdrop 1
BackdropColor 0 0 0
ZenithColor 0 40 80
SkyColor 120 180 240
GroundColor 50 40 30
NadirColor 100 80 60
FogType 0
DitherIntensity 1
AnimatedDither 0

RenderMode 2
RayTraceEffects 0
ClipRayColors 0
DataOverlayLabel
OutputFilenameFormat 1
SaveRGBImagesPrefix D:\Ian\Images\car000
RGBImageFormat 7
FullSceneParamEval 0

ViewMode 5
ViewAimpoint 0.683086 0.000000 -0.211467
ViewDirection -1.961750 0.450295 0.000000
ViewZoomFactor 0.856945
GridNumber 40
```

```
GridSize 1.000000
ShowMotionPath 1
ShowBGImage 0
ShowFogRadius 0
ShowRedraw 0
ShowSafeAreas 0
ShowFieldChart 0
```

Object file using materials

```
mtllib cube.mtl

v  1.0 1.0 1.0
v -1.0 1.0 1.0
v -1.0 -1.0 1.0
v 1.0 -1.0 1.0
v 1.0 1.0 -1.0
v -1.0 1.0 -1.0
v -1.0 -1.0 -1.0
v 1.0 -1.0 -1.0

vn 0.0 0.0 1.0
vn 0.0 0.0 -1.0
vn 1.0 0.0 0.0
vn -1.0 0.0 0.0
vn 0.0 1.0 0.0
vn 0.0 -1.0 0.0

vt 1.0 1.0 0.0
vt 0.0 1.0 0.0
vt 0.0 0.0 0.0
vt 1.0 0.0 0.0

g cube
usemtl redshiny
f 1/1/1 2/2/1 3/3/1 4/4/1
f 8/4/2 7/1/2 6/2/2 5/3/2
f 1/2/3 4/3/3 8/4/3 5/1/3
f 6/2/4 7/3/4 3/4/4 2/1/4
f 1/4/5 5/1/5 6/2/5 2/3/5
f 7/2/6 8/3/6 4/4/6 3/1/6
```

Object material file

```
newmtl redshiny
Ka 1.000000 0.000000 0.000000
Kd 1.000000 0.000000 0.000000
Ks 1.000000 1.000000 1.000000
illum 2
d 1.000000
Ns 20.000000

newmtl brick
Ka 1.000000 0.000000 0.000000
Kd 1.000000 0.000000 0.000000
Ks 1.000000 1.000000 1.000000
illum 2
d 1.000000
Ns 20.000000
map_Kd brick.jpg
```

References

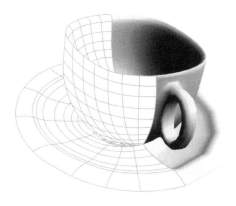

General Java

Essential Java 2 fast, J.Cowell, Springer-Verlag, 1999.
http://www.javasoft.com/

Java 3D

The Java 3D API Specification, H.Sowizral, K.Rushforth &
M.Deering, Addison-Wesley, 2000.

General graphics

Essential Computer Animation fast, J.Vince, Springer-
Verlag, 1999.
Computer Graphics, J.Foley, A.van Dam, S.Feiner,
J.Hughes, Addison-Wesley, 1995.

OpenInventor

The Inventor Mentor, Silicon Graphics, Addison-Wesley,
1993.

VRML

The VRML 2.0 Handbook, J.Hartman, Addison-Wesley,
1996.

Lighwave3D

Inside Lightwave3D, D.Ablan, New Riders, 1997.
http://www.newtek.com/

3D file formats

http://www.cica.indiana.edu/graphics/3D.objects.html

Index

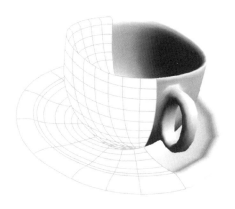